Film Parody

To Mom and Dad, and Andrew

Film Parody

Dan Harries

 Publishing

First published in 2000 by the
British Film Institute
21 Stephen Street, London W1P 2LN

The British Film Institute is the UK national agency with responsibility for encouraging the arts of film and television and conserving them in the national interest.

Copyright © Dan Harries 2000

Set by Fakenham Photosetting Limited, Fakenham, Norfolk
Printed in Great Britain by St Edmundsbury Press, Bury St Edmunds

Cover designed by Default/Lisa Swerling
Cover images: (front) *Austin Powers: The Spy Who Shagged Me* (Jay Roach, 1999); (back) *Abbott and Costello Meet Frankenstein* (Charles Barton, 1948)

British Library Cataloguing-in-Publication Data
A catalogue record for this book is available from the British Library
ISBN 0–85170–803–X (pb)
ISBN 0–85170–802–1 (hb)

Contents

Acknowledgments	vi
PART ONE – MAPPING FILM PARODY	1
1 Introducing the Anti-Canon-as-Canon	3
2 Spoofing Traditions	11
3 Transtextual Targets	22
PART TWO – SKETCHING FILM PARODY	
4 Reiteration	43
5 Inversion	55
6 Misdirection	62
7 Literalization	71
8 Extraneous Inclusion	77
9 Exaggeration	83
PART THREE – WATCHING FILM PARODY	
10 Reading the Parodic	93
11 Parodic Pragmatics	101
12 Conservative Transgressions and Canonical Conclusions	120
Filmography	135
Bibliography	139
Index	151

Acknowledgments

A number of people have provided valuable input into this book over the past few years and a big thanks goes out to them: Rhona Berenstein, Nick Browne, Jonathan Dawson, Thomas Elsaesser, Gordon Fletcher, David Gardner, Ron Gottesman, Anita Greenhill, John Heritage, Peter Lunenfeld, Tony May, Gerry Power, Diane Waldman, Peter Wollen and Justin Wyatt. Thanks as well to my colleagues and students at UCLA, Griffith University and Middlesex University for their contributions (subtle and not) to this on-going project. I would also like to thank Mouton de Gruyter, publishers of *Semiotica*, for their permission to reprint an altered version of an article by myself titled 'Semiotics, Discourse and Parodic Spectatorship' (vol. 113 no. 3/4, 1997). At the BFI, a big thanks to Andrew Lockett, Tom Cabot, Sophie Contento and Chantal Latchford for their assistance and support for this book. Finally, particular thanks is due to Andrew Fayé for his keen editing eye and true partnership.

Part One
Mapping Film Parody

1
Introducing the Anti-Canon-as-Canon

A few years ago, I was teaching a class of fourteen-year-olds, and we began tackling the question of genre and the disaster film. To get them situated with a 'classic' example, I screened the 1970 film, *Airport*. After the film, one student eagerly raised his hand and asked if this film was *based* on *Airplane!*. I smirked, informed him it was the other way around, and immediately wondered if any of these kids had ever even *seen* a 'classic' Hollywood film. I left class that day pondering if parodies and other similar forms of irony had replaced the canonized genres and 'classics' for a new generation.[1]

Film parodies have long been popular with film audiences, ranging from Buster Keaton's zany antics in *Sherlock Jr.* (1924) to Warner Bros.' classic cartoon parodies such as *Duck Amuck* (1953) to Mel Brooks' string of film spoofs including *Blazing Saddles* (1974) and *Dracula: Dead and Loving It* (1995). And with the tremendous success of such parody films as *Austin Powers: The Spy Who Shagged Me* (1999) bringing in large receipts at the box office ($205,526,345 total gross over its three-month first theatrical run and the twenty-sixth top-grossing motion picture in US history), such popularity is certainly still in place. The sparse critical acclaim these films have garnered has been centred not only on their effective dislodging of established film genres, but also on their ability to assault other film canons with humorous effect. While such claims are, to some extent, true, my observations of film parody over the years suggest a process more akin to canonization than any type of radical critique.

The central argument of this book hinges upon film parody's increasing transformation into its own canon; looking at how parodic discourse engages in its disrupting activities in a surprisingly standardized and predictable manner. While I would shy away from generating yet another totalizing grand theory of narrative, I am drawn to the notion that certain standardized processes of text and spectatorship are operating in contemporary film parodies, and that such processes are indicative of our ever-increasing levels of cultural irony. One can also draw certain correlations between parody's canonization and the substantial increase in the number of commercial film parodies released since the mid-1970s – making it an even more popular and profitable film mode.

Not only do films such as *The Naked Gun: From the Files of Police Squad!* (1988) prove to be big box-office draws, they also serve as cogent markers of a culture steeped in an ever-increasing level of irony; an era where postmodern activity has become more the norm than any sort of alternative practice. I characterize this as our culture's state of 'ironic supersaturation'. In fact, with newer generations being fed a daily diet of ironic and parodic discourse in every type of media, one could even posit the threatened relevance of 'classic' canons to people in the not-so-distant future.

This book additionally questions the 'subversive' and emancipating properties of parodic film (do we really become 'liberated' after watching an hour and a half of *Spaceballs?*) and concludes that the potential for both transgressive thought and action rests more in our heads than on the flickering image on a screen. Realizing the overlapping distinctions between media in this age of irony and the fact that additional volumes could well be written about parody in television, comic books, radio or literally any other medium, I focus this particular study on film parody – the manner in which it refers to its own film history and how cinematic texts and spectatorship have functioned in creating a parodic canon.

The subsequent chapters of this book are concerned with developing a theory of film parody which combines three central dimensions of parodic discourse: the textual, the pragmatic and the socio-cultural. By combining all three dimensions, we can gain a better understanding of how parodic processes function inter-relatedly – with all three dimensions operating simultaneously during any engagement with a parodic film text.

Although the modern parody has developed over the last century, there seems to have been a dramatic increase in the number of parodies produced since the late 1960s. Yet, even with such a long history of violating literary norms and up-ending reader expectations, until recently relatively little critical work has been done on how parody operates textually and what functions it serves in a socio-cultural context. In fact, many earlier writings on parody were either heavily descriptive or predominantly historical introductions to parody anthologies and provided useful insight into the relation between parody and source texts.[2] Over the past fifteen years, though, there has been an acceleration of theoretical work on parody (again, mostly by literary critics) that has generated more productive accounts of exactly what parody is and does.[3]

Unfortunately, such writings on film parody are often even more limited by both their slant toward film *criticism* rather than film theory and the corresponding laudable and exhaustive efforts in the location of parodic instances and the identification of their parodied sources (a kind of 'source archaeology').[4] In other words, much of the critical work done on film parody has dealt more with offering criticism around how well (or not) a particular parody has spoofed its target than with providing a model of how parody functions both textually and pragmatically. In the end, little remains understood from these studies about the larger organization of film parody and the processes in which it operates. In fact, Joseph Dane balks at the possibility of *any* theoretical account of parody, arguing that 'definitions of parody and various theories of parody should be regarded as useful tools only, as working hypotheses toward a history of parody. Each will fail when confronted with particular texts and with their particular literary and cultural contexts' (1988, p. 1). Although parodic criticisms such as Dane's have great descriptive power, they put forward and utilize few explanatory tools, especially in terms of parody's textual operations and the actual production/reception of such texts.

Encouraging efforts to theorize film parody have been conducted by both Robert Stam (1989) and João Luiz Vieira (1984) through their useful integration of Bakhtinian analysis into the study of parodic discourse. Drawing on Bakhtin's conceptions of the carnivalesque, dialogism and heteroglossia, Stam and Vieira have been successful in theorizing the co-optive (and even subversive) powers of film parody. However, as I will discuss later, much of their work is limited by a primary focus on the macro-functioning of parody (i.e. the ideological 'effects'), which often ends up neglecting the means by which parody functions ironically throughout such films.

Additionally, parody as a descriptive label has often been loosely applied to anything remotely satiric or ironic; typically evoked by film reviewers and trade publications with amazing fluidity. For example, in a review of the parody film, *Zorro, the Gay Blade* (1981), Merrill Shindler demonstrates this hyper-fluidity by describing the film as 'part spoof, part parody and part lampoon' (1981, p. 342). Interestingly, Shindler is essentially (and probably needlessly) evoking a number of synonyms for 'parody'. Trade magazines such as *Variety* and *Hollywood Reporter* constantly categorize parody films within a wide range of descriptive labels: satire, spoof, put-on, lampoon, comedy-satire, as well as simply: parody. In fact, I recall one particular review of *Young Frankenstein* (1974) in *Variety* (18 Dec. 1974) that seemed to avoid the film's overt parodic discourse all together by labelling it a 'period comedy thriller'.

Such fluidity suggests that it might be helpful to quickly trace how the term 'parody' has been defined and conceptualized over the years. Margaret Rose argues that parody has traditionally been defined in terms of: (1) its etymology or its historical and linguistic development as a concept; (2) its use as a rhetorical device; (3) its 'attitude' toward the parodied text and the reader; (4) its effect on the reader; and (5) 'the structure of the texts in which parody is not just a specific technique but the mode of the work itself...' (1979, p. 17). The breadth of these concerns underscores the importance of an 'elastic' definition of parody and its ability to stretch simultaneously in varied directions with each considered context.

Etymologically, parody can be traced to two earlier uses. Traditionally, parody has been defined as a derivative of the Greek term *paroidia*, a burlesque or 'counter-song'. Thus, the prefix 'para' creates the connotation of 'counter' or 'against', concepts that have had a considerable influence on how theorists conceptualize the process of parody. As a 'counter-text', parody has been viewed as a mode that essentially ridicules another text by mimicking and mocking it. Linda Hutcheon takes issue with this initial emphasis on parody's 'counterness', stating that 'para' can 'also mean "besides", and therefore there is a suggestion of an accord or intimacy instead of contrast' (1985, p. 32). While there is a great deal of accord in modern parody, one must not ignore the moments of difference (through textual ruptures, slippage and transformations) that create a strong 'counter'-element in the term.[5]

Taking both etymological roots into consideration, one can see how parodic textual systems continuously incorporate both roots by emulating texts ('besides') as well as mocking them ('against'). As a textual system, parody simultaneously says one thing while saying another, always acting as an ironic tease. Thus, it is probably more productive to think of parody as a term connoting both closeness and distance as well as the oscillating process that binds both discursive directions.

Due chiefly to its constant shifting of textual referents and contextual placements, it is quite difficult to saddle any definition of parody to a specific historical moment. With some theorists defining parody as a textual *object*, such trans-historical definitions are even more challenging. Instead, one would profit by defining parody across historical periods, considering it as a *process* (rather than an actual entity) that does indeed change and adapt to its historical moment. In other words, any text can be parodically reworked, and it is the status of process that allows for such flexibility.

Some of the earliest theorists to seriously consider parody as an examinable topic and to valorize its status as a rupturer of canons were the Russian Formalists. At the core of their theory of art is the centrality of convention and the establishment of canons. And a celebrated disrupter of these conventions is, of course, the parody; a text that exposes the structural configurations of any textual entity or canon. Textual form, then, could be 'deformed' by parody through the processes of 'defamiliarization', thus highlighting the text's social constructedness. In this manner, parody was designated as an excellent vehicle for critiquing aesthetic (and social) norms. By criticizing an artistic norm through transgressing it, the social norms that reinforce certain hegemonic relations are transgressed as well. The importance, the Russian Formalists argue, is centred not on the actual, parodic shift that occurs *within* the text, but 'the very fact that such a shift had occurred, that a deviation from the norm had been made' (Erlich, 1981, p. 178).

Although the Russian Formalists have long been criticized for being what one might term 'text-centric', they have also shown a remarkable concern for the pragmatic or spectatorial functionings of interpreting formal elements. Not only did they focus on the literary techniques of transgression utilized in creating parodic texts, they also found interest in the subsequent effects in readers of such writings. Maja Herman-Sekulic reaffirms this focus, commenting on how the Formalists 'showed that parodic cross-reading creates a semantic shift, a change in meaning and "inner reform", which accompanies the structural changes resulting from the comparison and the contrast of the two texts' (1985, p. 7). With this two-pronged focus, the Russian Formalists' theorization of parody – in terms of both textuality and pragmatic activity – serves as an excellent starting point for defining what parody is and does.

Paying particular attention to contextual determinants, I define parody as the process of recontextualizing a target or source text through the transformation of its textual (and contextual) elements, thus creating a *new* text. This conversion – through the resulting oscillation between similarity to and difference from the target – creates a level of ironic incongruity with an inevitable satiric impulse. It is from this position that I analyse the process of what makes a film a parody and how we view such films in contemporary culture.

Within this critical tradition, parody is lauded as an anti-canonical, incongruity-generating mechanism by obliterating conventionalized codes through disruptive, disunifying techniques. Although typically in agreement that parody serves an anti-canonical function, most writers have yet to agree on what type of textual category parody resides. Is it a genre or a form? Or is it a particular style? Such confusion is not surprising since film parody can spoof a variety of targets: film genre (the Western in *Rustler's Rhapsody* (1985)); film cycles (disaster films in *The Big Bus* (1976)); celebrated filmmakers (Ingmar Bergman in *The Dove* (1968)); individual films (*Top Gun* (1986) in *Hot Shots!* (1991)); or modes of film production (early silent film-making in *Silent Movie* (1976)). Because of this ability to transmutate into the target text's structure, some even argue that parody cannot actually constitute a distinct textual process or category itself.[6]

Although I agree that parodic discourse does indeed exhibit these properties of osmosis, I would contend that parody also takes on these qualities in quite specific, systemic patterns (and often without regard to the particular type of target). For these reasons, I prefer to describe film parody not so much as a 'meta-genre', or, conversely, as a textual anti-genre, but rather as a discursive *mode*. This perspective more clearly aims at the *functions* of parody rather than any specific content or thematic.[7] Employing a range of ironic, 'disrupting' techniques, parody therefore becomes more of a methodic 'approach' to recontextualizing target texts and canons than a particular text type.

Not only is parody a textual process and category, it is a strategy of spectatorship, much in the same vein as camp or 'counter-readings'. One of the distinct features of camp is centred on the viewer's awareness of certain moments of excess in a text and the reading of it in a specific way to accentuate that excess. For example, drag acts, long a staple of camp culture, are often read in terms of the way their performers exhibit excessive 'feminine' traits in the form of huge hairdos or overly expressive make-up. Similarly, parody can be read this way (which might also explain why a good deal of parodic texts are considered camp, or texts which foster a camp reading). As Dane points out, the fact 'that the reader has the power to read any text as a parody is something every reader knows' (1988, p. 10).

Looking at this from another angle, Terry Caesar argues that in order for one to read a text as parody, the text itself must be textually parodic. He states that 'parody has never merely been a way of seeing something. It is that something – which has been seen, and then written down.' Caesar further asks, 'is it possible to have parodic attitudes where there is no parody? Is it possible to have parody where there is not the formal character of the thing parodied?' (1979, p. 207). I would answer 'yes, sometimes'. For example, the television programme *Mystery Science Theater 3000* operates in this manner by screening old Hollywood B-movies while the show's characters (viewed in silhouette from behind while watching the movie) provide biting and ironic commentary throughout the film. Such activity, then, creates a sense of contextual displacement and possibly engenders a parodic viewing strategy.

Yet many theorists of parody (and, ironically, even those who devote entire books on the subject) seem reluctant to give any credence to the proposition that parody is itself a canonical process, thus reducing parody to a formless, random assault on established codes and conventions. This is evidenced in Dane's conclusion that parody is 'parasitic of its object and thus cannot be described formally' (1988, p. 5) or, to an even greater extreme, J. B. Price's contention that 'a true parodist does not really create anything...' (1951, p. 243).

In contrast, I argue that parody does indeed have fairly specific formal and structural characteristics which, operating in tandem, signal the process of parodic activity. These include a number of formal methods and patternings implemented to transform the primary texts, features that are both describable and indicative of parodic activity. Not only do parodies create 'something' (new textual configurations as well as modifications to pre-existing canons), they also foster 'ways' to view texts, developing and nurturing *critical* spectatorial strategies. While parody does indeed rely on and cannibalize other texts, its reworkings affect not only the viewing of previous textual systems but also the construction and viewing of future related canonical texts.

Probably one of the reasons why film parody is often viewed solely as a parasitic anti-canon is due to the amount of emphasis that is typically placed on the *difference* generated between the parody and its target. Hutcheon argues that 'parody is ... repetition with critical distance, which marks difference rather than similarity' (1985, p. 6). In this manner, Hutcheon (as well as other theorists of parody) is placing too much emphasis on difference rather than the *combination* of both differences and similarities. Rather, as I will develop further in the next chapters, in order to theorize parody productively, there must be a focus on how parodic texts simultaneously generate similarity to and difference from their targets in a regularized fashion – privileging neither and, therefore, not reducing parodic discourse to a solely difference-generating anti-canon.

In order to analyse the parodic process in films, I chose to use a methodology that can productively chart this textual movement between similarity and difference and its systematic repetition of technique. Based on a methodology for the analysis of film genre proposed by Rick Altman (1986 and 1999), this approach breaks the film text down into three central categories: the lexicon, the syntax and the film style. The lexicon is composed of the elements that populate any film text, such as the setting, the characters, the costumes and the various items comprising the film's iconography, like guns or horses. Such elements, therefore, produce effective markers that signal that a particular kind of text (genre, mode) is unfolding and create a viewing situation in which 'you don't have to see a whole film to know whether it is a Western...' (Altman, 1999, p. 89). The syntax, on the other hand, is the narrative structure in which the lexical elements reside, and functions by regulating the ways in which lexical units can be combined. In other words, the syntax is the film's plot. Both lexicon and syntax typically work together to generate sets of expectations by each connoting the presence of the other (e.g. the setting of a Western lexicon might connote an inevitable gun fight narrative syntax). Lastly, the film's style (including sound effects, camera movements and dialogue subtitles) weaves itself throughout the lexicon and the syntax to add additional sets of expectations based on that particular type of film text. Together, these components function to create any film's 'canonical knot'.

Rose uses a somewhat similar methodology in her analysis of parody but seems to favour a hyper-correlation between shifts in *both* lexical and syntactic dimensions. She writes that 'as in most cases of form and content relationships, semantic–syntactic dependency here means that a change to one aspect is accompanied by a change to the other...' (Rose, 1979, p. 28). I commend Rose's charting of parody's regularized, discur-

Fig. 1: *Blazing Saddles* (Mel Brooks, 1974)

sive movement, yet I disagree with her contention that an alternation of one dimension necessarily correlates with a change in the other. In fact, I argue quite the opposite, positing that one of the means by which parody generates both similarity and difference is by faithfully replicating either the syntax or the lexicon of the target text while altering the other dimension.

In order to flesh out this important distinction, let us quickly look at a few examples. In *Blazing Saddles*, one memorable scene features a pack of bad guys riding through the open plains (clearly evoking a Western syntax). Yet as they ride on, they come across an object rarely found in the Western: a toll booth in the middle of nowhere (see Figure 1). This is a clear example of a genre's syntax being relatively untransformed with the insertion of an extraneous lexical unit to generate both similarity and difference. Conversely, the story line can depart from the normative constrictions of that canon, yet retain lexical units within the newly generated narrative context. In *Transylvania 6-5000* (1985), the narrative from the classic 1931 *Frankenstein* featuring a little girl playing with the Monster near an idyllic pond is replicated, but with a lexical twist in which the setting of their exchange occurs in a smoke-filled room featuring an intense poker game. Rarely does one find both syntax and lexicon dramatically transformed at once since total departure from the target canon leaves little anchoring to generate incongruity; therefore creating only total difference. In other words, parody operates in terms of a system centred on 'logical absurdity', with one dimension needed to ensure a logic and another for difference-creating absurdity. This is the necessary oscillation between similarity to and difference from a target that allows parody to maintain either the lexicon, syntax or style while manipulating the others. By evoking and denying its selected target, parody becomes inevitably ironic – a quality that permeates all parodic efforts.

Film parody, by its very nature, is concerned with historical tradition; it is here where its potential targets reside. From early Porter films such as *Uncle Josh at the Moving Picture Show* (1900) to box-office hits like *Austin Powers: The Spy Who Shagged Me* (1999), film parody has created its own tradition and canon of films by recalling and playing with the codes and conventions of films past (see Figure 2). It is this developing tradition that we now turn to in charting how film parody has changed over the years.

Fig. 2: Website for *Austin Powers: The Spy Who Shagged Me* (Jay Roach, 1999)

Notes

1. There are various levels at which one can identify the use of irony by young people that move beyond such possible inadvertent instances of ironic thinking. Linda Hutcheon, for example, suggests that 'casual eavesdropping on young people would show any teacher that students of all ages are more than capable of deploying irony within their *own* discursive communities' (1994, p. 96).
2. See, for example, Edward Hope (1906) and Dwight Macdonald (1960).
3. See Margaret Rose (1979), Linda Hutcheon (1985) and Joseph Dane (1988).
4. An efficient example of 'source archaeology' can be found in Mark Siegal (1985).
5. Margaret Rose conducts a very thorough survey of the etymology of the term (and concept of) 'parody' in her 1993 book, *Parody: Ancient, Modern, and Post-Modern*, pp. 5–29.
6. Garabed Kiremidjian certainly thinks so, arguing that parody 'has no form, structure, or mechanism of its own, but must adopt, by its very nature, the form of the original to which it constantly refers and to which it even owes its existence' (1964, p. 7).
7. Terry Caesar agrees, writing that

   since parody has no subject matter other than what is parodied, since furthermore it is a relation and not the specific form that the relation takes . . ., it is always somewhat misleading to regard it as a genre and even to the Victorians it seems to have functioned as much as a mode. (1979, p. 11)

2
Spoofing Traditions

From its inception, cinema arose out of a discourse of intertextuality by recycling, reconfiguring and borrowing from other modes of entertainment. Novels became short films, vaudeville acts were re-enacted, and scenes of everyday life were captured through lenses of the cinematic camera. As cinema quickly developed its own canons and conventions, it also began to parody its own narrative scenarios and device. Buster Keaton's often overlooked film, *The Frozen North* (1922), is indicative of this developing self-reflexivity. From beginning to end, the film takes aim at a variety of Western film genre conventions. As David Robinson remarks,

> From vaudeville days Keaton had enjoyed parody; and in *The Frozen North* he did a cod on a W. S. Hart Western. The satire came sufficiently near its mark – particularly in its teasing of Hart's tendency to cry, in a manly way, in emotional crises – for the great Western idol to take offence. (1969, p. 66)

Capitalizing on its ability to spoof a recognizable movie star as well as a firmly-established film genre, *The Frozen North* cleverly exploits parody's characteristic oscillation between similarity to and difference from its target: Keaton arrives to the snow-bound 'Western town' by way of an out-of-the-way subway stop (see Figure 3); the local taxi glides on ski blades; and even Keaton's Hart-inspired 'sensitive' side is reflected by a hearty swig from a bottle – of Coca-Cola, that is. Such pin-pointed lampooning could only have occurred after the establishment of certain canonized

Fig 3: *The Frozen North* (Buster Keaton, 1922)

cinematic traditions that allowed for the generation of such similarity to and difference from recognizable targets.

As an intertextual discourse, cinema had already established a discernible pattern of transforming and borrowing from other film texts. In fact, many early film efforts are marked by their out-right piracy of contemporaneous film productions. For example, Edison filmed *Garden Scene* (1896) only a week after the Lumière Brothers released their *L'arroseur arrosé* (1895) in the United States (both featuring the simple plot of a man teasing a gardener by stepping on a water hose). Such early films (rarely exceeding a minute in length) derived much of their humour from fairly simple farcical plots by quickly establishing a social situation and violating their associated set of behavioural codes (as well as audience expectations).

The fairly rapid development of cinematic technique also created a new range of humorous possibilities through manipulating the medium itself by under-cranking, halting the camera to alter the *mise en scène*, or other filmic techniques. An early example of this occurs in the Lumière Brothers' film titled *Charcuterie mécanique* (1895), featuring a 'mechanized sausage maker' in which a pig is fed into one end of the machine, and sausages immediately emerge from the other. Similarly, Méliès made a name for himself through his employment of cinematic tricks to jolt the viewer's expectations, such as in *Escamatage d'une dame chez Robert Houdin* (1896) featuring a marvellous 'disappearance' of a woman created by simply stopping the camera, removing her from the scene, and rolling the camera again.

By the 1900s, a number of films became more self-reflexive by parodying cinematic spectatorship itself. Edwin S. Porter's series of 'Uncle Josh' films serve as excellent examples of early parodic activity. In *Uncle Josh at the Moving Picture Show* (1900), a man visits the movie theatre for the first time and becomes alarmed at the mistreatment of one of the female characters. Incensed, he 'leaps' into the film, tearing down the screen and falling to the ground. This 'reflexive' scenario would eventually be echoed in a number of films, including Keaton's self-reflexive masterpiece, *Sherlock Jr.* (1924) and later in Woody Allen's *The Purple Rose of Cairo* (1985).[1]

As cinema developed in terms of 'feature length' and multiple reels, greater screen time began to be utilized for generating complex narrative scenarios – setting up a wider range of intertextual, filmic references. One of the earliest parodists of the cinema was Max Linder, a successful stage actor who initially performed in the *Théâtre des Arts*. After a series of early films under the direction of Ferdinand Zecca at Pathé, Linder directed himself in *Les débuts d'un patineur* (1906) and established his well-known character of the *boulevardier* (a dandy donning a top hat and cane) by cleverly satirizing bourgeois mannerisms. Linder embarked directly into parody with his *Max médecin malgré lui* (1918), a witty and humorous parody of Moliére. By the end of 1919, Linder had moved to the United States to set up his own production company and in 1922, released the five-reel long *The Three Must-Get-Theres*, which parodied not only the Dumas classic but also the recently released Douglas Fairbanks film, *The Three Musketeers* (1921).

Although D. W. Griffith is probably best known for his epic melodramas of the silent film period (themselves targets for a good deal of early film parody), he also made a number of popular comedies, including the spot-on parody, *The Curtain Pole* (1908). Starring a young Mack Sennett, *The Curtain Pole* features the *boulevardier*-like character known as 'Monsieur Du Pont' (a reference and parody of Linder's then-popular character complete with top hat, cane and 'bourgeois' gestures). After a few years with Griffith, Sennett began directing his own films, including a number of farcical films. Interestingly, much of Sennett's parodic focus was aimed toward Griffith's melodramas as he poked fun at the films' often forced seriousness. Sennett's output of comedies was prolific and 'by 1911, Sennett had his own farce "unit" at Biograph and was given free play to his natural, unsubtle sense of burlesque, parodying Griffith's melodramas and sentimental comedies at the rate of two films a week' (Wead, 1976, p. 110).

In 1912, Sennett began directing films at the newly established Keystone Films and continued to spoof Griffith's now-clichéd melodramatic style. These films often featured overly-exaggerated acting gestures as well as titles lampooning Griffith's painfully poetic phrases by employing crass puns or exaggerated prose. Sennett's developing parodic style was also geared toward deflating Griffith's established technical film style. As George Wead mentions, 'Sennett's use of ludicrous inserts or close-ups was a parody of film's space–time continuum which Griffith's work so strongly depended on' (1976, p. 110). Additionally, Sennett took aim at current popular movie stars with films such as *His Bitter Pill* (1916) starring Ben Turpin as reigning cowboy star, William S. Hart.

During this period, Keaton began making films for Fatty Arbuckle's Comicque Film Company and, after three years, left to set up his own production company, Buster Keaton Productions. In a particularly interesting parodic gesture, Keaton renamed his company in 1921 to the differently spelled 'Comique Film Company, Inc.' – an affectionate, yet cutting jab at his former mentor. In his 1920 directorial debut, *The High Sign*, Keaton embarked on a series of clever film parodies. *The High Sign* also features an early instance of 'parodying the parodic' with Keaton spoofing Sennett's already mock-poetic titles by extending them even further into the absurd. For example, one title card in *The High Sign* reads:

> The brutal bungalow of the Blinking Buzzards, a bold bad bunch of bloodthirsty bandits who would break into a bank, blow a battleship to bits or beat a blue-eyed baby blonde.

In Keaton's 1921 film, *The Boat*, we see a continued effort to construct a filmic discourse that capitalizes on both parodic disjunction and other forms of intertextual linkages, such as the pun. A particularly funny example of a parodic pun centres on the boat in the film, which happens to be christened the 'Damfino'. At one point in the film, the boat springs a leak and is about to sink. Through a transmitted SOS, a radio operator is contacted who offers to help Keaton out. Yet through a witty exchange of miscommunications, each question asked by the operator receives the seemingly rude reply of '… Damfino!'

In *The Boat*, Keaton also pokes fun at the fairly conventional use of titles to indicate temporal ellipses, such as 'one week later'. Utilizing the comical form of the understatement, one title reads 'Ten seconds later' and remains for, well …, exactly ten seconds! Keaton uses a similar example of temporal title cards at the end of the film, *The Paleface* (1921) but makes his parodic point visually. Finally reunited with his Native American sweetheart, Keaton and the woman embrace, followed by a title reading 'Two years later'. In a twist of visual expectation, the immediate shot features the identical scene with the two still embracing.

In 1923, Buster Keaton's second feature length comedy, *The Three Ages*, was produced – one of the first 'sustained' feature length film parodies. In a send-up of Griffith's epic film *Intolerance* (1916), *The Three Ages* consists of three interwoven sequences telling basically the same humanistic story set in different historical periods (Stone Age, Roman and modern periods). Poking fun again at Griffith's propensity to utilize overly-dramatic title cards, Keaton throws in one of his own which attests, particularly within the context of a comedy film, the melodramatic ring of such words: 'a troubled heart ever yearns to know the future.' The middle 'Roman' period of the film also presents a perfect opportunity to parody another well-known film, the 1907 one-reeler, *Ben-Hur*, from the Kalem Production Company. Again, Keaton uses the altering of setting to create parodic transcontextualization by staging the exciting chariot race in a snow storm. Adapting to this new twist to an old story, Keaton's character improvises by hitching up four Huskies to pull his chariot!

One of Buster Keaton's best-known films, *Sherlock Jr.*, offers yet another dose of parodic activity, yet in a form less sustained than in *The Three Ages*. The film's title itself provides a parodic twist to the original Sherlock Holmes stories and suggests ways in which film parodies simultaneously announce both their parodic status and their intended target. Not only is the film aimed at John Barrymore's filmed version of *Sherlock Holmes* (1922) released only two years prior, it also finds an opportunity to self-reflexively parody the popular melodramatic films of the day. In a scene outside of the movie theatre, popular melodramas are lampooned by a poster announcing the film currently being exhibited:

To-Day
Hearts & Pearls
or
The Lounge Lizard's Lost Love
in Five Parts

We later find out from the projected movie that the film is made by the 'Veronal Film Co.' and is accented by over-exaggerated acting by the movie's performers. Recalling the self-reflexivity of earlier films such as *Uncle Josh at the Moving Pictures*, Keaton dozes off and dreams that he is entering the diegetic world of the movie being screened. Yet, as soon as he 'steps into' the film, he is immediately thrown 'out' by one of the characters, landing on the theatre's front stage. Not to be intimidated, he once again steps into the scene and initiates a hilarious sequence of setting and character displacement. Each time the Keaton character adjusts to the projected scenery, the background swiftly changes to a totally different locale: from a cliff top to a lion-filled jungle to a rock in the ocean. Each shift up-ends lexical expectations of narrative and setting continuity and dislocates not only the poor character, but also the viewer who 'safely' watches the sudden changes.

A particularly notable aspect of Keaton's parodic output is the development of his own self-parody. In the 1925 film, *Go West*, Keaton plays a character named 'Friendless'

Fig. 4: *Go West* (Buster Keaton, 1925)

in a cowboy movie that is literally about a '*cow* and a *boy*'. A clever scene which provides the perfect opportunity for self-parody involves Friendless in a not-so-friendly game of cards in the local saloon (see Figure 4). After being accused of cheating by Friendless, a man at the table pulls out his gun and recites (via a title card, of course) the famous line from Owen Wister's classic book, *The Virginian – A Horseman of the Plains* (1902): 'When you call me that, SMILE.' This, of course, presents Friendless (and particularly Keaton's own star persona – also known as 'The Great Stone Face') with an uncomfortable dilemma: how to literally form a smile. After gesturing his discomfort with this problem, Friendless raises up two fingers and creates a fake smile from the corners of his mouth. Such mimicking not only pokes fun at the classic poker scene of the Western, it also rebounds upon itself and constructs a jibe at Keaton's own filmic personality. Another moment of parodic self-referencing occurs in Keaton's 1927 *College* where he plays Ronald, the cox on the college crew team. At his first outing with the team, Ronald leaps with gusto into the boat and smashes through the bottom of it. The name of the sinking boat? 'Damfino!'

In 1928, Keaton went to work for the then-growing MGM studios; a move that marks the decline of Keaton's career. At MGM, Keaton lost much of his production independence and made only a few films before being relegated to gag writer for the studio. Yet even at MGM, Keaton continued to develop outlandish film ideas that he constantly pitched to Irving Thalberg, head of production at MGM. One of his more wacky projects was to be a parody of MGM's *Grand Hotel* (1932) starring Marie Dressler donning a pink tutu and proclaiming into a mirror, 'The public thinks I'm too old to dance. The Fools!' (Blesh, 1967, p. 331).

Other film parodies made in the 1920s and 1930s featured such screen comedians as Laurel and Hardy and Will Rogers. In 1922, Stan Laurel starred as 'Rhubarb Vaselino' in *Mud and Sand*, a hilarious spoof of Rudolph Valentino's *Blood and Sand* made that same year. Other film parodies made by the duo include *Dr. Pyckle and Mr. Pryde* (1925) and *Way Out West* (1937), a Western parody featuring Stanley singing in a saloon with an over-dubbed woman's voice. Popular box-office draw, Will Rogers, starred in no less than three 1924 films that spoofed popular contemporary targets: *The Cowboy Sheik* (another parody of Valentino as well as Rogers' own Western genre), *Big Moments from Little Pictures* and *Uncensored Movies*. The latter film contains a very funny scene that sends up the popular 'swashbuckling' films of the day, such as *The Mark of Zorro* (1920). In the film, Rogers performs such amazing feats as shooting consecutive arrows into each other's tips or acrobatically leaping up on to huge tree branches. The film then delivers the parodic punch line by exploring what *really* happens behind the scenes as Rogers lifts off his various safety harnesses and gingerly tries to get down from the tree.

Film parody in the 1930s is also characterized by the prolific output of cartoon spoofs, particularly those made by the Warner Bros. Studio. Similar to the form of 'borrowing' evidenced in early cinema, many of Warner Bros.' first cartoons feature characters that are based on (and clearly parodies of) other popular cartoon characters, such as the early cartoons featuring Foxy (the star of the first Merrie Melodies cartoons and a parody of Disney's Mickey Mouse), Bosko (also a take-off of Mickey), Honey (Minnie's parody), and Brunno (looking very similar to Pluto). In *Porky's Movie Mystery* (1939), a parody of the 'Mr Moto' series of films starring Peter Lorre occurs. This form of parodic borrowing is overtly announced with a title stating: 'Any resemblance this story has to the one it was stolen from is purely coincidental.' Such acknowledgments only add to parody's reputation as 'flippant' and unconcerned with 'conventional decor'.

Many of these cartoons also exhibit a heightened sense of self-reflexivity as they poke fun at their own cinematic and narrative apparatus. For example, in *Ride Him, Bosko* (1932), Honey is caught on a runaway stagecoach with Bosko on his horse trying to save her. As the camera pulls back, we see Bosko's creator, Rudy Ising, and two associates watching the cartoon itself as they discuss the best way to end the film. Many of the cartoons of the 1930s and 1940s also parodied the developing technical conventions used in Hollywood film-making. In *The Bear's Tale* (1940), we watch Red telephone Goldie through the now-clichéd cinematic convention of the diagonal split-screen. Yet in this instance, at the end of the conversation, Red literally *reaches* across the 'divider' and hands Goldie a note. In *Duck Amuck*, poor Daffy Duck faces a barrage of cinematic, self-reflexive transgressions with strangulating irises, dislodged film frames and rapid shifts in background scenery (see Figure 5). Such violations, within the context of a film mode where the suspension of disbelief is already paramount, display the relative instability of any filmic convention and the ease by which they can be transgressed.

Fig. 5: *Duck Amuck* (Chuck Jones, 1953)

Cartoons also self-reflexively tackled the Hollywood institution itself – lampooning various film modes, movie stars and popular genres. *Bosko's Picture Show* (1933) is an exemplary tour de force of cinematic parody with an entire 'evening at the movies' as its parodic target. With Bosko serving as the theatre's organist, we are treated to a variety of topical film spoofs: the *Out-of-Tone* newsreel that 'sees all – hears all – smells all', a short featuring caricatures of the Marx Brothers, and a feature film titled *Spite of Everything* starring 'Haurel and Lardy'. A similar jab at a contemporary popular film series occurs in *I Haven't Got a Hat* (1935), which cleverly parodies Hal Roach's 'Our Gang' comedies by featuring a group of animals (including Porky Pig in his film debut) putting on their own backyard variety show.

Early cartoon parodies also took aim at the popular movie stars of the time. A particularly funny example of star spoofing occurs in *The Coo Coo Nut Grove* (1936), with a host of Hollywood stars mingling at a fancy night club. One of the highlights of this cartoon features 'W. C. Squeals' making a move on a very uninterested 'Katharine Heartburn'. Among the many other examples of Warner Bros. star spoofs include *A Sunbonnet Blue* (1937), with singing by the 'Three Ratz Brothers', and *A Star Is Hatched* (1938), featuring a star-struck hen with a Katherine Hepburn-sounding voice and caricatures of Freddie Bartholomew, W. C. Fields and Dick Powell ('Dick Fowl').

Warner Bros. cartoons later lampooned specific well-known films with amazing precision and humour. For example, the 1961 *D' Fightin' Ones* parodies the then-popular film, *The Defiant Ones* (1958), while *Bunny and Claude* (1968) features Bugs Bunny robbing carrot patches. Beginning with their early usage of the Foxy and Bosko characters to parody Mickey Mouse, Warner Bros. cartoons have always been eager to spoof their key animation rival, Walt Disney. Such efforts produced *Coal Black and the Seben Dwarfs* (1943) and two classic spoofs of *Fantasia* (1940): *A Corny Concerto* (1943), complete with a telling juxtaposition of Disneyesque frolics with scenes of shootings and death, and *What's Opera, Doc?* (1957), featuring an ever-versatile Elmer Fudd self-reflexively 'sketched' into operatic scenes.

As Hollywood film-making in the 1930s continued to build upon its staple of surefire genres, cartoon parodies took appropriate aim at popular genres, particularly the Western. In *The Lone Stranger and Porky* (1939), Porky the Pig reconstructs the lore of the famous masked man with his partner, 'Pronto'. What makes this cartoon even more notable is the timing of its release – only a few months after the launch of Republic's successful serial. The Western is also parodied in *Saps in Chaps* (1942) with all of the characters (including the animals) walking in a stereotypical bow-legged fashion. Later cartoons such as *Drip Along Daffy* (1951) feature parodic scenarios of traffic light-controlled gun fights and the ringing of those familiar words, 'Hi-Ho, Tinfoil!' Other notable cartoon parodies of genres and film modes over the next few decades include horror spoofs such as *Transylvania 6-5000* (1963); Warner Bros.' parody of nature documentaries with *Wacky Wildlife* (1940); and the now classic sci-fi parody, *Duck Dodgers in the 24 1/2th Century* (1953).[2]

With the onset of the Second World War and the subsequent 1946 peak in US cinema attendance, parodic output in film dramatically declined. Much of this drop correlates with three central factors: Hollywood's ensuing economic instability and the 'security blanket' afforded by its film genres; the related demise of non-feature length films; and, finally, the shift of various discursive modes to the newly competitive television medium.

Huge film attendance in 1946 delivered a boom year to the major Hollywood studios, yet this honeymoon was short-lived as post-war attendance slumped and company profits sharply declined. One reaction to this decline was the use of 'sure-fire' genre formats (particularly the Western and the musical) to secure at least a minimal level of profit. And while many genres began to spill over into modes of self-reflexivity and critical re-evaluation in what Schatz calls the 'progression from transparency to opacity', they rarely dipped into a total parodic mode until the early 1970s (Schatz, 1981, p. 38). This, in turn, suggests that the concept of 'deconstructing' narrative models of money-making genres was probably seen as nothing short of financial suicide by the studios.

One of the results of Hollywood's reshuffling was, therefore, a reduction of non-feature length films, especially the short subject and the cartoon (until then the two central formats of film parodies). Nevertheless, there were a few notable film parodies during the 1940s and into the 1950s that continued the tradition of spoofing and increased self-reflexivity. For example, many popular comedy teams from the 1930s continued to parody popular films and genres. Shifting from the farcical to the parodic, the Marx Brothers starred in MGM's *Go West* (1940) and performed their typical disruptive antics within the setting of the Western. Interestingly, the Marx Brothers were often fodder for parody themselves – spoofed a year earlier in Gracie Allen and George Burns' *Honolulu* (1939) and later in *Hollywood Steps Out*, a classic 1941 cartoon featuring the hilarious scene of Harpo striking a match under Greta Garbo's enormous shoe (to which she replies with a very uninspired 'ouch'). The Western genre was also parodied, including Bob Hope's 1948 film *The Paleface* (a spoof of the 1929 film, *The Virginian*) followed by *Son of Paleface* in 1952.

The arrival of the Second World War additionally fostered a limited number of film parodies aimed at those film modes most closely aligned to 'serious' reportage: the newsreel and the instructional short subject. The famous newsreel segment in *Citizen Kane* (1941) particularly stands out as a clever parody of the newsreel format with its booming narrator (à la 'March of Time') and over-the-top, 'serious' musical score. Cartoons also spoofed the newsreel, with such releases as the *Weakly Reporter* (1944), making fun of the typically dour presentations. Not only were these types of film parodied by fictional and animated film, they were also, at times, created in a parodic mode, and found to be an effective means for getting serious points across to a war-weary audience. For example, the US Ministry of Information sponsored a film titled *Germany Calling* (1944) which provides a humorous example of taking newsreel footage and giving it a parodic twist through the addition of sound and visual effects. In one segment, Hitler is seen delivering a fiery speech while the background soundtrack swells with football-type cheers of '*Eins, Zwei, Drei, Vier*'. Sound effects are also added and are carefully timed to Hitler's quirky gestures and the crowd's '*Zeig Heil*' salutes. The funniest scene of this short film is made possible by utilizing an old projectionist's trick: goose-stepping Storm Troopers perform a 'dance' by the forwarding and reversing of a film loop.

Yet the champions of film parody in the 1940s must arguably be awarded to the popular comedy team of Abbott and Costello (who themselves were parodied in a

Fig. 6: *Abbott and Costello Meet Frankenstein* (Charles Barton, 1948)

series of Warner Bros. cartoons, including the 1942 *A Tale of Two Kitties* featuring two mice named 'Babbit and Catstello'). *Abbott and Costello Meet Frankenstein*, released by Universal Pictures in 1948, is by far the team's most important film spoof and stands as a classic example of a sustained film parody, that is, a film which operates within a parodic mode from start to finish. This film is even more remarkable in the way that its studio, Universal, parodies a number of its own profitable properties including Dracula, the Wolf Man and Frankenstein. And within the spirit of successful parodies generating both similarity to and difference from their target, this film also stars the original actors reprising their now-famous monster roles: Bela Lugosi as Count Dracula, Lon Chaney, Jr as the Wolf Man and Glenn Strange as Frankenstein (see Figure 6). In fact, it is their ability to play the monsters 'straight' that makes this film so effective in critiquing the horror genre itself. Abbott and Costello went on to make other film parodies, including the jungle picture spoof, *Africa Screams* (1949), the pirate movie parody *Abbott and Costello Meet Captain Kidd* (1952), and the sci-fi lampoon, *Abbott and Costello Go to Mars* (1953), but none seem to affectionately embrace their target as does the *Frankenstein* picture. Beyond these limited examples of film parody, few notable parodies were produced during the 1940s and early 1950s.

Film parody in the 1950s and 1960s fared little better with only a few scattered attempts at spoofing Hollywood genres and popular films. Again, much of this can be tied to a declining domestic market and the move toward large, epic blockbusters designed to save the major studios from financial disaster. Rare exceptions can be found in the 1950s, as a couple of budding comedy teams began to utilize generic backdrops to perform their antics. The Western genre was tackled in 1956 by Lewis and Martin in *Pardners* (a remake of Bing Crosby's 1936 *Rhythm on the Range*) while Rowan and Martin starred in *Once Upon a Horse* (1958) with cameo appearances by Western stars Bob Steele and Tom Keene. Another notable parody from the 1960s is *Casino Royale* (1967) with its uneven spoof of the James Bond films.

Another major change occurring in the 1950s is the shift in parodic targets, with a noticeable move toward parodying newly competitive television programmes and stars. For example, cartoons which often lampooned famous movies began to spoof popular television programmes: *The Honey-Mousers* (1956), *The Mouse that Jack Built* (1959) and *Bonanza Bunny* (1959). Television not only began to provide material for some limited film parody activity, it, too, began to take on the role of mass media parodist. This is, of course, in line with Hollywood's movement away from the non-feature length film and additionally capitalizes on television's own conducive, shorter format. This ability to create skit-based comedy would become even more highlighted with the premiere of the hit television programme, *Laugh-In*, in 1967 and subsequent parody-themed programmes including *The Carol Burnett Show*, *Saturday Night Live* and *Second City Television*. In fact, Robert Stam seems to suggest that television might be more suited for parodic activity since its pervasive heteroglossia provides a fertile arena for creating swift, cultural parody. Any quick glance at today's television screen would attest to this, from the mega-intertextual pitches offered by American advertising to the ironically kitsch programming of such TV channels as Nickelodeon (with its 'Nick at Nite' series featuring the rebroadcasts of classic 1950s and 60s programming), MTV and Fox (a network built around such parodic shows as *The Simpsons* and *Married...With Children*). Yet one cannot completely divorce the tandem ironic positioning which American cinema was also experiencing during this period as it, too, crept towards a state of ironic supersaturation.

American cinema's leaning toward the parodic can be seen in a number of films in the 1960s, as film-makers began to tackle not only the popular genres ported out of Hollywood over the previous forty years but also the fairly recent influx of 'foreign' art films being screened in the United States. The 1968 short film, *The Dove*, takes as its target the films of Swedish director, Ingmar Bergman and stars the soon-to-be queen of film parody, Madeline Kahn. Set in the stark, Swedish countryside, *The Dove* evokes many of Bergman's classic movies (particularly 1957 films *Wild Strawberries* and *The Seventh Seal*) as characters wander between flashbacks and flashforwards contemplating how 'worn and brittle these woods look now'. At one point, Kahn's character offers a man a cigar, stating in hilarious fake Swedish, '*Phalicon Symbül?*'

Other film-makers began to parody and deconstruct the Hollywood model in general; reworking and re-examining accepted notions of film narrative and style. For example, Bruce Conner's 1958 *A Movie* (the title is itself parodic in its over-determined declaration of its status) is comprised of found footage assembled to create the 'narrative' within a musical context of a Hollywood film. As Robert Stam aptly describes, the film 'begins with epic Hollywoodean music that makes us expect something heroic and grandiose; instead, we are given a disorienting sequence of film leader, found footage, and titles reading "start", "head", and "end of Part IV"' (1992, p. 264).

Yet by the late 1960s, a new generation of film-makers began to playfully parody Hollywood genres and the celebrated auteurs so revered in college film courses. One specific film-maker who flourished during this period within the realm of film parody is Woody Allen. As Maurice Yacowar notes, 'In the beginning was the parody. From *What's Up, Tiger Lily?* (1966) through *Sleeper* (1975), Woody Allen developed his film artistry through forms of genre parody' (1987, p. 29). Actually, Allen only occasionally targets film genres in his parodies ('English-dubbed' Japanese films; the documentary in *Take the Money and Run* (1969) and *Zelig* (1983); or the science-fiction film in *Sleeper*). Instead, Woody Allen seems to focus on particular auteurs or classic films for his parodic exercises. Ingmar Bergman gets the once-over in *Love and Death* (1975) while Roberto Rossellini gets his poking in Allen's 1972 *Everything You Always Wanted to Know about Sex* (*But Were Afraid to Ask)* – as the hand-held camera swishes past every inch of the screen. Woody Allen also sends-up the film classic, *Casablanca* (1942) in *Play It Again, Sam* (1972), with Allen's character seeking advice from the on-screen Bogart.

Another film-maker to embark on a series of film parodies was Mel Brooks, former *Your Show of Shows* writer and creator of the popular TV spy spoof, *Get Smart* in 1965. Beginning with the 1974 release of his highly influential Western parody, *Blazing Saddles*, Brooks went on to make a number of clever film parodies including *Young Frankenstein* (1974), *Spaceballs* (1987) and *Robin Hood: Men in Tights* (1993). These films serve as signposts for a period of increased parodic film-making on a number of production fronts ranging from independently-produced shorts such as *Porklips Now* (1980) to studio-produced films like the *Naked Gun* series. This is also a time when we witness a number of films parodying television genres (such as the 1991 *Soapdish*) or particular canonical programmes (*The Flintstones* (1994) and the 1995 film, *The Brady Bunch Movie*).

It is this period of film-making (1974 to the present) which this book is mostly concerned with – a period steeped in the cynical and wrapped-up in the intertextual. In a sense, the age of irony is a time when the parodic itself has become so marketable and so predictable that its status has mutated into the very thing it has long assailed: a canon. The following chapters investigate this process of canonization by looking at the multiple intersections of parodic production and consumption and by charting out the specific characteristics of a discursive mode so pervasive on today's cultural landscape.

Notes

1. See Robert Stam (1992) for more on self-reflexive cinema.
2. So classic, in fact, that George Lucas requested that *Duck Dodgers* be shown with the San Francisco premiere of *Star Wars*.

3
Transtextual Targets

Postmodernism, it is argued, hinges upon a process of double-coding in which the modern, aesthetic core is preserved as well as transformed into a new, recontextualized entity.[1] Such heightened transtextuality, then, functions to foreground the inherent instability of any canonized text as well as the ease at which such altering can occur.

Within this vein, parody has long been championed as a particularly potent mode of postmodern intertextual discourse which seems to get its verve from such disruptions. By taking established canons and transforming them through various techniques of recontextualization, parody cements its status as an effective 'double-coder'. Yet, what happens when such recontextualizing activity becomes normalized itself, generating predictable and standardized discursive shifts? Looming here is one of the central contradictions of postmodernism itself, namely the implosion of signification, and its recuperation into canonicity. This, I believe, demonstrates a much larger cultural shift from an invigorating historical instance of instability to the maturation of the ironic.

As discussed in Chapter 2, parodic discourse has been around for a long time, yet its development into a fairly major mode of Hollywood film-making has occurred only within the past twenty years. A quick glance across the contemporary cultural landscape also suggests that parodies have made their mark in other forms of media such as television, radio, magazines and the Internet. Generations of kids raised on television have developed a certain 'knack' for appreciating the ironic, and such sensibilities are built into a number of marketing campaigns aimed at the 'under forties'. The popularization of parody makes the irony of postmodernism less threatening, less radical and, dare I say, more marketable to the general public.

As the postmodern cultural psyche continues to gel, it becomes increasingly difficult to think of cultural objects and activities which are *not* imbued with some sort of hyper-transtextuality; Baudrillard's infinite spiral of referencing is becoming a clear reality for a culture supersaturated in the ironic. Throughout this chapter, I examine this hyper-transtextualization of film parody, paying particular attention to parody's evocation of various modes of transtextuality, film parody's utilization of 'target' texts, and the narrative processes that regulate the operation of parodic discourse. Since very little has actually been written about the process of film parody, I will additionally sort and synthesize the work of a number of cultural theorists in order to construct and flesh out the basic parameters of parodic discourse in terms of both film text and viewing strategy. Finally, I will introduce the six primary methods used in film parody to create ironic discourse in a standardized manner.

Yet before examining film parody's heightened trans- or intertextuality, we should first acknowledge that, to some extent, *all* texts are intertextual.[2] Not only are texts read by spectators in relation to their previous textual experiences, the texts themselves are constructed out of previous works. Stam suggests that 'since all words, including literary words, always come from "the mouth of another", artistic creation is never *ex nihilo*; rather, it is premised on antecedent texts' (1989, p. 199). In this manner, then, it is not a radical step to confirm the potential for pluralistic readings of any text; that floating sense of non-closure with which literary and film theorists have long grappled.

Not only are texts intertextual reincarnations of previous constructions, they foreshadow future constructions – providing the 'stuff' for subsequent generations of discourse. Todorov maintains that 'intentionally or not, all discourse is in dialogue with prior discourses on the same subject, as well as with discourses yet to come, whose reactions it foresees and anticipates' (1984, p. x). It is this dualistic nature of looking both back and forward that film parody exploits in its heightened intertextual manner: challenging the old, reconfiguring the present and forecasting the new.

Such discussion brings to mind the many useful elements proposed by Mikhail Bakhtin in conceptualizing the plurality of meanings that any text engenders. Much of Bakhtin's writings reflect upon the pervasive presence of intertextuality involved in any textual encounter and that text's denial of univocal meaning. According to Bakhtin, all texts by their very nature are intertextual, that is, they are always based on previous texts in some form. In one major swoop, Bakhtin sheds the binary oppositions so favoured in structuralist theory and creates a shift from the dialectic to the dialogic or the relational context of any cultural object or activity. Robert Stam adds that

> in the broadest sense, intertextual dialogism refers to the infinite and open-ended possibilities generated by all the discursive practices of a culture, the entire matrix of communicative utterances within which the artistic text is situated and which reach the text not only through recognizable influences but also through a subtle process of dissemination. (1989, p. 15)

Not only are all texts dialogic in one form or another, they are invested with many meanings, what Bakhtin refers to as a text's heteroglossia. The task of securing a single meaning for a text becomes a futile exercise for Bakhtin who reckons such an explosion of meaning is what precisely makes language dynamic and alive. What keeps texts from moving into a total anarchistic arena is the continuous struggle between heteroglossia and canonization. Constructively, Bakhtin posits that every text embodies two poles: the conventional system of signs or language manifested in the text (and recognized within specific interpretive communities) and the moment of performance, the utterance.

It is this space between both poles that film parody exploits by engaging the intertextuality of both texts and spectatorship. By constructing signifiers which inter-relate with past film texts, parody generates textual incongruity and highlights the heteroglossia of that text. For example, a gangster spoof such as *Bugsy Malone* (1976) must both evoke and avoid its target genre. Such shifts of referencing must then be *recognized* by the spectator. This incongruity, therefore, drives the interpretive process and moves beyond specific textual encounters as well as interrogating the validity of normative systems in general. Through an examination of films that initiate the parodic spectatorial process, we can see how film parody functions by inscribing both similarity to and difference from its target texts and constructs an incongruity that evokes both ironic and pluralistic meanings.

Scholars have described parody as a specific mode of intertextuality that capitalizes on its ironic play *between* texts. Peter Wollen suggests that 'parody constantly veers towards the hybrid, towards the graft, both compatible and incompatible with its apparent model!' (1985, p. 39). As a hybrid text, parody is charged with an especially potent intertextual activation. This commingling of multiple texts within a single textual system generates a bitextual structure comprised of a set of 'target' texts and their reformulation in a parodic text.

As a mode of heightened heteroglossia, film parody proudly displays its multivoicedness by appropriating from a variety of preformed sources. For example, a film parody such as *Hot Shots!* not only targets the single film, *Top Gun*, but an entire cycle of 'fly-boy' films including *Devil Dogs of the Air* (1935) and *Angels One Five* (1952). Thus, a parodic signifier (based on previously established normative signifiers) produces a number of potential signifieds relating to the parodied text(s) and to those arising from the parody's transformational activity. Spectators of film parody must then simultaneously engage with both the foregrounded text (the parody) and the backgrounded target through a singly-demarcated system of signifiers.

Additionally, it is important to note that this 'doubleness' needs to be *noticed as double* in order for the text to be read specifically as a parody. Hutcheon comments that

> both irony and parody operate on two levels – a primary, surface, or foreground; and a secondary, implied, or background one. But the latter, in both cases, derives its meaning from the context in which it is found. The final meaning of irony or parody rests on the *recognition* of the superimposition of these levels. (1985, p. 34, my emphasis)

In other words, if the spectator does not pick up on the many references to James Bond films in *Spy Hard* (1996), there is a risk that they might simply read the parody as comedy and 'miss' the parodic level. Thus, the context of the potentially parodic situation greatly influences the interpretation of the system of signifiers.

I must admit, I am uneasy with Hutcheon's separation of parody into 'background' and 'foreground' texts. As Hutcheon clearly points out above, it is the *superimposition* of these texts that is important. The newly generated parodic text *absorbs* the preformed texts and then 're-presents' them within its own discourse, leaving some elements intact and reformulating others.[3] Film parody is not only the latter; it is performing both tasks of creating similarity and difference within the parodic text. Thus, the background exists merely as a memory of past textual experience, while the new parodic text generates a new text using the previous texts as its models. I argue that in order to theorize parody productively, one needs to focus on how parodic texts simultaneously generate similarity to and difference from their target texts, privileging neither. Margaret Rose recognizes this distinction as well, suggesting that parody consists of 'combining two codes (code B being familiar to the decoder, and code A which "estranges" the message of text B, strange) and irony by juxtaposing at least two messages in the one code' (1979, p. 61).

Parodic discourse, therefore, operates through its juxtaposition of both familiar and 'strange' appropriated elements.

A particularly productive means for discussing the intertextualization of texts has been proposed by Anton Popovic in his 1976 article, 'Aspects of Metatext'. Popovic makes the important distinction between a 'prototext' (the previously constructed text that serves as the 'target' or 'object' of mimicry) and a 'metatext' (the model based on the prototext) and argues that one can trace the textual distance between the prototext and the metatext by measuring how much variance is generated within the metatext. He writes that

> within the semantic aspect, we ought to distinguish between meaning invariants, which are those meaning components of the prototext which are kept intact in the metatext (intertextual invariants) and meaning variants, which are among those meaning components of the prototext which are realized in the metatext through semantic shifts. (Popovic, 1976, p. 227)

Thus, his proposed continuum runs from almost exact replication (meaning invariants) to total reformulation (meaning variants). The relationship between proto- and metatexts then becomes centred on the degree of similarity and difference that occurs between the two. Parodic discourse fluctuates between these two extremes, not only with each new textual encounter, but also within the text itself as the ebb and flow of transformation occurs along the narrational trajectory. As part of the metatext, the prototext is evoked with differing amounts of variance throughout the text, ranging from replication to total transformation. For example, *The Brady Bunch Movie* moves from near replication in terms of the characters (with intact individual traits) and similar story lines to complete transformation with a 1990s setting.

Intertextual reading strategies are typically instigated by both intertextually-signalled texts and viewing contexts. In this manner, 'intertextual reading is the perception of similar comparabilities from text to text; or it is the assumption that such comparing must be done even if there is no intertext at hand wherein to find comparabilities' (Riffaterre, 1980, p. 626). Thus, even when a parodic text is not present, a text can be determined a parody from its viewing context (such as watching a 'weepie' at a comedy film festival). As Barbara Klinger adds, 'without the authority of the text to invoke, the exterior sphere of intertextual relations suddenly appears strategically relevant to the queries of the social contours of text and subject-reader' (1986, p. 93). This suggests, though, that the viewer needs to have some familiarity with the target text in order to appreciate the parodic activity. It would surely be difficult to comprehend the occurring parody in a film such as *Repossessed* (1990) if you had never seen its central target, *The Exorcist* (1977).

Owen Miller argues that parody operates on the basis of an 'obligatory' intertextuality where knowledge of the previous texts becomes necessary for any comprehension of the newly generated metatext. Miller states that obligatory intertextuality 'imposes several important constraints on the connections the reader makes in his choice of intertexts and in his choice of relational procedures' (1985, p. 30). Such constriction attempts to channel the spectator's meaning construction by relying on pre-established codes which the spectator needs to know in order to 'get' the full extent of the parodic intertextuality. Thus, parody's evocation of specific prototexts generates an obligatory intertextuality, which makes familiarity with that system almost crucial for a parodic viewing of the text. Yet as I discuss in Chapter 11, the plurality of readings evoked from any textual encounter demands a more dynamic and fluid spectatorial system than one based merely on either 'getting it' or not.

This combination of intertextual texts and reading strategies creates a sort of heightened 'intertextual dialogism' and demonstrates the importance of examining not only the textual qualities of a text based on another but also the contextual factors involved, including the viewer's previous experience with texts. Thus, parody processes produce texts that rely on preformed, previously constructed texts as well as the recognition of these texts.

While we often talk about the concept of 'intertextuality' when discussing film parody, a shift toward Gérard Genette's categories of a broader 'transtextuality' might prove beneficial and serve as a more precise method for analysing a film parody's dialogic relation with other texts. In his highly influential book, *Palimpsestes*, Genette proposes five types of transtextuality: intertextuality, paratextuality, metatextuality, architextuality and finally hypertextuality. Together, these categories help sort the subtle nuances which occur between, through, and around textual relations.

Intertextuality, according to Genette, refers to the co-presence of two texts, often in the form of quotation, allusion and plagiarism. At the heart of parodic discourse is its function as an *imitative* form of intertextuality: a previous text is reformulated in the new, parodic text through a strategy of repetition that incorporates and refashions the texts. On Popovic's continuum of proto- and metatextual relations, the intertextual form of quotation lies closest to the ratio of greatest similarity. Popovic characterizes this as 'imitative continuity' in which 'the metatext refers to a concrete object – metatext *sensu stricto* – and imitates its patterns …' (1976, p. 231). This differs, of course, from parody in that no (or little) difference from the prototext is generated within the metatext.

Yet, while quotation and parody differ in the amount of transformation they perform, they both share many similar qualities, with quotation often being used in film parodies to generate the similarity needed for successful parodic identification. This is evident in the use of quotation at moments where there is no transformational activity within the text, in order to generate the recognition of similarity to the prototext.[4] This can be seen in the use of specific sets or locations found in the target films such as the use of the original *Frankenstein* (1931) laboratory equipment props in Mel Brooks' *Young Frankenstein*. As Margaret Rose states,

> while non-parodistic quotation may be described as leading the reader to make associations between two related but contingent texts, the function of the quotation in the parody might be said to be to connect and contrast disparate texts so that either their concealed identity or their concealed discrepancy will be foregrounded. (1979, p. 49)

This is an essential operation in parodic activity in order to ensure some recognition of the prototext and to secure an initial viewing strategy based on that prototext.

One could also argue that 'true quotation' placed within a different context might be considered parodic as well. Thus, a segment of a film may be reproduced with absolutely no transformation other than the material before and after it (therefore producing a contrasting transformation out of context through juxtaposition). When one exhibits a serious film (e.g. a 1950s melodrama) in a non-serious context (e.g. a comedy film festival), it can have the effect of making the film a parody (possibly even a self-parody).

David Bennett adds that such considerations problematize basic theories of parody which rely too heavily on difference as the source of parodic functioning. He writes that 'quotation as parody puts into question traditional, so called "intrinsic" definitions of parody as a function of rhetorical inflation or of manifest fault-lines, incongruities, within a text' (D. Bennet, 1985, p. 193). Such parodic uses of quotation are seen in parodic films such as *Dead Men Don't Wear Plaid* (1982), where actual old film clips are incorporated into a newly constructed parodic narrative, or *Zelig*, which places the fictitious Woody Allen character into archival footage of 'real' historical events.

Robert Stam, Robert Burgoyne and Sandy Flitterman-Lewis suggest that one can augment Genette's notion of the intertextual by dividing it even further into five sub-categories that further differentiate the particular nuances of intertextual referencing. The first proposed sub-category is that of 'celebrity intertextuality', which they define as a 'filmic situation where the presence of a film or television star or celebrity intellectual evokes a genre or cultural milieu...' (Stam et al., 1992, p. 207). We see this in a number of film parodies, from the clever use of Susan Sontag as herself in the pseudo-documentary *Zelig*, to Linda Blair's recreation of her role of Regan, the young girl from *The Exorcist*, in *Repossessed*. The humour evoked with this type of intertextuality partially arises from being familiar with their extra-textual performances and the witnessing of their juxtaposition in the film parody.

A similar form of intertextuality can be referred to as 'genetic intertextuality' in which the appearance of famous star's offspring (or close relatives) evokes memories of their parents. A good example of this occurs in *Rustler's Rhapsody* (1985), which features Patrick Wayne (John Wayne's son) as a cowboy and creates a familiar nod to his legendary father. Parody films also play around with familial relations on the character level as well. Thus, a film noir spoof such as *The Black Bird* (1975) can feature Sam Spade, Jr, 'son' of the famous 1940s character.

'Intratextuality', according to Stam et al., is the process by which a film refers to itself within the text in an overtly self-referential manner. This is evident in a number of parody films, such as *Spaceballs* – when the Yogurt character takes the other lead characters to his small boutique featuring a variety of *Spaceballs* merchandise. Other films refer to themselves intratextually by displaying their stylistic devices, such as Daffy Duck's battle with various film techniques (a closing iris, sync-sound, the zoom) in *Duck Amuck* (1953). Each of these build on their dialogic status by overtly exposing their own construction and flaunting this display.

A fourth sub-category of intertextuality can be referred to as 'auto-citation' – those moments when a film-maker refers to his or her own previous films in the text. One can see such auto-citation with the use of inside jokes in Keaton's *The Three Ages* with the baseball team roster in the film consisting of the names of Keaton Studio employees. On another level, one can often see studios poking fun at themselves by referring to their

Fig. 7: *Airplane!* (Jim Abrahams, 1980)

Fig. 8: *Airplane II: The Sequel* (Ken Finkleman, 1982)

previous movie output, such as Universal Pictures' classic parody, *Abbott and Costello Meet Frankenstein*, in which the studio retools one of its most profitable properties for parodic purposes. An interesting example of auto-citation occurs in *Airplane II: The Sequel* (1982) as the film evokes its parodic predecessor, *Airplane!* (1980). In *Airplane!*, a funny use of set props features the Lloyd Bridges character standing in front of a framed photo of himself in the exact pose. In *Airplane II: The Sequel*, the photo and pose are recalled, yet this time with an additional 'layer' of his image within the frame (see Figures 7 and 8).

Another sub-category that features texts that create their own pseudo-intertextual references is 'mendacious intertextuality'. A prime example of this is the fake newsreel which operates by utilizing a familiar newsreel mode and filling them with jibes at current topical events. *Citizen Kane* exhibits this technique with its opening 'March of Time' inspired pseudo-newsreel creating a doubling-back reference to the fictitious lead character of Charles Foster Kane. Such 'fake newsreels' also make numerous appearances in Warner Bros. cartoons, including *The Weakly Reporter* and *Bosko's Picture Show* (featuring the 'Out-of-Tone News').

Genette's second category of transtextuality is what he terms 'paratextuality', the interconnection generated between the text and its associated extra-textual elements such as film posters, soundtracks, reviews and promotional material. Film parodies often utilize such prototextual references to both situate the viewer into a 'parodic spectatorial mode' as well as to indicate the target text being parodied. For example, *High Anxiety* (1977), a parody of various Hitchcock films, was advertised with a tag line referring to it as a 'Psycho-Comedy' – thus making a clear reference to one of its intended targets. Alternatively, a film parody's paratext is also used to cloak the film's parodic nature, such as the promotional material accompanying *This Is Spinal Tap* (1984) that makes no reference to the film's parodic nature and refers to the band as a 'genuine' item. Such contextual examples are important elements for understanding parody since they acknowledge the spectatorial process of reading a film as parody.

The third type of transtextuality outlined by Genette is that of 'metatextuality', which can be described as the relation between one text and another text in which one is typically evoked at a larger, institutional level of discourse. In other words, a parody film might take aim at the more macro film-making conventions of the 'Hollywood style' while also parodying a particular genre or film title. An excellent example of this occurs at the end of *Blazing Saddles* when the camera cranes upward into an aerial shot which exposes the Western locale as Warner Bros.' Burbank back lot. The film, *Silent Movie*, is completely based on spoofing early modes of film-making including the use of title cards, the lack of sound, slapstick scenarios, and expressive acting. Such metatextuality is also present in virtually all documentary spoofs – such as *Take the Money and Run* where Woody Allen parodies the institutional stylistic modes of documentary film-making (hand-held camera movement, grainy 16mm film texture, sound mishaps, etc.). This form of parodic transtextuality is far too often overlooked in analyses of film parody with most attention usually paid toward finding the particular targets or sources for the parodic jibes and discounting the larger, institutional critiques being proposed.

'Architextuality' is Genette's fourth type of transtextuality and is described as a category that 'refers to the generic taxonomies suggested or refused by the titles or intratitles of a text' (Stam et al., 1992, p. 208). Such titles are often utilized self-reflexively to critique both their specific targets as well as the general modes being evoked. For example, the lead character in Warner Bros.' Western parody cartoon, *Drip Along Daffy*, is introduced by way of a title stating 'Western-type Hero'. This not only spoofs the Western genre and its propensity to focus on the efforts of a sole, rugged hero, but it also challenges the stereotypic nature of most characters found in any Hollywood produced genre film.

Genette's fifth and final type of transtextuality is what he deems as 'hypertextuality', in which one text (the 'hypertext') transforms another text (the 'hypotext'). Most film parodies utilize this form of transtextuality as they rework and spoof recognizable genres, modes of film-making and particular films. Therefore, a parody film such as *The Dove* evokes and transforms a host of clichéd attributes found in most of Ingmar Bergman's classic film corpus.

In total, I find Genette's proposal of five types of transtextuality (intertextuality, paratextuality, metatextuality, architextuality and hypertextuality) highly useful in categorizing the number of ways in which film parodies construct their similarities to and differences from other texts as well as their ability to differentiate a range of textual borrowings.

As a transtextual actualization, parody is often collapsed or confused with other forms of intertextuality that have different and discreet (although often compatible) qualities that both separate and align themselves with parody. One of the essential elements located in parodic discourse is the operation of irony and its generated level of incongruity. The ironic typically involves the transformation of a conventionalized code into another code, an activity that results in the possible recognition of incongruity between the two codes. Irony is often thought of as the juxtaposition of meanings from a 'background' text with those of a 'foreground' text. A semantic contrast occurs between what is said and what is meant. This, then, creates a two-tiered potential message within a single signifier that embodies the incongruous elements. Rose writes that 'the term irony generally describes a statement of an ambiguous character, which includes a code containing two (or more) messages, one of which is the message of the ironist to his "initiated" audience, and the other the "ironically meant" decoy message' (1979, p. 51). The 'initiated' message (what is meant) is juxtaposed with the 'decoy' message (what is said, but not directly meant).

This textual configuration is, of course, integral to parody's bitextual structure.[5] As an incorporated mode within parody, a closer comparison would be 'irony's patent refusal of semantic univocality matches parody's refusal of structural unitextuality', although any discussion of parody should already assume (and subsume) irony's ability to engender semantic shifts (Hutcheon, 1985, p. 54). In other words, film parody operates on both semantic and structural levels in creating a text with ironic layering.

Irony is also seen as an activation device for signalling parodic activity. Hutcheon writes that 'irony appears to be the main rhetorical mechanism for activating the reader's awareness of this dramatization ... and participates in parodic discourse as a strategy ... which allows the decoder to interpret and evaluate' (1985, p. 31). Thus, ironically-generated incongruity cues the spectator into activating his or her textual memory and, in turn, aids in the viewer's appreciation of both the similarity and difference created by the parodic text. An ironic reading of the incongruity created by the multiple signifieds generates a possible actualization of the parodic text and therefore becomes an essential element in any parodic encounter.

With its eye firmly placed on the irony of the postmodern, probably the closest transtextual cousin to parody is pastiche. By compiling and 'pasting together' preformed texts into a new text, pastiche obviously functions in a very similar manner to parody. On Popovic's intertextual scale, both parody and pastiche operate within a mode of 'selective continuity' where 'the metatext makes use of a selection of certain elements of the text, e.g. the rules of construction of the prototext, in a broader, modelling sense ...' (1976, p. 232). Much of this reformulation is motivated in both parody and pastiche by a willingness to juggle and play with preformed texts; possibly sharing the same *intentional* quality.

Hutcheon argues that 'both parody and pastiche not only are formal textual imitations but clearly involve the issue of intent. Both are acknowledged borrowings' (1985, p. 38). Yet pastiche seems to differ from parody in the tone or mood it produces through its imitative processes. Hutcheon maintains that while parody imitates a preformed text in order to transform and generate critical distance, pastiche imitates for the sake of mere imitation, creating more similarity than difference between the proto- and meta-texts.

One could argue, then, that the amount of critical distance created by a transformational activity might be measured by the manner in which a metatext assembles the prototextual material. The parodic process takes apart the prototextual unity and recreates a new text modelled after the prototext. Likewise, pastiche collects various, already-fragmented elements and recreates them into a new context, a metatext. As Ramona Curry aptly puts it, 'parody deconstructs, pastiche reconstructs' (1990, p. 29). Although this distinction does address both modes' core of operation, it must not be forgotten that while parody does deconstruct its target, it actively reconstructs the material into a new text. Or for that matter, one cannot ignore how pastiche deconstructs as it tears elements out of their original contexts and reinserts them into a new assemblage.

Because pastiche is said to pick and choose from a greater pool of sources – thus unsettling fewer unities as parody – it is often described as having less of a 'critical effect' than parody. Fredric Jameson has called pastiche 'blank parody, a statue with blind eyeballs' and is critical of how pastiche operates as postmodern play. He writes that 'pastiche is, like parody, the imitation of a peculiar mask, speech in a dead language; but it is a neutral practice of such mimicry, without any of parody's ulterior motives, amputated of satiric impulse, devoid of laughter…' (Jameson, 1984, p. 65). Thus, pastiche is argued to be less of a co-ordinated critique of the prototexts and more of an indiscriminate appropriation of elements which lacks depth and coherence. Pastiche is also seen as a practice which does not transform actual content signifiers but rather juxtaposes assorted elements within the same metatext. It will be demonstrated in subsequent chapters how pastiche often works within a parodic mode by creating incongruity through incorporating elements that are unrelated to the transformation of the prototexts, therefore engendering absurd connections between unrelated elements and aiding the creation of critical distance from the prototextual system.

Probably one of the most confusing (and debated) intertextual relationships is that between parody and satire. As an effective mode of critique in the arts, satire has often been collapsed and equated with the mode of parody. This has generated a great deal of confusion around parody's relation to satire and prompted such questions as: Is parody always a form of satire? Are all satires also parodies? What is a parodic satire?

In order to address these queries, let us first discuss the general qualities of satire which affect parodic discourse. Satire is typically linked to some form of critique that is often embodied in the artistic product. Shannon Antoine defines satire as 'criticism which is presented through indirect methods which are entertaining as well as enlightening' (1979, p. 3). Such criticism typically focuses on the inherent weaknesses found in the social order through exposing their constructedness and highlighting their contradictory nature.

While satire functions by way of critiquing social mores, it also seems to be driven by the wish to change (or correct) such social configurations and motivated by specific aims that are either persuasive or punitive in nature. While there does seem to be a destructive tendency in satire, there is also an 'implied idealism' in its effort to not only critique, but to improve. Not surprisingly, one of the main methods for generating such critiques is through irony. This is done by creating critical distance, which produces a recognition of such disparity and possibly even proposes how to 'fix' such problems. As we will see, such aims, although often present in many film parodies such as *Zelig* or *Germany Calling*, are not *essential* for parodic activity.

There has also been some confusion over the focus of critique utilized in both satire and parody. While satire has long been associated with a critique of larger, macro-level, social institutions, parody has been relegated to strictly 'artistic' or literary levels of critique. This is clearly evident in analyses such as those of Bertel Pedersen, when he argues that 'in satire the norms which are held up and shown in their limitations are extraliterary (religious, philosophical, moral, social, and so forth), whereas in parody the direction is intrinsic toward literary standards' (1972, p. 21). Thus, it is posited that parody questions only aesthetic norms which are somehow dissected from social norms in general. Hutcheon also makes this distinction, differentiating between satire's critique of 'extramural' norms (social/moral) and parody's 'intramural' norms of aesthetics (1985, p. 25). Such distinctions, of course, simply foster the illusion that 'intramural' aesthetic norms are somehow removed from the realm of social discourse. Artistic norms, like any set of norms, are social, enforced and regulated within the social order. Margaret Rose persuasively argues that

> in refunctioning the preformed language material of other texts and discourse parody not only creates allusions to another author, another reader, and another system of communication, but to the relationship between the text, or discourse, and its social context. Thus while parody may be distinguished from other forms of satire as a form dealing with the refunctioning, or criticism, of other preformed literary and linguistic material, such a definition need not imply that parody is therefore only concerned with literary norms. (1979, p. 44)

What is important here is the notion that the violation of *any* norm has social and political consequence.

As Dane correctly points out, 'when parody calls attention to the norm, it criticizes the very system on which its own plane of expression depends' (1980, p. 153). It can be said that normative disruption might somehow jar the spectator into questioning norms in general – taking a more critical stance toward 'every day' normative assumptions. Satiric discourse is a form of critique, and thus all parody (which always critiques) can be subsumed under a more general mode of satire. For example, *All You Need Is Cash* (1978) is a hilarious satire of the rise and fall of the Beatles as told through a stylistically-parodic 'mockumentary'. At times, the film turns to even more specific parody as it evokes particular films featuring the Beatles, including *Help!* (1965) which becomes *Ouch!* and *Yellow Submarine* (1968) which is transformed into *Yellow Submarine Sandwich*. Overall, the film, including its moments of targeted parody, is satiric as it takes a critical position toward the Beatles and the eccentricities of rock music in general.

As stated previously, at the base of parody's generation of similarity and difference is the prototext which serves as the parody's 'target'. Prototexts have syntactic, lexical and stylistic properties that have been conventionalized within a 'boundary'. Such boundaries can be referred to in a fairly inclusive manner as 'logonomic systems', defined by Hodge and Kress as 'rules prescribing semiotic production' (1988, p. 266). These textual systems operate based on rules of inclusion and exclusion in creating textual boundaries or paradigms and provide parodies with an excellent springboard for recontextualization.[6] Thus, logonomic systems become unsettled with parodic reappropriations and in turn engage new framing strategies based on parodic spectatorship.

There are various levels of logonomic systems in filmic discourse that parody utilizes as prototexts. On a macro level, parody often utilizes the conventions of modes of filmmaking practice to create its lampooning such as the 'documentary', 'cartoon', or even film movements which share particular traits (e.g. Italian Neorealism or American Direct Cinema). For example, a film parody such as *Zelig* evokes and critiques various documentary film forms. As David Denby describes the film, 'for its entire length, [*Zelig*] is a mock documentary, a brilliant, loving parody of the "serious" style of historical film investigation, complete with stock footage, archive stills, period music, newsreels, and interviews with savants...' (1983, p. 51).

Probably the logonomic system evoked most often in film parodies is that of genre. As logonomic systems, genres are composed of various shared elements such as setting, iconography, character types and story. And although films in a particular genre share many traits, they also reformulate these traits, creating variation from the shared core.[7] Some of the more celebrated film genres include the Western, musical, science fiction, horror, gangster, hard-boiled detective and the screwball comedy. Quite often, though, film parodies spoof more than one established genre at a time. For example, *UHF* (1989) parodies not only the science-fiction genre, but also the historical epic, horror, adventure and television game show throughout its narrative. *The Rocky Horror Picture Show* (1975) refers not only to its primary target genre, horror, as well as individual films with the genre (*King Kong* (1933) and the 1932 James Whale film, *The Old Dark House*), it also parodies other genres (musical, science fiction and detective) as well as other specific films (the 1951 sci-fi classic, *The Day the Earth Stood Still*).

Most genres can be differentiated even further into sub-genres that are more narrow in their constellation of shared elements. Margaret Byrne (1988) argues that sub-genres are often connected to narrative 'worlds' rather than just story formulae. In this manner, the Western can be further divided into such sub-genres as 'California gold rush', 'cavalry outpost', 'singing cowboy' and the 'spaghetti' Western. Thus, a Western parody such as *Rustler's Rhapsody* not only targets the more general Western genre but also specifically targets the 'singing cowboy' sub-genre.

Closely connected to the level of sub-genre is the film cycle which tends to be more temporally specific and tied to a specific period of production. Byrne defines a cycle as a group of films that are 'connected to topical themes, thus historically limited to a timeframe reflecting audience interest (usually two to seven years); a cycle may be charted through identification of themes or iconographic elements' (1988, p. 445). Examples of film cycles which have been parodied over the last twenty years include the disaster film (*The Big Bus* (1976) and *Airplane!*), the martial arts films (*They Call Me Bruce?* (1982)), and the 'blaxploitation' film (*I'm Gonna Git You, Sucka* (1989)).

Additionally, one might add another logonomic system loosely determined by the work of certain auteurs of the cinema, such as Alfred Hitchcock or Fredrico Fellini. These logonomic systems often overlap with other systems (for example, Hitchcock and suspense) and are comprised of idiosyncratic thematic and stylistic concerns. As mentioned before, a film like *High Anxiety* parodies many of the films directed by Hitchcock as well as the more general mode of the suspense film. One may even argue that single film texts (and specific scenes) constitute particular logonomic systems that are composed of certain arrangements of story elements, characters, setting and dialogue. For example, *Porklips Now* is almost exclusively focused on the Francis Ford Coppola epic, *Apocalypse Now* (1979).

What one usually finds when analysing film parodies is that they draw from a variety of logonomic systems, at once employing prototexts based on form, genre and single films. *Blazing Saddles* not only parodies the Western and musical genres as a whole, but also transforms scenes from specific canonical films that are constituent members of that genre, such as *High Noon* (1952). Again, the common feature of all logonomic systems is that they are constituted by a particular set of conventionalized signs.

Not only do film parodies rely on logonomic systems to create their central discourse, they typically must also choose target texts with which spectators are familiar. In other words, limited genres or unknown prototexts do not usually generate enough of an anchor from which the parody can deviate effectively. Akin to the Russian Formalists' notion that parodies must provoke both familiarity and defamiliarity, Caesar adds that parodies must also create a sense of attraction and repulsion in the spectator. This is difficult to achieve if the prototext itself is not vested with certain qualities that make the spectator care if the prototext is being transformed. He argues that 'the particular admixture of attraction and repulsion in parody breaks apart if the object is too banal to be attractive, or too naive to be repulsive' (Caesar, 1979, p. 211). A 'banal' prototext more likely leads to an unnoticed (or unidentified) target than would a decreased amount of attraction. In this manner, some critical distance needs to be generated from the prototext but not to the degree that the prototext becomes unidentifiable by the spectator.

With a target or prototext that has enough idiosyncratic qualities to exploit in its recontextualization (and therefore is distinctive enough to elicit a certain memory of it), parody is then able to generate its oscillation between similarity to and difference from that target. While a certain degree of closeness is necessary to anchor the spectator into identifying with the target text, parody must also produce enough difference to actually recontextualize the prototext (and thus avoid becoming just an exaggerated form of quotation). As J. G. Riewald warns in his 1966 article, 'in order to remain effective as parody, parody should not come too near its original. It should stop short of complete illusion' (1966, p. 127).

Although parodic discourse typically engages with its familiar target text in a somewhat affectionate manner, it also demonstrates a certain degree of disdain towards its target. With its connection to both the burlesque and travesty, it is not difficult to see parody's position as a critical mode of discourse that reformulates its target in order to expose its constructedness. Yet this critique is often focused more on the mocking of aesthetic norms in general rather than the texts themselves, therefore reasserting parody's role in postmodern discourse as a critique of representational systems.

Hutcheon has suggested that parody might be conceptualized as exhibiting an attitude situated between disdain and admiration – one which is 'a more neutral or playful one, close to a zero degree of aggressivity toward either backgrounded or foregrounded text' (1985, p. 60). Although parody may not demonstrate an over-aggressivity toward its prototexts, it is far from ever being neutral in its attitude. The mere *choice* of a target text constitutes an attitude. In line with its narrative functioning, parody may be characterized as producing admiration during its moments of similarity to and as creating critical distance as it generates difference. Overall, though, parody's attitude is a critical and satirical one grounded in its juxtapositioning of such moments. In the final analysis, I would conclude that such notions of intertextual 'attitude' may not be terribly relevant to analyses centred on how parody is used by contextually-placed spectators.

While examining how film parodies create this satiric oscillation between similarity and difference, it is necessary to look at the particular narrative functioning of parodic texts. As the site of textual structure, the syntactic plane therefore becomes an important factor in analysing how the narrative elements are arranged in a signifying chain. The syntax determines how the text progresses in terms of narrative movement by providing the rules for the combination and arrangements of narrative elements. In fact, Leland Poague argues that 'the rules of syntax provide the "anticipated sense of the whole"' by following patterns of construction based on established logonomic systems' (1978, p. 154). And one of the central features of this 'anticipated sense of the whole' is how the syntactic plane unfolds narratively along a diachronic trajectory. As we will see, this diachronic dimension is highly utilized in parodic texts by fulfilling or subverting viewer expectations that are propositioned knowing the conventional rules of the normative system. It is this movement between contiguity and change which propels the narrative. Thus, at the heart of any narrative text lies the process of transformation, the constant element of change needed for discursive activity. As John Ellis adds, 'filmic narration is an economic system: balancing familiar elements of meaning against the unfamiliar, it moves forward by a succession of events linked in a causal chain' (1982, p. 74).

Parody exploits this transformational basis by violating the grammatical rules that dictate that narrative construction. Recalling Hutcheon's definition of 'repetition with difference', parody functions in terms of oscillating between such processes as transformations and slides. As Hodge and Kress indicate, one may even argue that repetition *is* difference, with mere repetition necessarily operating on the distinction between similarity and difference. Film parody's repetition of textual elements from established prototextual systems decontextualizes them as well as alters their composition, thus generating multiple levels of ironic incongruity.

Previous writers have often privileged the structural dimension of the text as the primary site for parodic transformation – the core of parodic discourse. Bakhtin writes that

> it is the nature of every parody to transpose the values of the parodied style, to highlight certain elements while leaving others in the shade: parody is always biased in some direction, and this bias is dictated by the distinctive features of the parodying language, its accentual system, its structure – we feel its presence in the parody and we can recognize that presence.... (1981, p. 75)

Yet as we will see, while structure is indeed a very important aspect of parodic texts, its constituent lexical elements as well as its stylistic treatment, are equally involved in parodic transformation. Parody takes familiar structures, narrative elements and stylistics and recontextualizes them through certain operations of transformation and recollection, thus 'defamiliarizing' them. Although a film such as *Johnny Dangerously* (1984) clearly evokes the gangster genre, overall it seems to function more as a comedy than as a constituent of the genre since so much narrative effort is placed on delivering 'the joke'.

A constructive way to conceptualize how parody transcontextualizes logonomic systems is to analyse the functioning of genre rules and how they help guide and cue spectatorial processes. In this manner, genre rules provide the interactional web often necessary for a communicative act to occur. As an elemental factor in social semiotics, logonomic systems

> often operate by specifying genres of texts (typical forms of text which links kinds of producer, consumer, topic, medium, manner and occasion). These control the behaviour of producers of such texts, and the expectations of potential consumers. Genre-rules are exemplary instances of logonomic systems, and are a major vehicle for their operation and transmission. (Hodge and Kress, 1988, p. 7)

In fact, one could even argue that generic structure is a factor in all discourse (as a frame) and agree with Derrida that 'a text cannot belong to no genre, it cannot be without or less a genre' (1986, p. 65). Genre, then, becomes a generalized form of transtextuality.

Much of the current work in film and literary genre theory echoes this wider scope, emphasizing the issues of context, audience reception and rules of structure and grammar. Film genre theory itself is helpful in conceptualizing four central issues of film parody: the notion of a collective, standardized body of work; the 'contract' established between production options and spectatorial expectation; the 'enforcing' nature of ensuring the stability of norms; and the diachronic development of generic forms.

The fact that most parody films have targets that are popular genres should be of no surprise since both operate by way of 'contracts' between film-makers and viewers in terms of the control of possible meanings. Rick Altman argues that these genre elements arise not merely as detached, textual processes, but result from audience/producer interplay. He states that 'far from postulating a uniquely internal, formal progression, I would propose that the relationship between the semantic and the syntactic constitutes the very site of negotiation between Hollywood and its audience, and thus between ritual and ideological uses of genre' (Altman, 1986, p. 35).

In this manner, there is the constant interplay between generating and fulfilling spectatorial expectation while also modifying other expectations by postulating various derivations (typically still cemented in the generic core). Over time, these expectations settle into an identifiable paradigm for producers and viewers. Altman further argues that

> spectator response, I believe, is heavily conditioned by the choice of semantic elements and atmosphere, because a given semantics used in a specific cultural situation will recall to an actual interpretive community the particular syntax with which that semantics has traditionally been associated in other texts. (1986, p. 38)

Not only is there some form of 'contract' in use, but genre is also used to 'guide' the viewer's experience of the film. By engaging with particular canonized structures, the viewer is able to become 'genre literate' from previous exposure and in turn is able to generate meaning based on the satisfaction and up-ending of expectations. Recalling the importance of the interplay between both the lexical and syntactic plans of discourse as outlined by Altman, the repetition and transformation of narrative material propel and guide the viewing experience. As Thomas Schatz adds, the 'viewer's negotiation of a genre film thus involves weighing the film's variations against the genre's pre-ordained, value-laden narrative system' (1981, p. 10). By referring to a tradition of previous texts (logonomic systems) while simultaneously creating new variations, genre operates by contesting any singular contextual anchoring.

As somewhat fluid logonomic systems, genres are constantly in flux, always changing due to new additions and new expectations. Thomas Schatz states how a

> film genre is both a static and a dynamic system. On the one hand, it is a familiar formula of interrelated narrative and cinematic components that serves to continually reexamine some basic cultural conflict.... On the other hand, changes in cultural attitudes, new influential genre films, the economics of the industry, and so forth, continually refine any film genre. As such, its nature is continually evolving. (1981, p. 16)

As the genre develops, it is constantly in need of redefinition. Film parody typically emerges when the dynamic nature of the logonomic system begins to overtake the static dimension, with established conventions becoming exhausted.

All of these processes of generating similarity and difference work in a structured fashion to stabilize a normative patterning of aesthetic product and response. And it is exactly these structured processes that eventually lead to parody's predictability and normalization. In order to achieve this, film parody employs six primary methods along the lexical, syntactical and stylistic planes: reiteration, inversion, misdirection, literalization, extraneous inclusion and exaggeration. Utilizing these methods, film parody has created a formulaic means to generate its discourse in a standardized fashion.[8] In other words, the anti-canon has become quite canonical in the way that it both textually functions and is read.

Contrary to the focus most theorists have placed on the operation of parody, the first of the central methods employed is that of reiteration. In other words, elements are evoked or quoted from the prototexts to generate a connection to the target text as well as to aid in the creation of syntactic expectation. For example, *Frankenweenie* (1984) reiterates the classic 'animation of the monster' scene from *Frankenstein* complete with laboratory and lightening. This method is especially essential in setting up the other five methods by establishing a norm off of which to play.

The second important method which does rest on the process of transformation within parodic discourse is inversion. This method modifies either the lexicon, syntax or style by way of creating a signifier that connotes an opposite meaning from its previous usage. In her *A Theory of Parody*, Hutcheon provides an example of such an inversion from the film, *Carny* (1980), which she argues is a parody of the film, *Freaks*

(1932). Here, a central character is inverted from being a 'negative' character to a 'positive' character. Although many instances of parody are indeed predicated on a normative inversion, I argue that other, if not most, shifts of signification occur in degrees – oscillating between similarity and difference, but not in total congruence or contrast to the preceding signifier. Thus, many methods for creating incongruity have been previously left underdeveloped or completely ignored by other scholars.

One such method is that of the misdirection, which creates a degree of ironic incongruity through both reiteration and transformation of the target text. This occurs when specific elements are evoked, and initially played out in a manner similar to the target text, but then are transformed to deliver an unexpected turn in the eventual parodic presentation. A good example of this occurs in *Spy Hard* (1996) as Dick Stelle throws his hat toward the hat rack in a manner similar to that done numerous time by James Bond. Yet this action (and its associated expectations) are misdirected when the hat unexpectedly tips the rack into a glass bookcase rather than landing perfectly on the hook.

Literalization is the fourth method used by parody to create its oscillation between similarity and difference. This is often achieved by utilizing the pun (both verbal and visual) as well as self-reflexively pointing to the ways in which any film is a constructed cultural product. For example, in *Fatal Instinct* (1993), the *femme fatale* character, Lola, is constantly shadowed by a jazz saxophonist who continuously plays her signature theme music. The soundtrack score, therefore, is literalized into a diegetically-placed visual and aural element.

Not only does parody reiterate, invert, misdirect and literalize, it also transforms its target through the method of extraneous inclusion. This is often seen in terms of the inclusion of foreign lexical units into a specific, genre-based syntax (such as the appearance of a Santa Claus character in the 1977 film *The Last Remake of Beau Geste*), or the insertion of scenes along the narrative axis which is associated with neither the target's set of lexical units nor the general conventions of that logonomic system.

Exaggeration – a parodic method that has been recognized (although not systematically explained) by numerous scholars – is the last fundamental means for parodic disruption that I will be discussing. Syntactic, lexical and stylistic features of the prototext are targeted and extended far beyond their conventionalized, expected limits. Such disruptions are often created within film parodies through changing perspectives and other altered quantitative relations. For example, Dark Helmet's helmet in *Spaceballs* is well over three times the size of the already large helmet worn by Darth Vader in *Star Wars* (1977). Exaggeration is also achieved by an excessive repetition of filmic elements that goes beyond parody's general repetition and reiteration of established logonomic systems.[9]

As one can see, parody's functioning as a 'double-coder' and a form of postmodern transtextuality is a complex and often tedious process. As parodic texts reconfigure canonized logonomic systems, they generate a range of narrative patterns which constantly teeter between 'similarity to' and 'difference from' the target or prototext. This activity can be charted by examining the distance which is created between the prototext and the parodic metatext as well as the various means used to borrow textual elements as proposed by Genette's five types of transtextuality. Yet what clearly stands out from all of these systemic elements is the manner in which parody goes about its business in a fairly predictable and standardized way. As mentioned above, parody itself is becoming a canon of canons.

In Part Two, I will examine how parody operates textually in an increasingly standardized fashion by focusing on the methods of parodic coding: reiteration, inversion, misdirection, literalization, extraneous inclusion and exaggeration. Within each of these chapters, specific film parody examples will be assessed at the levels of the lexicon (e.g. sets, costumes, iconography, characters), syntax (e.g. narrative development, temporal progression of the plot) and style (e.g. visual technique, sound, titles) to explore the construction of the parodic and ironic metatext. Such a review will demonstrate how the consistent and predictable employment of these six parodic methods now provides a standard way to examine how parody constructs its metatext across different modes and genres. We will see how parody's development into canonicity is not evidenced by a shared lexicon, syntax or style. Rather, the means by which all parodies engage with these elements have become so systematic that the once revolutionary anti-canon has become regularized and formulaic.

Notes

1. See, for example, Charles Jencks (1989).
2. As Umberto Eco reminds us, 'no text is read independently of the reader's experience of other texts' (1979, p. 21).
3. Interestingly, writing nine years later, Hutcheon does place more emphasis on the juxtaposition of levels when she writes about how irony functions by the 'simultaneous perception of more than one meaning . . . in order to create a third composite (ironic) one' (1994, p. 60).
4. Thus, as with parody, 'the idea of quotation is linked irresistibly with, above all, a knowledge of sources' (Morawski, 1970, p. 690).
5. Not everyone agrees. John A. Yunck argues that 'irony is subdued, when it is present at all' in modern parody (1963, p. 30).
6. In this manner, 'parody capitalizes on the uniqueness of these styles and seizes on their idiosyncrasies and eccentricities to produce an imitation which mocks the original' (Jameson, 1983, p. 113).
7. As Paul Petlewski states, 'a Western must be like all other Westerns, only different' (1979, p. 19).
8. Margaret Rose (1993) lists a similar catalogue of parodic 'markers', yet neglects to look closely at how these markers affect each other across semantic and syntactic planes of discourse.
9. Stamos Metzidakis (1986) makes the useful distinction between inter- and intra-repetition which relates to parody. All parodic discourse is a form of inter-repetition by recalling past logonomic systems and evoking them through repetitions of similarity and difference whereas intra-repetition consists of repeating shots or scenes within the parody to create narrative disjunctures in the syntax.

PART TWO
Sketching Film Parody

4
Reiteration

As discussed in Chapter 1, theorists of parody have often placed a great deal of emphasis on the difference generated between the parody and its target text rather than the similarity. Since parody essentially functions as a process of oscillation between similarity to and difference from a target, it is very important to understand the means by which film parody evokes such similarity. One of the parodic methods to achieve this is through 'reiteration' – evocation or quotation of particular elements from the targeted text to both create an association between the prototext and the parody as well as to establish conventional narrative expectations. Relatedly, such associations serve as the foundations or norms from which the other methods of parodic discourse will play off of.

Lexicon

Since lexical elements such as setting, characters or costumes are essential for creating conventional filmic systems, they are particularly important for the parodic method of reiteration. The establishment of setting in any logonomic system often serves the crucial function of historically situating the narrative. This is especially important in specific genres (such as Westerns, science fiction and certain horror sub-genres) that are tied to historical periods. As a key lexical unit, setting is often reiterated intertextually in order to anchor the parody to its target texts. For example, in homage to Hitchcock's *Vertigo* (1958), the parody *High Anxiety* contains a particular scene shot at the base of the Golden Gate Bridge that echoes the exact location used in the classic film. In *Rustler's Rhapsody* (1985), one of the frontier sets utilized was originally built by Sergio Leone in Almeria, Spain almost twenty years prior for his own series of 'spaghetti Westerns'. A third example of anchoring reiteration occurs in *Young Frankenstein* (1974), with much of the scientist's laboratory equipment on the set (originally created by famed set designer, Ken Strickfaden) coming out of studio storage from the original *Frankenstein* film (see Figure 9). Together, these examples demonstrate the effort many parodies make in generating almost exact similarity to their targets by not only creating faithful reproductions of sets, but also utilizing the actual sets themselves.

Probably the most highly coded lexical item in any filmic text is its cast of characters. With their actions, the constellation of characters propels a narrative forward. One means for devising parodic characters that the spectator will find familiar is the reiteration of characters clearly recognizable from the target text. Two qualities that make such characters recognizable are their particularity and autonomy. Richard Dyer argues that characters generally must go beyond the mere serving as plot elements and become

Fig. 9: *Young Frankenstein* (Mel Brooks, 1974)

identifiable 'people' in the narrative. He writes that 'precisely because they are no longer representatives of ideals or ideas, they must not appear to be merely a part of the design of the text, whether that be a thematic structure or simply a plot' (Dyer, 1986, p. 105). Parody capitalizes on this notion of autonomy by reaffirming and deconstructing a character's existence within both the target and parodic texts.

As a type of reiteration, characters in parody films often exist as continuations of past characters, at times being a relative of previously presented characters. In *The Black Bird*, the lead character is Sam Spade, Jr – the son of earlier film noir figure Sam Spade. The Dr Frankenstein character in *Young Frankenstein* is narratively presented as the grandson of the famous Dr Frankenstein (as seen in many old horror films). In *Zorro, The Gay Blade* (1981), the lead character is not only the son of the famous Zorro, but also the twin brother of the apparent heir to the Zorro legend. Each of these examples exhibit the length some parodies will go to in order to narratively legitimize the main characters and to secure them as a point of reference in recalling past constructed characters.

Previous film characters are also directly targeted for spoofing in film parodies. One thing to keep in mind is that characters can be conceptualized as paradigms of traits that hold together various possibilities in creating autonomous characterhood. Parody exploits this paradigm by reiterating some of the traits to generate recognition and similarity while simultaneously altering and eliminating others to create difference. For example, in *Dead Men Don't Wear Plaid*, the character of the butler is a direct parody of director Erich von Stroheim's German butler in the 1950 film *Sunset Boulevard* (with the parody film's director, Carl Reiner, playing both a butler and a Nazi officer).

In order to examine this further, let us look at some of the stock characters generally found in the disaster film cycle. Maurice Yacowar argues that 'there is rarely a religious figure in the disaster film, because Faith would temper the dread, a sense of God's abiding support would nullify the suspense' (1986, p. 229). Yet one of the more memorable characters in the classic disaster film, The *Poseidon Adventure* (1972), is Gene Hackman's 'doubting' priest which allows for the 'lack of faith' component often needed for narrative suspense in disaster cycle films. Hackman's priest is parodied in *The Big Bus*, with a priest who is not only in doubt, but very rude about it. On the brink of death, one woman asks him for a prayer, to which he replies, 'No! If I pray for you, I'll have to pray for everyone!' Another religious figure often found in disaster films is the nun who seems to always be flying somewhere. In *Airplane!*, the presence of a nun character is highlighted by a scene depicting a nun casually reading a copy of the magazine, *Boy's Life* followed by a shot of a young boy reading *Nun's Life*. Often stock characters developed in one parody film are doubly parodied in another. Two of the passengers on the plane in *Airplane!* are Hare Krishna followers who satirize the presence of such persons in airports but otherwise serve no significant function in the advancement of the film's plot. Yet in *Airplane II: The Sequel* (1982), the two men reappear; this time as operators of 'Transcendental Airlines'. Other stock characters find recurring appearances in a number of parody films, such as the often seen 'lounge lizard' piano player, making appearances in *The Big Bus*, *High Anxiety*, and *Hot Shots!* (and all played by the same actor, Murphy Dunne).

The evocation of famous, particularized characters is also utilized for lexical reiteration through a process of condensation in which character roles are constructed out of a number of past characterizations as well as played by the same actor. In *The Cheap Detective* (1978), Dom Deluise's role as an informer combines past characters immortalized by Peter Lorre in *The Maltese Falcon* (1941) and *Casablanca* (1942). In *Blazing Saddles*, the character of Lilly von Schtupe singing 'I'm So Tired' is a dead-on parody of both Marlene Dietrich's Lola-Lola character in *The Blue Angel* (1930) and her saloon singing character in the Western, *Destry Rides Again* (1939).

A final example of reiterating similar character types for parodic purposes is evidenced in the documentary parodies *This Is Spinal Tap* and *Zelig*. Both employ the conventionalized technique of interviewing people who are either related to the film's subject or called upon as experts in their field. In *Zelig*, real contemporary cultural heroes (including Susan Sontag, Saul Bellow, Irving Howe and Bruno Bettelheim) are interviewed and offer their interpretations of the 'Zelig phenomenon'. As Robert Stam describes, 'the figures interviewed in *Zelig* vary substantially in their fictive status ... [as they] enact their own personae under their own names, making plausible comments reflecting what we know to be their real-life preoccupations' (1989, p. 203). Thus, as stock constituents of the documentary film mode, such interviewed characters function to create a source of similarity with the parodied form. The fact that they are famous people playing themselves also adds an element of similarity to the parody. The transformation occurs in the role they serve as commentators on a fictional person, thus disrupting the level of validity aimed at the character's credibility.

A related form of reiteration is the re-use of actor's themselves to reprise conventional roles they are well known for as well as to generate a sort of self-parody. This often produces a large amount of incongruity by an ironic teetering between the star's past roles and his or her current role. As Maurice Yacowar correctly points out, 'often the stars depend upon their familiarity from previous films, rather than developing a new characterization' (1986, p. 225). Such casting works to secure a familiarity with the target text. Often, the self-parody is directly from past work within the parodied logonomic system. For example, the casting of Leslie Nielsen in the *Naked Gun* films relies on parodying the many television roles Nielsen played in 1970s police action programmes such as *Cannon*, *S.W.A.T.*, *Hawaii Five-O* and *The Streets of San Francisco*. In *Top Secret!* (1984),

Omar Sharif, well known for his spy character portrayals, is cast as spy character Cedric. Two of the band member characters in *This Is Spinal Tap*, Viv Savage and Mick Shrimpton, are played by real-life rock band members David Kaff (Natural Gas) and R. J. Parnell (Atomic Rooster).

Probably one of the most unique examples of reiteration is the casting of Linda Blair to reprise her *Exorcist* role in *Repossessed*. Similarly, every time John Astin appears in a scene in *Silence of the Hams*, all of the other characters stop and snap their fingers to the 'Addams Family' theme music, paying homage to Astin's previous role as Gomez in the classic television programme. Additionally, Slim Pickens recreates many of his past roles in old Western films in *Blazing Saddles*. In *The Cheap Detective*, Charles Bastin repeats his role as 'Croupier Number Two' from *Casablanca*, while Douglas Wilmer (the British actor who played Sherlock Holmes on BBC-TV) plays Holmes in *The Adventures of Sherlock Holmes' Smarter Brother* (1975). Lastly, most of the characters in *I'm Gonna Git You, Sucka* had roles in previous 'blaxploitation' films.

Particular scenes can be constructed around a star's self-parody to generate reiteration. As Lone Starr and Barf sit in a space diner waiting to be served in *Spaceballs*, the camera scans the room to pick up a conversation between a group of space pilots. One of the pilots is identifiable as actor John Hurt, remembered for his role in *Alien* (1979) where a monster pops out of his stomach. In a quick 'hit and run' reference to the original, Hurt's new character begins to have stomach cramps and announces: 'Oh no, not again!' as another alien rips through his abdomen and dances across the counter. Such a characterization not only presents a form of cross-pollination between film texts (thus destabilizing textual boundaries), it also spoofs Hurt's own star persona, creating a sense that his *Alien* character will follow him throughout his acting career.

This same sort of self-parody occurs in *Naked Gun 33 1/3* as both characters and the actors who originally played them make cameo appearances that spoof roles that they have yet to shake. For example, one scene features Lt Frank Drebin undercover in a prison cell and penning a letter to his estranged wife. In the letter, Drebin reminisces how they always wanted to have the perfect housekeeper. The visuals then show them driving up to their house and waving to their trusty housekeeper – played by Ann B. Davis reprising her role as Alice (complete with dowdy blue uniform) from the popular television show, *The Brady Bunch*.

The casting of actors to reiterate representations made famous by one of their relatives serves to generate a sense of organic connection to the logonomic system, while remaining ironically distanced from the actual characterization. In *Movie, Movie* (1978), the 'Dynamite Hands' short (a parody of the 1954 classic, *On the Waterfront*) contains a character named Momma Popchick played by Jocelyn Brando. As Marlon Brando's sister, the casting of Jocelyn links the parody's narrative to its target by way of relational reference. This can also be seen in *Rustler's Rhapsody* with the casting of Patrick Wayne (son of John Wayne) as a cowboy.

While often employing characters that fit neatly within the target prototexts, parodies also use costumes and make-up to create connections to the target texts. For example, Edith Head, long known for her design of Hollywood costumes (especially during the 1940s), designed the costumes for the film noir parody *Dead Men Don't Wear Plaid* (ironically her last film). The costumes in *Rustler's Rhapsody* were created by

Wayne Finkelman to faithfully reproduce celebrated film costumes – including Dietrich's famous black satin net can-can costume in *Destry Rides Again* and Smiley Burnett's sidekick outfit from the early Roy Rogers film, *Under Western Stars* (1938). In *Love at First Bite* (1979), the Dracula character even laments over his 'typical' costume, stating 'How would *you* like to go around dressed like a head waiter for the last 700 years. Just once, I'd like to go to dinner dressed in a turtleneck and sports jacket.' Such employment of conventionalized costumes helps define characters by closely identifying them to their respective target texts.

Film theorists often contend that iconography serves a paramount function in determining the boundaries of genre since iconography 'involves the process of narrative and visual coding that results from the repetition of a popular film story' (Schatz, 1981, p. 22). Thus, certain items become generically charged through convention – cowboys have faithful horses, haunted houses have creaky doors. As with many of the other lexical elements, icons are reiterated in parody film to generate a connection to the target text as well as to aid in the creation of syntactic expectation. Thus, *Young Frankenstein* features such clichéd horror items as creaky doors and a revolving book case (although, through the method of inversion, this one is hard to operate). Documentary parodies use certain items to increase their perceived validity as capturers of reality, with *Zelig* featuring a wide array of 'Leonard Zelig-inspired' dolls, toys and watches, while *This Is Spinal Tap* features a photo montage of the band's 'previous' album covers.

Syntax

The incorporation of scenes based on similarity from the target texts creates what Hodge and Kress call 'slides' in the syntax – narrative progressions based on repeating stated scenarios. One of the means by which parody generates such slides is by reiterating scenes from specific target texts. Once a familiarity with the scene is registered (often by way of recognizing the constituent lexical units), the units are rearranged in order to create an incongruous effect based on how the scenes initially were played out. For example, in one of the pivotal scenes in the classic 1931 film, *Frankenstein*, the monster plays with the little girl and eventually throws her into the pond, drowning her. This scene is effectively echoed and parodied in two particular films. In *Transylvania 6-5000*, the lexical units of a monster and a little girl playing are repeated, yet their interaction is located not next to a pond, but rather in an intense game of poker in a smoke-filled room. The same scene is repeated in *Young Frankenstein* as the monster and the girl throw flower petals into a well. After the last flower has been thrown in, the little girl turns to the monster and says, 'All gone. What should we throw in now?' Playing off of the previously established scenario, the monster sheepishly looks directly into the camera and flashes a 'knowing' smile.

Another evocation of a classic *Frankenstein* scene occurs in *Frankenweenie* as Viktor attempts to 're-animate' his dead dog, Sparky. Reiterating the scenario with a suburban twist, Viktor sets up a laboratory in his bedroom using various household objects, including an electric blender, toaster, bicycle and trash can lid. As the lightening lights up the sky, the dog is raised through a hole in the roof where an electrical current animates his body. Although the various lexical items have been altered in this scene, the basic structure of the syntax from the original is left intact.

Parody also reiterates narrative situations and extends them to logically absurd conclusions. Maurice Yacowar notes that 'the disaster film is predicated upon the idea of isolation. No help can be expected from the outside' (1986, p. 226). Thus, planes are airborne, boats are underwater, and large, burning buildings are high above the ground. A parody such as *The Big Bus* plays off of this narrative situation by making the bus literally 'non-stop' – unable to stop after a bomb blows up the rear – and isolating the victimized passengers in an absurd fashion. Oddly, *The Big Bus* came out nearly twenty years *before* another popular film with a very similar narrative scenario, *Speed* (1994). Another narrative situation carried out to its logical absurdity is based on a central motif found in the Western – the famous ride into the sunset at the end of the film. This situation is evoked, yet given a logically modern twist, in *Blazing Saddles*, when the heroes jump off of their horses and into a waiting limousine that whisks them away into the sunset.

Parody also reiterates material that can be decontextually quoted in order to create ironic juxtapositions. Thus, a parody such as *Dead Men Don't Wear Plaid* functions primarily by way of the juxtaposition created between the literal incorporation of old film noir clips and the newly staged footage which comments on the quoted material. A particular cinematic method exploited in this film to achieve this is the shot-reverse-shot editing convention of classical Hollywood cinema which can then create a conversation between characters in the quoted shot and those in the new material. For example, the Steve Martin character, Rigby, picks up the phone and places a call, saying 'Hello, Marlowe?' to the respondent. This is followed by a quoted shot of Humphrey Bogart (from the 1946 classic, *The Big Sleep*) picking up the phone and replying, 'Oh, hello, Bernie?' In a narrative move that not only parodies the ease in which one could manipulate the creation of new material to correctly respond to the borrowed material, but also film noir in general, the Steve Martin character responds, 'No, it's me, Rigby!' (see Figures 10 and 11).

Often, quoted material is worked directly into the parody through some form of narrative motivation. In *The Last Remake of Beau Geste*, Digby enters a 'mirage zone' and begins to hallucinate on the desert sands. He then sees the opening credits of the 1939

Fig. 10: *Dead Men Don't Wear Plaid* (Carl Reiner, 1982)

Fig. 11: Scene from *The Big Sleep* (Howard Hawks, 1946) in *Dead Men Don't Wear Plaid*

Beau Geste and carries on a conversation with Gary Cooper's original character over a table, again using the shot-reverse-shot style to link their discussion. Much of the humour here is derived from Digby posing questions to the original Beau in which his previously established dialogue answers in correspondence to the questions. A similar example occurs in the 'Video Pirates' sequence in *Amazon Women on the Moon* (1987) which juxtaposes previous footage from an old, pirate-themed B-movie with similarly-shot footage to create a seamless narrative bridged by newly dubbed dialogue. Thus, syntactically, the narrative generates a level of incongruency through the recognition of both the borrowed, previously established texts and the newly created texts which match (or overtly mismatch) the quoted material.

Through trickery of optics, parodic juxtapositions can be created within quoted material by way of superimposing newly staged material into borrowed material. In one particular scene from *Zelig*, a borrowed segment of Adolf Hitler making a speech includes the figure of Leonard Zelig lurking in the background. A sense of incongruity emerges from the recognition of the original footage, the identification of Woody Allen playing a character, and the historically impossible juxtaposition that results. As Robert Stam mentions, *Zelig* has a sort of ' "freedom from historical limits" (the film's unlikely neighboring of a contemporary actor with long-deceased public figures) ...' (1989, p. 198). Thus, juxtaposition of old and new material created through editing and superimposition provides parodic discourse another avenue for syntactically altering the expected, non-problematized response one might have based on the target logonomic system.

Additionally, similar scenarios from a logonomic system can be utilized in an exaggerated form to create a sort of 'familiar overload'. As a parody of the disaster cycle, *The Big Bus* features elements from virtually *every* disaster that has been filmed including earthquakes, bombs, fire, floods (of soda pop) and small planes flying into jets (transformed here into an old Chevy pick-up ramming into the side of the bus). Similarly, *High Anxiety* is constructed as a compilation of famous scenes from a number of Hitchcock films. In a particular scene that both evokes and parodies *The Birds* (1963), Dr Thorndyke is followed by a massive number of birds who prefer to 'drop' on him rather than peck. The lexical units are repeated, but their actions within the narrative are transformed. Re-enacting the famous shower scene from *Psycho* (1960), *High Anxiety* contains a scene featuring Thorndyke taking a shower in his hotel room. The parody moves into a stylized close-up of the nozzle and then cuts to various parts of his body. A shadow then begins to appear beyond the shower and suddenly, the bell-boy appears and 'stabs' Thorndyke with his requested newspaper. This scene is additionally accompanied by a high-pitched, shrieking voice mimicking the original's Bernard Herrmann score. Startled, Thorndyke falls in the tub, pulling the shower curtain down with him. The camera then focuses on the newspaper ink as it goes down the drain. The scene ends humorously with Thorndyke declaring, 'That kid gets no tip!' As this example clearly demonstrates, the narrative syntax and action can be repeated, yet with their lexical units quite altered.

Style

Bakhtin posits that parodic texts can transform a target's text style in a fashion that captures the spirit of the original. He writes that 'the other's style can be parodied in various directions and may have new accents introduced into it, but it can be stylized essentially only in one direction – in the direction of its own particular task' (Bakhtin, 1984, p. 193). Again, he reaffirms the importance of retaining some similarity in order to generate difference. Anton Popovic adds that the mere replication of a target text's style connotes some level of critical evaluation – a level more closely determined by the degrees of transformation that take place. He writes that 'the stylistic aspect of the metatext is at the same time an axiological aspect, since it embodies evaluation of the prototext, as well as of its means of expression' (Popovic, 1976, p. 229). By centring their analyses on narrative content and structure, previous writings on parody have not focused on stylistic reiteration and, therefore, have neglected a major element of the parodic process.

From the early days of cinema, titles have been used to present written information to the audience through either superimposed titles or inter-title cards. Some films often begin with a dedication that thanks some great influence on the making of the film. Due to parody's intertextual nature, dedications seem prime for spoofing. Two particular films reiterate the use of dedications so as to immediately clue the audience in on the source of the parodies. *High Anxiety* begins with a title reading, 'This film is dedicated to the Master of Suspense Alfred Hitchcock,' while *Zorro, the Gay Blade* presents a dedication to Rouben Mamoulian, the director of the classic 1940 film, *The Mark of Zorro*.

Opening titles are also used to evoke the narrative tradition of the film or to present some narrative context in order to situate one's viewing. This often includes the reiteration of previous narrative elements or the historical placement of the narrative context. *The Big Bus* utilizes such titles in evoking its narrative tradition (the 1970s cycle of disaster films) as well as signalling its parodic approach with the title reading:

> There Have Been Movies About Big Earthquakes . . . There Have Been Movies About Big Boats Sinking . . . Movies About Big Buildings Burning . . . Movies About Big German Balloons Bursting. And Now A Movie About . . . The Big Bus!

This title effectively evokes past films from the disaster cycle (*Earthquake* (1974), *The Poseidon Adventure*, *The Towering Inferno* and *The Hindenburg* (1974) respectively) and signals the comparatively absurd magnitude of the film's subject – a nuclear-powered, transcontinental bus. The use of ellipses in the text of the title also contributes to the anticipation of the next disaster topic and the eventual drop in magnitude with the words, 'big bus'.

Another use of titles, often seen in documentaries, is the initial thanking of filmed participants for their co-operation during the production. In the same vein as creating a 'legitimate' logo which connotes an appearance of extra-cinematic existence (*This Is Spinal Tap*), such titles are used to evoke a sense of 'realness' to the film. The documentary parody, *Zelig*, begins with a title thanking the film's primary subjects (characters) for their involvement with the project: 'The following documentary would like to give special thanks to Dr Eudora Fletcher, Paul Deghuee and Mrs Meryl Fletcher Varney.' Not only does the film announce its parodic target by stating its status as one (a documentary), it also refers to the fictitious characters as if they possessed an extra-cinematic existence. Both *This Is Spinal Tap* and *Bob Roberts* (1992) begin with similar titles in the opening credits. The former film announces that the director of the 'rocumentary' is Marty De Bregi (a clever reference to director Martin Scorsese); *Bob Roberts* states that the film is 'A Documentary by Terry Manchester'. These titles function parodically by explicitly referring to their prototextual targets and alluding to their inclusion within the logonomic systems parodied.

Along with titles being used for crediting actors, they are also used in identifying film subjects through the use of informational subtitles. This is typically seen in documentaries when identifying an 'expert' or witness and their credentials or affiliations. *This Is Spinal Tap* and *Zelig* utilize subtitles to identify their subjects, yet in different ways. In *This Is Spinal Tap*, the subjects are fictitious, yet given 'convincing' names and titles, such as 'Sir Denis Eaton Hogg, President of Polymer Records'. In *Zelig*, the subtitles reinforce the validity of the subjects, reinforcing their actual extra-textual existence. Thus, when the interviewed subject is Susan Sontag, the subtitle reads 'Susan Sontag' (see Figure 12). The film's discourse teeters between fictional construction and documentary validity by identifying subjects who have an extra-textual existence but are actively discussing fictional subjects without a blink. Similarity (titles identifying known personalities) brushes against difference (fictional discourse) with ironic incongruity as the result.

Fig. 12: *Zelig* (Woody Allen, 1983)

Creating film title graphics which reiterate particular styles are often employed for transtextual referencing. Falling under Genette's category of architextuality, some parody films closely replicate the style of title presentation, such as the horror spoofs *Haunted Honeymoon* (1986) and *Young Frankenstein* with their overtly 'gothic' lettering. In *The Black Bird*, the letters 'drip' in the same manner as the letters do in the targeted text (*The Maltese Falcon*), while the film *Hot Shots!* begins with a title logo that closely resembles the red, white and blue military patch-looking logo of *Top Gun*. As a parody of Warner Bros. programmers of the 1930s, in its credits the film *Movie, Movie* (1978) replicates the older convention of referring to its actors as 'Players'. *Dead Men Don't Wear Plaid* utilizes the convention of introducing each actor over a shot of one of their scenes. What makes this example especially interesting is that the credits also include the actors from the various old film clips used in creating narrative juxtapositions with the newly shot material. Thus, not only is Steve Martin billed, but so is Fred MacMurray for his role in *Double Indemnity* (1944). As these examples demonstrate, the near replication of title graphics functions to immediately engage the spectator into the genre or target film and to create a source of similarity to the prototexts with very little effort to deconstruct its target.

The soundtrack is often used in the creation of parodic counter-points to juxtapose visual and aural elements in order to generate textual similarity. As its name implies, *Silent Movie* uses the soundtrack in the silent movie tradition by having musical accompaniment and no spoken dialogue. This creates a sort of meta-commentary by utilizing fifty-year-old sound techniques in a contemporary film.

One of the more stylistic aspects of the soundtrack, of course, is the use of music in film. In garnering enough similarity to anchor spectators into a specific logonomic system, parody films often use music that reiterates the target texts. *Blazing Saddles* opens with a typical Western genre song crooned by Frankie Laine, the original singer of a similar theme song in the classic Western film, *Gunfight at the O.K. Corral* (1957). The use of the same singer to sing an alike song evokes a clear connection to the Western and, specifically, to the *Gunfight* film. One of the scores which has been often repeated is the music from *Airport*. The 1970s, brassy, suspenseful music is heard throughout *The Big Bus* and *Airplane II: The Sequel*. Its use in *Airplane!* is described by Vincent Canby as 'pricelessly awful' (1980, p. D-15).

The actual quality of sound is sometimes reiterated by parodies in order to generate a sense of realness to their discourse, especially seen in documentary parodies. For example, *Zelig* is a film constructed as a historical compilation documentary by using a great deal of fictional 'archival' footage from the early 1920s. In order to replicate the historical authenticity of such recordings, the audio is modified to 'sound' old. Thus, a record playing a song about 'Zelig the Chameleon' is scratchy and hollow sounding, while radio transmissions are full of interference. In its evocation of the filming style of Direct Cinema, *This Is Spinal Tap* has a soundtrack full of over-lapping dialogue and hand-held microphone mishaps. All of these manipulations of sound quality function to ensure the identification of the target logonomic system – in this case, two types of documentary film mode.

In order to evoke the specific 'look' of parodied logonomic systems, parody films utilize a wide variety of visual techniques in order to generate similarity to the prototext.

Because many of the target texts are older films from Hollywood's classical period of production, the choice of whether to use colour or black-and-white film stock becomes an effective way for the parodies to reiterate their targeted texts. As a spoof of 1950 spectacle films, *The Last Remake of Beau Geste* is filmed using the dated Technicolor process, producing the rich oranges and pale blues often seen in faded Technicolor films. In creating a look that closely resembles past gothic horror films, *Young Frankenstein* is shot in black and white to create the murky grey images often associated with such films. This form of style mimicking even leads Charles Eidsvik to declare that *Young Frankenstein* 'looks more like a horror film than most horror films do …' (1978, p. 72). Other examples of parodies using black-and-white film to connote their older targets include *Dead Men Don't Wear Plaid, Frankenweenie*, and the 'Dynamite Hands' segment in *Movie, Movie*.

A number of films mix types of film stock to carefully mimic their prototexts, including *Amazon Women on the Moon* and *Medusa: Dare to be Truthful* (1992). In *Who Framed Roger Rabbit* (1988), the classic 1930s cartoon character, Betty Boop, is presented in black and white even though all of the other characters are in colour. In generating a film which looks like a contemporary historical compilation documentary, *Zelig* mixes black-and-white 'historical' footage with current-day interviews filmed in colour.

Image quality is another means for replicating the look of the targeted texts. *Zelig*'s filmic quality is often scratchy and grainy, therefore producing an old newsreel look to it (echoing the famous 'Xanadu' newsreel in *Citizen Kane*). At times, one is left guessing as to the source of the film footage: Is it newly shot material that 'looks' old, or is it an old clip culled from some film archive? This parodic destabilizing is not merely achieved from the 'success' of historical replication of technology (taking black-and-white film and stomping on it in a lab easily creates the 'scratchy effect') but arises from its juxtaposition to the clean, colour filming of the contemporary subjects.

Another example of stylistic appropriation occurs in *This Is Spinal Tap*, which replicates two central types of quality in its presentation. In one scene, the group is seen performing on television during the mid-1960s, captured with the quality of a kinescope recording of the live transmission – complete with a stretched horizontal plane and vertical transmission lines. Most of the film, though, has the 16mm grainy quality often found in Direct Cinema. In order to get this look, *This Is Spinal Tap* was originally shot on 16mm and then blown up to 35mm giving it an even greater exaggerated amount of graininess. Additionally, the replication of filmic frame size also works to secure a specific look. Both *The Big Bus* and *The Last Remake of Beau Geste* were filmed in scope in order to capture the essence of their epic-oriented prototexts. On the other end, *Young Frankenstein* was shot in 1: 85 frame size in order to emulate the film frame size of the 1930s.

A variety of film techniques can be utilized in reiterating particular film styles and eras. For example, specific camera angles can often be parodied if they have an idiosyncrasy that makes their source identifiable. The 'Baxter's Beauties of 1933' segment in *Movie, Movie* parodies the back-stage musical by reiterating an over-head camera shot of dancers forming an immense roulette wheel, therefore looking very similar to any one of Busby Berkeley's trademark over-head shots. Similarly, lens focusing can also be reiterated in order to create a certain stylistic look. In *This Is Spinal Tap*, the Direct Cinema look is created by constant moments of rack-focusing – the on-screen adjustment of focus. Many films also utilize filmic grammar devices that are closely associated with a specific genre or period of film-making. Films such as *Movie, Movie* and *Young Frankenstein* utilize a wide array of outdated devices from the 1930s including superimpositions, horizontal and vertical wipes, heart-shaped irises, and quick reaction shots to make a parodic connection to their prototexts. Similarly, *This Is Spinal Tap* mimics the technical codes associated with Direct Cinema and other forms of cinéma vérité documentary film-making – i.e. the 'mishaps' associated with being 'at the moment of the happening' – by employing an array of whip pans, shaky hand-held camera movements and uneven lighting to create the look of a 'camera in the field'.

As we have seen outlined above, it is essential to analyse the various means by which film parodies evoke their targeted texts through reiteration. Such anchoring is needed in order to ensure an established norm to play off of as well as to cue the viewer into a particular conventional viewing pattern. Let us next turn to the second parodic method of 'inversion' and investigate the ways in which it takes these established norms and turns them up-side-down.

5
Inversion

In her essay on parody and the work of Bakhtin, Linda Hutcheon argues that 'ironic inversion is a characteristic of all parody ...' (1989a, p. 88). While this parodic method functions closely with the other five methods discussed in this book, it is, indeed, a major means for up-ending established norms. Inversion is utilized as a parodic method to modify either the lexicon, syntax or style by way of creating a signifier which ironically suggests an opposite meaning from its employment in the target text.

Lexicon

A film's setting serves as a perfect target for inversion since parody can exploit and transform the often thematic dependence a film's narrative might have on its setting and historical period. Thus, horror spoofs such as *Young Frankenstein*, *Love at First Bite*, *The Rocky Horror Picture Show* and *Transylvania 6-5000* dislocate their historical setting out of the late nineteenth century and into a contemporary setting. This also provides ample opportunities to create parodic juxtapositions by bringing together elements from a variety of historical periods. For example, in line with the contemporary setting of *Transylvania 6-5000*, the traditional Gothic castle sports an 'Opening Soon' banner as well as a plaque next to the door reminding visitors that the American Express card is always welcomed there. *Love at First Bite* inverts the conventional use of mist and fog hovering around the castle as seen in hundreds of old horror films by having an impenetrable amount of fog *inside* the castle.

The traditional use of projected back-drops to create the illusion of an exotic or specific setting provides another element of setting for parodies to manipulate in a meta-textual manner by misdirecting the spectator to its artifice while creating a meta-critique of Hollywood film-making conventions. In a scene from *Airplane!*, Rex Kramer drives to the airport to guide the jet's landing. As his car moves along the highway, the projected background of the passing road (as seen through the rear window) is poorly focused and faded – overtly announcing its status as a projected back-drop and appearing as well-worn stock film footage. This is emphasized even further when the back-drop suddenly changes from a roadway to a pursuing band of Indians on a chase (footage probably used in hundreds of Republic Westerns). The syntaxes remain stable in these examples (the drive to the airport by an expert pilot and the emergency landing of a jet, as well as the classic chase scene found in the Western), while the lexical unit of setting is transformed by the addition of extraneous sets.

Similar to the parodic method of reiteration, a film's characters can be evoked, yet with a few of their traits inverted from typical genre conventions. For example, the 'arrival' of a new sheriff is a common narrative motif often found in classical Westerns. *Blazing Saddles* retains this syntax (the arrival) and lexical unit (the sheriff character), but inverts some of the traits of the sheriff character, primarily by casting an African-American actor for the role. In order to construct further contrasts, the sheriff speaks in a dialect that departs from the few past representations of African-Americans in Western films. Yet, his characterization 'reminds' the viewer of past stereotypes by reverting to a 'servant' persona in order to escape the irate white citizens. Thus, the narrative shifts from a lexical alteration, in which part of the character's traits are changed, to a syntactic alteration, in which the character reverts to past, stereotypical behaviour and dialect. Another example is the transformation through inversion of monsters in science-fiction spoofs. Aliens become clowns in *Killer Klowns from Outer Space* (1988), while invading monsters are depicted as crazed tomatoes in *Attack of the Killer Tomatoes!* (1979).

In a similar fashion, the self-reflexive use of stunt doubles and extras functions to deconstruct and invert conceptions about the consistency and constellation of particular character types. A particularly funny example of stunt exposure occurs in *I'm Gonna Git You, Sucka*, as Ma Bell begins to fight two thugs in a diner. As she punches and roughs up the men, it becomes evident that Ma Bell is now being played by a stuntman, wearing the same dress, but also donning a poor fitting wig and a black mustache. Although there is no acknowledgment of this obvious use of trickery by the characters themselves, the switch is easily noticed. In another example, the switching of stunt doubles is even worked directly into the narrative of *Spaceballs*. As the main characters perform some daredevil manoeuvres in eluding the evil troopers, the fact that stunt doubles are doing the work becomes obvious due to their lack of *any* physical similarity to the central actors, again with a mustached man standing in for the female character, Princess Vespa. When the commanding officer notices that these characters are not the real ones, he admonishes his soldiers for 'only capturing their stunt doubles'! Extras are even referred to diegetically by characters within films which invert, yet reaffirm their supposed anonymity. For example, in *Hot Shots! Part Deux* (1993), Topper Harley asks the colonel: 'Who are those two people?' to which he replies: 'She's CIA, he's an extra.'

Character lexical units can also be inverted by violating conventional wisdom governing the use of stars in certain roles. Dyer suggests that the mere presence of a star in a film often supersedes any attempt to slot that character into a 'type' role. He writes that

> no star could be just a type, since all stars play central characters. (It may even be a rule that where the central character in a film is constructed by all other means as just a type, then the 'individuality' of the star masks this just as it does her/his image's typicality.) (Dyer, 1986, p. 117)

Parody uses this general conception and inverts it by placing stars in stock character roles, yet relying on the audience's recognition of the 'inappropriateness' of such placement.

The recognition of stars in typed roles functions to disrupt the lexical positioning of stock characters as backgrounded and non-attentive. A particularly clever example of such casting is in *Airplane!* with Ethel Merman playing a shell-shocked soldier who thinks he is, well, 'Ethel Merman'. In *The Big Bus*, the disaster cycle stock character of an old lady (made famous by Helen Hayes' Oscar-winning portrayal in *Airport*) is played by Ruth Gordon who fashions her representation more on her own past characterizations than on Hayes' character – thus capitalizing on the confusion many film viewers have in differentiating the two actresses. Joan Rivers lends her recognizable voice to the robot, Dot Matrix, in *Spaceballs*, and even reaffirms her role by using such trademark lines as 'Can we talk?'

Inverted casting in parody films is further bolstered by the inclusion of non-acting 'stars' in character roles. Quite often, the casting is so subtle that recognition of the 'star' is by an elite few. For example, the character of Arthur Brisbane in *High Anxiety* is played by Albert Whitlock – special effects wizard whose career started in England working on early Hitchcock films. Possibly a bit more noticeable is the casting of Isaac Hayes (who sang the title song in the 1971 *Shaft*) as the character, Hammer, in *I'm Gonna Git You, Sucka*. In *Airplane!*, many non-actors make cameo appearances in roles that directly satirize their own professions while also producing lexical incongruity by their mere presence as a character. Maureen McGovern (who sang the Oscar-winning tune in the 1974 disaster pic, *The Towering Inferno*), plays a guitar-swinging nun with a poor voice; California tax reformer Howard Jarvick, long known for his criticism of governmental waste, plays a character who is left stranded in a driverless taxi with a running meter; and basketball great Kareem Abdul-Jabbar plays pilot Roger Murdoch whose status as a pilot is questioned by a young boy – informing Murdoch that he is actually Kareem and that his Dad thinks he doesn't hustle enough down the court 'unless it's the play-offs!' (see Figure 13). In a Brechtian manner, Jabbar steps out of his Murdoch character and grabs the boy by the collar, stating: 'You tell your Dad to try dragging Walton up and down the court.' Later in the film, after Murdoch has passed out and is being dragged to the rear of the plane, we see him donning a Los Angeles Laker basketball uniform and signature playing goggles. These self-reflexive markings of Kareem's uneasy placement as a character actor in a film works to problematize the casting of any recognizable non-actor in such a film role.

Counter-casting is another method for using characters to destabilize the lexical configuration of a logonomic system; instances where the casting of an actor makes the character *exceed* standardized narrative expectation. For example, the inverted casting

Fig. 13: *Airplane!*

of an all-kid cast for gangster spoof, *Bugsy Malone*, creates an interesting juxtaposition to the typically adult-oriented themes of the gangster genre. The counter-casting of Andy Griffith as the evil colonel in *Rustler's Rhapsody* completely undercuts Griffith's past established persona as the tame, likeable Mayberry sheriff of TV's *The Andy Griffith Show*. And just in case one possibly forgets Griffith's connection to past 'likable roles', the colonel uses clichéd folksy quips such as 'Gee whiz!' to remind the spectator. A similar example of counter-casting is the 'jive-speaking' airline passenger in *Airplane!* played by Barbara Billingsly – better known for her portrayal of Mrs Cleaver on the classic, 1950s television programme, *Leave it to Beaver*, than as a woman fluent in urban English. Gender counter-casting can also disrupt expected lexical patternings. In both *Haunted Honeymoon* and *Lust in the Dust* (1984), the characters of Aunt Kate and Rosie are played by male actors, Dom Deluise and Divine, respectively. Such casting highlights the fictional construction of character in the cinema and functions to create a sense of irony with a man playing a woman character. The character may look like a woman, but the spectator's knowledge that a male actor is playing the part generates an iconic/symbolic split within a single signifier. Probably one of the more unusual parodic casting choices was that of Ray Charles as the bus driver in a scene from *Spy Hard* which spoofs the runaway bus in *Speed* (1994). As the bus gathers speed and begins its wild run, the Ray Charles character barks out: 'Sunset Blvd . . . I *guess* it's Sunset Blvd,' and reinscribes the fact that both the character and the actor are blind.

Through the method of inversion, parodic dialogue can be created by inverting the syntactic time period and the lines delivered to generate a heightened level of historical disjuncture. For example, long before the valorization of 'politically-correct' language, Rex O'Herlihan in *Rustler's Rhapsody* defends his pressed outfit, declaring that 'How one dresses is *his or her* own business.' Such language use would never be found in the targeted logonomic system of the 'singing cowboy' Western. In *Blazing Saddles*, the Indian chief does not speak in a stereotypical Native American dialect, but rather speaks in Yiddish. Another play on expected Indian dialogue occurs in *Hot Shots!* as the phoney Indian language is composed primarily of decontextualized Indian words and other 'Indian sounding' words, such as 'Winnebago', 'LaToya', 'Tito' and 'Jermaine' (the last three being names from the singing Jackson family).

Dialogue also generates irony through inversion by directly referencing the narrative process itself. In the first scene of *Haunted Honeymoon*, a woman opens up a window of the castle and immediately slumps forward – exposing the knife that has been placed in her back. As the wind picks up, the wig blows off of the character's head and reveals the actor to be a man. In a husky male voice, the man directly addresses the camera, stating 'It's not what you think. . . . Well, it's partly what you think, oh, it's so complicated.' Thus, the dialogue and representation self-reflexively disrupt the cinematic illusion of character, make-up and the narrative enigmatic quality of horror-suspense films.

As important constituent elements of any logonomic system, icons can be inverted not only to take on new narrative meanings, but also to trouble the conventionalized status of the icon in its original form. A clever example of this occurs in *Repossessed* as Nancy prepares dinner. Playing off of the infamous scene in *The Exorcist* where Regan vomits a substance resembling split pea soup, Nancy announces that they are indeed having split pea soup for dinner. Thus, this usage not only parodies the possible use of split pea soup as a prop in the original film, it also translocates the icon into a new context within the narrative by serving now as food intake rather than purged food.

Gothic films, for their part, often feature the common icon of long taper candles used to guide characters through the dark castle's corridors. Yet, these candles take on a different meaning in *Young Frankenstein* when they are used for navigational purposes, but oddly, are left unlit. As a partial parody of *Casablanca*, *The Cheap Detective*'s narrative revolves around the securing of papers, yet this time it is not visa documents but rather ownership papers for a new restaurant (often as difficult to obtain as a visa!). In *Fatal Instinct*, the often seen detective genre icon of the slowly-turning ceiling fan is found not only in the place where we would expect it to be – Ned Ravine's detective agency office – but also on the ceiling of his car. Further examples include Zorro's famous 'Z' slashing sword becoming an equally effective 'Z' slashing whip in *Zorro, The Gay Blade*, and the peace pipe featured in *Dances With Wolves* (1990) becoming a pipe for inhaling coloured helium balloons in *Hot Shots!*. Lastly, the ever-so-important light sabres used in the *Star Wars* trilogy become mere flashlights in *Hardware Wars*. All of these examples illustrate that the basic form of the icons can be repeated (the light sabre in *Star Wars* does indeed look like a flashlight), but that certain details about them can be altered, or inverted, to create an incongruity of meaning attached to them.

Another common icon ripe for inversion is the much-trusted radar found in many space and flying adventure films. This is parodied in a number of films by transforming the radar into a variety of other mechanisms. In *Hot Shots!*, the radar becomes a 'Super Mario Nintendo' screen; in *Airplane!* it literally becomes a 'radar range' for cooking; and in *Spaceballs*, Dark Helmet mistakes the radar screen for a 'Mr Coffee' machine. He is then informed that the radar is located next to the coffee machine and is appropriately called, 'Mr Radar'.

Beyond one shot disruptions, inversion also generates difference by introducing, in a consistent manner, transformed icons into fairly stable syntaxes. *Killer Klowns from Outer Space* transforms the majority of its 1950s science-fiction icons into circus icons – the 'pods' from *The Invasion of the Body Snatchers* (1956) become cotton candy pods; the space ship from *War of the Worlds* (1953) becomes a huge circus tent; martian laser guns shoot popcorn instead of dangerous alpha rays; and alien beings become grotesque clowns. Due to its casting of an all-kid cast, the characters in *Bugsy Malone* shoot gangster-type machine guns which shoot whipped cream rather than bullets. In *Closet Cases of the Nerd Kind*, children's toys appear: flying saucers are depicted by flying Frisbees and binoculars are replaced by Viewmasters, complete with faded travelogue photos of Greek ruins. The various space vehicles in *Hardware Wars* become appropriately common household appliances: irons, toasters and blenders (see Figure 14). In *Spaceballs*, the two primary space vehicles are made by well-known vehicle makers, Mercedes Benz and Winnebago, while Bart's saddle in *Blazing Saddles* carries the designer label of Gucci. As two men begin to fight in *The Big Bus* during a bar room brawl, one man breaks off the end of a milk carton (as one would typically do to a glass beer bottle) and brandishes it as a weapon, only to be matched by a man toting a broken candle.

A particularly funny employment of an inverted icon that exhibits elements taken from outside of the expected logonomic system is seen in *Love at First Bite*. Convinced that his friend is dating Dracula, the psychiatrist attempts to expose the man's true ident-

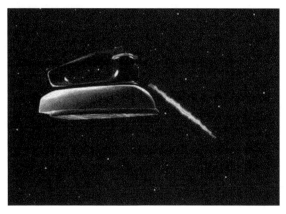

Fig. 14: *Hardware Wars* (Ernie Fosselius, 1978)

ity. Sitting at a table in a fancy restaurant, the man finally brandishes an icon to scare off Dracula, yet fails to get a reaction. Rather than holding up a crucifix, he hoists up a Star of David. Thus, the basic idea of a religious icon is indeed replicated, but the actual icon is inverted to where it has no vested meaning within the conventionalized narrative.

Syntax

The reiteration of plot with eventual inversion is an effective means for syntactic shifting. A good example of this occurs in a scene from *Amazon Women on the Moon* titled 'Son of the Invisible Man' which spoofs the classic 1933 film, *The Invisible Man*. In the parody, shot in black and white and utilizing emblematic high contrast lighting, the syntax rolls out in much of the same fashion as the original except for one major factor: the invisible man (played by Ed Begley, Jr) is *very* visible, yet does not know it. Therefore, when he decides to strip naked and parade around the local pub for a bit of a laugh thinking that the other patrons cannot see him, we get a reversal in the plot in which the patrons can, indeed, see him, but have decided *en masse* to play along and act as if he is invisible. This results in an initial establishment of the general syntax based on the original which must reverse its progression based on the alteration of his visible status.

Similarly, in the 1931 version of *Frankenstein*, the monster enters the room of the doctor's fiancée, frightens her and then flees. In *Young Frankenstein*, rather than frightening the fiancée, the monster's visit turns into a sexual encounter, with the woman waking up the next day donning a *Bride of Frankenstein* grey-streaked hairstyle. Another example of narrative reversal occurs in *Love at First Bite* as Dracula's victim decides to bite *him*. Probably one of the more clever inversions of plot can be found in *The Last Remake of Beau Geste*, during the scene of the missing sapphire at the estate. In the original version of the film, the mother turns out the room's lights and requests that the jewel be returned in the anonymity of the dark. When the lights come up, the sapphire remains missing. In the parody, when the lights come on, the jewel is still missing, but so is the table on which it sat. They repeat the procedure; resulting in the table being returned but Digby's pants being removed. Such shifts in narrative action depend on the audience's foreknowledge of the procedure performed in the older version of the film and subsequent recognition of the absurd actions that result in the parody.

Style

In terms of stylistic inversion, the use of graphics and titles to identify locations with greater specificity within a film is another means for generating parody. This identifying role is inverted by presenting location titles that actually *lack* such intended precision. In *Hot Shots!*, a title superimposed over an aircraft carrier at sea identifies its location as 'Somewhere in the Mediterranean', while another title over a desert landscape in *The Last Remake of Beau Geste* states, 'Somewhere in Morocco'. A third example occurs in *I'm Gonna Git You, Sucka* with the title 'ANYGHETTO, USA'. Other times, titles are used to *overstate* the obvious. For example, a title over a scene at an airport in *Spy Hard* states: 'The Airport'. Again, the titles work to both understate and overstate any narrative function by presenting little actual narrative information.

Parody films can also operate through inversion by signalling their parodic operations at the very beginning of their texts, if not just before. As we know, many films released in the United States start with the production (or distribution) company's logo. *Blazing Saddles* opens like most films produced by Warner Bros. with a short shot of the Warner Bros. company logo (the WB crest). This creates an identifying element of recognition with past uses of the logo. Yet, in line with the title of the film, the logo in *Blazing Saddles* begins to ignite and burn, a pointed comment on the forthcoming film's attempt to 'burn' past Western clichés. In *The Fearless Vampire Killers (or Pardon Me, But Your Teeth Are in My Neck)* (1966), the MGM lion morphs into a green vampire cartoon character with huge, blood-dripping fangs. Similarly, the opening credits for *The Silence of the Hams* parodies 20th Century-Fox's identity by featuring a logo with a howling wolf and inscribed with 'Thirtieth Century Wolf'.

The inversion of expected sounds and music is another productive means for creating parodic transformation. Within certain genres and cycles, specific groups of stereotyped characters commonly share musical heritages and tastes. For instance, many old Western films feature token African-Americans who sing nothing but traditional spirituals. This stereotypical situation is parodied in *Blazing Saddles* as the railroad crew foreman tries to convince the African-American workers to sing while they work. When they do sing, it's not the expected 'Swing Low Sweet Chariot' but the jazzy Cole Porter song, 'I Get a Kick Out of You'. Baffled, the foreman tries to convince them to sing one of their 'own' songs, breaking into his own version of 'Camptown Lady'. The workers watch in amazement as the foreman and his men get heavily involved in the song. Again, this transformation is based on inverting stereotypical musical numbers between stereotyped and non-stereotyped groups.

Although the parodic method of inversion is, indeed, an important means for creating ironic incongruity as discussed within this chapter, it is important to consider it in conjunction with the other 'transformational' methods which we will next turn to, first examining the parodic method of 'misdirection'.

6
Misdirection

The third parodic method of 'misdirection' functions by creating ironic incongruity through both the reiteration and transformation of the target text. This occurs when specific conventional elements are evoked and initially played out in a manner similar to the target text, but are then transformed to deliver an unexpected turn in the eventual parodic presentation.

Lexicon

Spectatorial misdirection is often generated through the misleading use of setting in parody films. A viewer of a parody is presented with a setting which looks very similar to the one in the prototext, yet turns out to be a complete fabrication. For example, in a fashion very similar to its target, *The Maltese Falcon* (1941), *The Black Bird* opens with a panoramic shot of the San Francisco skyline. Yet after a few seconds of anchoring the spectator to the target text, the fantastic skyline is exposed to be simply a mural painted on the side of a building. This same method of misdirection is utilized in changing the scale of certain sets. One scene in *The Last Remake of Beau Geste* opens on a lone fort standing in stark contrast to the open desert. As the camera pulls back, we notice that the fort is actually a small sand castle as soldiers on horses go riding by, smashing the little construction (see Figure 15).

Similarly, misdirection through the use of setting can also expose a film's artifice by incorporating part of its own filmic discourse (as a film) into the parody itself. For example, towards the end of *Blazing Saddles*, the main characters break out of their

Fig. 15: *The Last Remake of Beau Geste* (Marty Feldman, 1977)

Western set on the Warner Bros. lot and start a major fight on the set of a new musical being filmed in an adjoining sound stage. Finally, they arrive at the Chinese Theater in Hollywood (which, of course, has *Blazing Saddles* advertised on its marquee). Bad guy Hedley Lamarr enters the theatre and sits to watch the ensuing conclusion of the film. What he sees on the screen is an exterior shot of the Chinese Theater with the good guys arriving outside. He then gets up and exits the theatre to meet his match.

Misdirection additionally subverts lexical expectations by exposing the constructedness of the sets and breaking the illusions Hollywood crafts people work so hard to perfect. In *Top Secret!* (1984), a scene ends with the characters looking out of the train's windows as the station passes by. Yet suddenly, the station goes by, and we are clued in that the station was merely a painted mobile set being pushed by the train's window by the film crew. A similar exposure of the set occurs in *Blazing Saddles* during the climactic fight between the bad guys and the people of Rockridge as the camera cranes upwards to expose the Western locale as one of many different sets on the Warner Bros. Burbank backlot.

Misdirection and disruption of the filmic illusion are further accomplished through the breaking of the 'fourth wall' and exposing the film crew. During the fight scene between Dark Helmet and Lone Starr in *Spaceballs*, the action gets rough as they battle with their 'schwartz' swords, accidentally swiping a nearby sound technician. In *Closet Cases of the Nerd Kind* (1979), a similar example occurs as the camera pans left to expose the movie crew with the director frantically yelling, 'We're rolling!'

Dialogue is another lexical element that can be transformed through misdirection. One of the ways this is achieved is through the use of overly correct grammar in a grammatically-incorrect context to misdirect the viewer. Here, the target text can be disrupted by casually following its established dialogue patterns, only to jolt the viewer with a valid dialogue inter-play that is made ridiculous solely by the viewer's expectations. For example, in *Airplane!*, one scene features a doctor, attending to a sick passenger, stating 'We've got to get him to the hospital,' to which the flight attendant asks, 'A hospital? What is it?' Correctly responding, yet in a manner outside of the established pattern, he replies, 'A large white building with doctors and nurses inside, but that's not important now.' A similar example occurs later in the film as a passenger takes over the plane's controls. Another character proceeds to ask him, 'Surely you can land this plane?' to which he replies, 'Yes I can, and stop calling me Shirley!' Each of these parodic references is disruptive since each contains an unexpected answer to a question lifted from the target text. Yet this disruption is heightened by the film's ability to validate the answer through cleverly correct, though wholly inappropriate, grammatical structure.

Similarly, make-up and costuming can be effective evokers of a parody's prototext while being utilized in unexpected ways through misdirection. For example, the narrative of *Frankenweenie* revolves around the re-animation of a pet dog named Sparky in a similar fashion to the re-animation of the monster in the classic film, *Frankenstein*. After the dog comes back to life, his head plays host to two electrodes while his neck exhibits a ring of huge stitches (which constantly leak as he drinks water from his dog dish). Later in the film, Sparky finally meets his mate – a poodle sporting *Bride of Frankenstein* (1935) white streaks through her hair. In this example, the lexical elements

Fig. 16: *Spy Hard* (Rick Friedberg, 1996)

of make-up and hairstyle that are seen in the prototexts are re-utilized and reiterated, yet are now used in conjunction with very different types of character whom you would least expect them to be used on.

Make-up is also used inconsistently in parody films to highlight their fakeness and call attention to their actual mobility as film props while misdirecting the viewer's expectations. A scene in *Spy Hard* features Dick Steele meeting a female character in a groovy-looking dance club. In a matter of seconds, Steele's hair has transformed into a pony-tail and the woman's into a rigid bob style while they dance together on the dance floor – a pointed reference to John Travolta and Uma Thurman's hairstyles in *Pulp Fiction* (1994) (see Figure 16). In *Young Frankenstein*, Igor's hump constantly changes from one side to the other. At one point in the film, Dr Frankenstein notices the shift, but then shrugs off the idea with a baffled look. Similarly, a mole on the king's face in *Robin Hood: Men in Tights* changes facial location with every scene. Adding even greater self-reflexivity to this technique, Sergeant Markov retires to his room in *The Last Remake of Beau Geste* and removes the duelling scar from his face, storing it in a box labelled 'scars'. Again, the constructedness of the film is made evident by alterations of costume and make-up.

Syntax

As the narrative trajectory progresses forward in time, parody often locks the spectator into a familiar scenario and then adds a narrative twist to thwart expectation. Specific scenes are evoked and initially played out in a manner similar to the target text, but are then transformed to deliver an unexpected turn in the eventual narrative presentation. A simple example occurs in the animated short film, *Bambi Meets Godzilla* (1969). The film opens in an almost narratively understated fashion with a Bambi-like deer nibbling on some grass. This narrative action is accompanied by a flute-heavy soundtrack and the rolling of opening credits and obviously plays off of our expectations of how an animated short featuring Bambi might begin. Just as the credits finish, a huge dinosaur foot comes down and crushes Bambi as the familiar ending chord from the Beatles' 'A Day in the Life' rings out. The film ends unexpectedly with the final fade of the musical chord.

MISDIRECTION

Another example of syntactic misdirection spoofs a specific scene in *Star Wars* featuring Obi-Wan Kenobi's reaction to his feeling of a disturbance in the force at the same time a planet is disintegrated by the evil empire. In *Hardware Wars*, the scene is initially replicated as a planet is destroyed, followed by a cut to Augie 'Ben' Doggie groaning in pain. Fluke Starbucker then turns to him and asks: 'Did you feel a great disturbance in the force – as if millions of voices cried out in terror and were suddenly silenced?' Looking surprised, Augie responds, 'No, just a headache.' A similar example of narrative misdirection of action occurs in *Repossessed* which relies more on visual cues than dialogue. Repeating a memorable scene from *The Exorcist*, Nancy is on her bed being violently thrown around and yelling 'Make it stop, make it stop!' In a twist from the original, her violent actions are not caused by evil spirits as her husband walks in and turns off the vibrating bed controls. Finally, *Fatal Instinct* contains a scene which evokes the famous 'shower scene' from *Psycho* in terms of both lexical elements (the figure of the woman behind the shower curtain) and syntactic direction as Jane vigorously enjoys the rush of water from the shower head. Yet when 'mother' tries to stab her in the parody, the narrative alters its direction as she continuously misses – over and over. Finally, 'she' pulls out a hand gun and begins shooting, yet once again misses and ends up using a machine gun to complete the task. All of these examples demonstrate how a familiar syntax can be initially offered (full of similar lexical units) and then transformed to create an unexpected result.

Parody also uses the misdirection of narrative information to create incongruities within an initially stable syntax. A common cliché found in many films centred around prisons is the action of placing chalk marks on the cell wall to denote days behind bars. In *Top Secret!*, Nick Rivers is seen locked up in an East German jail, with twenty chalk marks stroked on the wall. In an unexpected twist of information, Rivers then informs his visiting manager that he has been locked up for twenty *minutes*! Another narrative cliché which is evoked and parodied is the fleeing criminal who tries to climb a chain link fence but gets pulled down by one of his feet. In *Fatal Instinct*, the scenario begins as expected, yet rather than pulling the guy down by his foot, Ned Ravine removes the criminal's shoe and 'tickles' him to the ground.

Narrative misdirection can also occur as the story tumbles into self-reflexive examination. In *Robin Hood: Men in Tights*, Robin unexpectedly loses the bow and arrow competition at the fair. Disbelieving this odd turn of events, Robin pulls out the script of *Robin Hood* to find out what exactly went wrong. Realizing that he does, indeed, have one remaining shot, Robin motions to the royal court that he has found the error which is confirmed by both the king and the prince as they check their own versions of the script. Again, the expected syntactic progression is stalled and redirected by the violation of expected, conventionalized codes.

Other films internally remind spectators that they are watching a cinematic construction through an actual declaration that is juxtaposed with the film's actual narrative text (and identified by Margaret Rose (1993) as a major signal of parodic activity). As a prologue to the film *Movie, Movie*, George Burns directly addresses the audience, stating, 'I'd like to say a few words before the picture starts. This is not the picture. Not yet. I'm not in the picture.' By disassociating itself from the rest of the film text, this segment subtly reminds the spectators that although this prologue is indeed part of the film, it is not part of the narrative; the scene thus misdirects and challenges the expectations that revolve around when the film is actually starting. An even more direct reference to the film's status as a film is seen in *Hardware Wars*. As their ship is being pulled into the evil space station, Fluke Starbucker cries out to the captain of the ship, Ham Salad, 'You've got to get us out of here' to which Ham replies, 'Take it easy kid, it's only a movie!'

As fictional worlds, Hollywood films attempt to create their own, enclosed *vraisemblance* which often resemble, but do not replicate, the real, extra-textual world. One method for destroying this illusion in the narrative is by employing elements of reality that are usually unevoked in the Hollywood tradition to misdirect and subvert viewer expectation. Thus, the incorporation of a high degree of realism into a generally fictitious syntax creates incongruity between the factors. Many of these are based on the physical limitations of the characters. While performing all sorts of super hero feats, characters rarely have time for day-to-day physical maintenance. In *I'm Gonna Git You, Sucka*, tough man Slammer is slowed by his tender, swollen feet (poking fun at the ageing actor replaying a past character). In *This Is Spinal Tap*, the world of rock and roll and its accompanying sexual promiscuity is manifested in a scene where all of the characters sport herpes sores on their lips. While performing a daring feat in *Zorro, The Gay Blade*, the main character turns his ankle and cannot continue his actions. Probably one of the most famous bodily intrusions of reality in a parody film occurs in *Blazing Saddles*. John Cawelti describes the scene:

> The cowboys sit around a blazing campfire at night, a scene in which we are accustomed to hearing mournful and lyrical cowboy ballads performed by such groups as the Sons of Pioneers. Instead, we are treated to an escalating barrage of flatulence. Anyone who knows the usual effect of canned wilderness fare is likely to be delighted at this sudden exposure of the sham involved in the traditional western campfire scene. (1976, p. 192)

Thus, the inclusion of a lexical element that is typically excluded from that particular syntax functions to misdirect and disrupt the entire cohesion of the narrative by producing gaps in the fictional *vraisemblance*.

Other actions can be introduced into a syntax that reflect how the scene would *probably* work out in real life. For example, in *Lobster Man from Mars*, an alien specimen is brought into the professor's laboratory for examination. Nervous that it might still be a functioning organism, John hysterically yells out: 'It might attack us any moment! What could we do?' Reacting in a manner which highlights the often contrived nature of all-knowing authorities in many films, the professor replies: 'I saw it for the first time five minutes ago. You expect a whole big analysis? How should I know?' In *The Cheap Detective*, the characters have a very difficult time unwrapping the paper around the Maltese Falcon icon; this results in a noticeable arresting of narrative progression. Mimicking the rough and ready riding style of many old cowboy film characters, Rex O'Herlihan, leaps off of his horse onto a large horizontal tree branch in *Rustler's Rhapsody*. Rather than using the branch for further leverage in his leap forward, the branch cracks and he falls haplessly to the ground. Repeating the exciting action of fighter jets flying upside down, as seen in *Top Gun*, *Hot Shots!* provides a more 'realistic' glimpse at what really happens when they make such a manoeuvre as the contents of the pilots' pockets (e.g. gum, coins and a driver's licence) fly out and cover the interior of the jet's domed wind shield. Parodying an action seen in many James Bond films, Dick Steele throws his hat towards the office coat rack in *Spy Hard*. But rather than landing perfectly on one of the hooks, the hat instead tips over the rack which falls and shatters a glass bookcase. As all of these examples demonstrate, the introduction of elements of realism functions to disrupt the stable syntax of the logonomic system and creates an ironic counter-point to compare the fictional content with its realistic results.

Narrative misdirection also utilizes the direct address by a character for generating self-reflexive comment. For example, in *Blazing Saddles*, a short scene features an old woman being held back and punched by a group of bandits. Not only is this an inversion of conventional character activity relations, it also becomes self-reflexively a misdirection when the woman turns toward the camera and exclaims: 'Have you ever seen such cruelty?' Another scene in *Blazing Saddles* features Hedley Lamarr talking to himself in his office as he ponders how to locate a sheriff who would 'offend' the citizens of Rockridge. Typically, the omniscient camera takes on an invisible status and such talking to oneself is viewed as normal. Lamarr continues, stating 'How would I find such a man? Why am I asking you?' as he acknowledges the presence of the imposing camera and by extension, the audience.

Quite often, parodies will paratextually refer to their own extra-textual discourse through the use of misdirection. For example, in a scene from *Spaceballs*, Colonel Sandurz wonders what they should do next in the film and suggests, 'I have an idea. Get me the video of *Spaceballs: The Movie*.' The camera then pans across a video collection of past Mel Brooks films (a good example of auto-citation intertextuality) until we see the *Spaceballs* videocassette. Sandurz then explains that these are 'instant' cassettes that are 'out on video before the film is done'. He puts the video in and fast forwards through past scenes of the film until they arrive at the current point of the film. The video monitor then displays them looking at the monitor – a sort of 'live action feed'. Both of these examples parody the traditional self-containment of Hollywood films and self-reflexively refer to their own status as filmic constructions by misdirecting the spectator through the juxtaposed worlds of fiction and cinematic constructedness.

Style

The parodic method of misdirection is employed stylistically through the use of titles seen on the screen. In particular, parody can reiterate a specific identifying logo and then transform it for ironic effect. For example, the beginning of *Dead Men Don't Wear Plaid* features the older spinning Universal globe logo rather than the new, modern Universal Pictures logo. This historical translocation not only signals the period of the parody film, it also comments on old Universal films of this genre by its recontextualizing activity. Another Universal Pictures film, *The Last Remake of Beau Geste*, opens with the Universal spinning globe, yet adds a comical twist. As the film opens with the globe spinning (typically using the 'stock' logo footage), the star of the film, Marty Feldman, can be seen lurking behind the globe, thus immediately identifying that this is not stock footage. He then proceeds to grab the globe and crush it, again signifying a certain element of destroying products of the past.

Misdirection is also employed to undercut the story-telling function of titles when used for initiating the narrative discourse. For example, *The Cheap Detective*, a spoof of *The Maltese Falcon* and other films noir, opens with the following title: 'In the Philippines, a small band of native guerrillas prepared secretly for the inevitable conflict that would engulf the east. ... This has nothing to do with our story.' Such narrative misdirection works not only to signal a disruption of the logonomic system, but also to acknowledge such disruption by downplaying the seriousness of the film presentation. A similar example occurs in *The Last Remake of Beau Geste*, based on the 1939 classic, *Beau Geste*, starring Gary Cooper. As with the original, the narrative takes place in two locations: England and Morocco. Yet in the parody, this locational transition is performed in an overt and misdirecting fashion. Echoing the original, the parody opens with a scene of an evacuated fort in the middle of the desert. Rather than using a brief title to connote a flashback, the title reads: 'This story appears to start here in the Sahara Desert – But it really started some years earlier – in England.' Thus, the narrative transition of the original is preserved, but the 'signals' are overtly manifested and transformed, causing an internal disruption and acknowledgment of the cinematic modes of temporal and spatial transition.

Another use of subtitles to misdirect is the translation of non-native languages for the viewing public or the clarification of muddled or heavily-accented dialogue. *Airplane!* utilizes such subtitles when two African-American men begin to speak in 'jive' to each other. Creating an interesting juxtaposition centred on race (and, arguably, racism), words such as 'baby' and 'shit' become overly 'cleansed' and translated to 'Mrs' and 'Golly'. The disjunction between what is said by the characters and what is written in the subtitles becomes the source of incongruity within the text and is parodic due to both its utilization for a conventionalized purpose and its subsequent clashing of visual and aural planes. In the 1993 parody, *Fatal Instinct*, one scene features Lana and Frank sitting on a park bench and planning a murder. In order to hide their discussion, Lana suggests they speak in Yiddish (accompanied by English-translated subtitles). After a lengthy conversation, a nearby man on another bench responds in English to one of their concerns about the murder. Alarmed, Lana asks the man: 'Do *you* speak Yiddish?' to which the man replies: 'No, I can read the subtitles!'

Dialogue titles also occur in parodies by evoking the silent film tradition of intertitles, yet misdirecting their use within a contemporary film. For example, in *Silent Movie*, title cards are employed not only to create a general sense of disruption with their presence throughout an entire contemporary film, but also to parody the use of such titles to faithfully convey the 'stated' dialogue. In one scene, Mel Funn begins to scold Marty with the words 'You dirty son-of-a-bitch' clearly emanating from his lips. Yet as the titles appear at the bottom of the screen, an obviously toned down statement comes across as the title reads: 'You bad boy,' thus creating an ironic juxtaposition between what is presented visually and textually.

Another interesting example of parodying this practice is seen in *The Last Remake of Beau Geste*. Looking beyond the fort's walls into the open desert, a soldier sees another figure approaching. We soon see that the figure is a superimposed black-and-white shot reminiscent of Rudolph Valentino from the silent classic, *The Sheik* (1921). The soldier yells out to Rudolph to identify himself and Valentino replies by way of an intertitle card.

They converse back and forth, verbally and through intertitles, until Valentino 'teaches' the soldier how to 'speak in intertitles'. After he accomplishes a few title card words, he, too, becomes black and white and rides away with Valentino, still talking through intertitles. These self-reflexive uses of title cards not only disrupts the technological dominance of the sound film and creates an unstable commitment to cinematic technology, it also misdirects viewer expectation based on how such titles have been traditionally employed.

Through various applications of misdirection, parody films use musical scores that begin as conventional to secure recognition and then parodically transform them. For example, *Love at First Bite* starts with a traditional violin score that soon changes into a contemporary dance score with electrical guitars and contemporary percussion. A similar misdirection is heard in *Closet Cases of the Nerd Kind* when the four note signature tune from *Close Encounters of the Third Kind* rings out and then speeds up until it becomes a full, 1920s sounding jazz tune. When Beau takes over playing the bugle for a fallen soldier in *The Last Remake of Beau Geste*, the tune is not the expected reveille, but rather a jazzy trumpet solo. In a final example, the theme song for *I'm Gonna Git You, Sucka* might sound familiar since it was written by Curtis Mayfield, who also penned the music for one of the original 'blaxploitation' films, *Superfly*. The song replicates the theme from *Shaft* – a song that conveniently covered up lyric profanity with back-up singers and instrumental swells. This is parodied in *I'm Gonna Git You, Sucka* as the lead male singer croons to the likes of 'Watch out, you dirty mother . . . ' and the female background singers quickly chime in: 'Don't say that!' The music becomes a condensation by evoking past uses (type of song, instruments and even the same musician) with a transformation at the level of 'literalizing' the covert profanity cover-ups found in the original *Shaft* theme song.

The use of mismatching sound sources can also contribute to a sense of misdirection through a film's narrative. For example, as a control operator studies the radar screen in *Spaceballs*, the expected sounds of computer beeps and blips can be heard. When the radar begins to malfunction, the sounds become stranger. When the commanding officer orders the operator to explain the malfunction, we find out that the sounds are actually being verbally emitted by the character himself (played by sound effects wizard, Michael Winslow). Not only does this source mismatch subvert expectations centred on diegetic sound source, it also up-ends further (or more analytic) expectations that the sounds have been added through post-dubbing in order to create the illusion of actual radar sounds.

The mismatching of the visual source of a sound and the actual sound can additionally be used to create ironic juxtapositions through misdirection. For example, in the film *Hot Shots!*, a fighter jet passing another jet sounds its 'car horn', while a doorbell rings inside of a Native American 'teepee'. In *Hardware Wars*, the rocket flying through space is accompanied by the sound of a race car. Both *Airplane!* films perform a particularly clever act of sound source mismatch. In *Airplane!*, the exterior shot of the flying airline jet is supplemented by the whirl of a plane's propeller. In *Airplane II: The Sequel*, the exterior shot of the space shuttle flying through space has the sound of a jet. Both soundtrack tricks probably rely more on technical competency than cinematic literacy.

In terms of visual cinematic conventions, misdirection is utilized to both evoke and transgress the ways in which they are used in the prototext. A telling example occurs in *High Anxiety* as Hitchcock's penchant for shooting certain shots from unexpected angles is evoked and misdirected. In one particular scene that directly evokes a similar scene in *Notorious* (1946), nurse Diesel and Montegue are discussing their plans for Dr Thorndyke and the Institute. The scene is shot upward through a glass-topped table, yet the camera must constantly shift positions due to the placement of cups, trays and sugar bowls that block the camera's view of the characters. Thus, the technique is replicated, but the resulting actions by the characters in the film function to expose the novel nature of the camera angle.

A similar effort to parody the stylistically-fluid camera movements of Alfred Hitchcock is seen in *High Anxiety* as it constantly exposes the camera's presence through camera movements gone awry. In one scene, the camera looks in on two people talking in bed. As the camera begins to track back, the voice of a crew member can be heard saying 'pull back – nice – we're going too fast!' At that moment, the camera crashes through the wall of the room and leaves a gaping hole, accompanied by a voice-over stating 'keep going, maybe no one will notice'. In another scene from the film, the camera replicates a particular shot found in Hitchcock's *Foreign Correspondent* (1940). In the original, the camera cranes in on the exterior of a flying plane and then 'through' one of the windows to enter the plane and film two people talking. In *High Anxiety*, the camera begins to crane in on the exterior of a house to film through a pane glass window a group of people dining at the table. As the camera gets closer to the window and begins its 'magic' entrance into the house, it instead crashes through the window, accompanied by the sound of shattering glass and the shocked expression of the guests. Thus, the incongruity occurs by replicating a filming scenario (including an idiosyncratic technique) and then misdirecting the spectator by altering it through an acknowledgment of the physical limitations of set design and camera movement.

A final example of stylistic misdirection occurs in *Top Secret!* as the technique of using deep focus is cleverly parodied. In a scene that takes place in the East German military board room, the entire area is in focus, with a German general speaking in the background and a phone featured in the foreground. Due to focal perspective, items in the foreground appear to be disproportionately larger than those in the background. When the phone rings, the general enters the foreground and picks up the phone receiver. Thwarting expectation, the receiver is four times as large as a normal phone and its 'illusionary' size was not created by visual perspective but, rather, by its sheer mass alone.

Misdirection operates, therefore, by reiterating an expected convention along lexical, syntactic and stylistic paths and then transforming that convention in a way that is both unexpected and 'inappropriate'.

7
Literalization

Another method for creating parodic difference is 'literalization' in which the targeted text is transformed through the use of the pun (visual, aural and textual) as well as through specific formations of self-reflexivity to 'literalize' the film-making process.

Lexicon

Richard Dyer suggests that character names generally function as 'personality signals' in conveying narrative information, suggesting that 'the character's name both particularises her/him and also suggests personality traits' (1986, p. 122). The transformation of character names in parody seems to play off of this notion by altering names systematically either to change the character's personality profile or merely to draw attention to the specificity of names established in the logonomic systems.

Utilizing the parodic method of literalization, both *Spaceballs* and *Hardware Wars* (1978) transform many of the character names from the *Star Wars* trilogy through clever shifts in phonology – which in turn define the transformed characters. For example, Darth Vader becomes both Darph Nader and Dark Helmet; R2-D2 mutates into Artie Deco, while Yoda becomes Yogurt. The character name of Han Solo takes two notable turns: Ham Salad in *Hardware Wars* and Lone Starr in *Spaceballs*. Probably the most clever of the *Star Wars* name shifts is based on the gluttonous leader of the gangsters and bounty hunters, Jabba the Hutt. In *Spaceballs*, Jabba's layers of fat become a pile of melting cheese, tomato sauce and pepperoni – appropriately named 'Pizza the Hut'.

Often, the literalizing pun is derived from a specific source associated with the targeted film or logonomic system. Thus, the wolfman in *Transylvania 6-5000* is named Lawrence Malbot – a transformation of the Lon Chaney, Jr film character named Lawrence Talbot (while also indirectly parodying Chaney's own original role as the wolfman). The attorney general in *Blazing Saddles* is named Hedley Lamarr, closely resembling the name of actress Hedy Lamarr. So close, in fact, that Ms Lamarr filed a $10,000 invasion of privacy lawsuit during the film's production against the director, Mel Brooks, for exploiting her name without permission. Humorously, the suit is even referred to within the film as the governor accidentally calls Hedley 'Hedy' and is quickly corrected by Hedley. Without missing a beat, the governor, also played by Brooks, retorts: 'What the hell are you worried about? This is 1874. You'll be able to sue *her*!'

Additionally, character names can be transformed by shifting based on literalizing either a particular trait or by borrowing from a lateral source. For example, the already peculiar character name of 'Oddjob' from the James Bond film, *Goldfinger* (1964) becomes 'Random Task' in *Austin Powers: International Man of Mystery*. In *The Cheap*

Detective, the character, Paul, gets his namesake (in a convoluted fashion) based on the actor who played Paul's model, Paul Henreid's Victor Lazslo character in *Casablanca*. Another example occurs in *Repossessed*, a parody of *The Exorcist*. The main character in the target film is named Regan and becomes transformed into Nancy in the parody, thus playing off of the name of Nancy Reagan. Finally, in *The Silence of the Hams*, the lead male character is named Jo Dee Fostar and parodies the name of the female actress who starred in *The Silence of the Lambs* (1991), Jodie Foster.

Similarly, characters can speak in mixed metaphors and puns to create literal transformations. In *The Big Bus*, for example, the character of Dan Torrance reasserts his confidence in Shoulders O' Brien for taking over the bus's wheel for his injured co-driver by stating: 'Shoulders can fill his shoes!' to which 'bus attendant' Kate replies: 'But can he fit into his uniform?' Another clever example of punning occurs in the 'Dynamite Hands' segment of *Movie, Movie* when Joey exclaims: 'You know what they charge to fix eyes? An arm and a leg!' Often, puns are formulated in order to work extraneous scenes into the syntax. In *Airplane!*, the doctor gives Ted Striker a pep speech by urging him to forget his past mistakes that led to the death of George Zipper and to take control of the situation to land the plane safely. As the speech progresses, the soundtrack begins to fill with the Notre Dame fight song, followed by the encouragement to 'win one for the Zipper!' – a direct parody lifted from *Knute Rockne All American* (1940).

Syntax

Within the syntactic progression of a narrative, actions and objects can often be transformed based on certain principles of literalization by playing off of a word's double meaning and punning. One direction of transformation is the changing of a physical action (a verb) into an object (a noun). When Lone Starr tells Barf to 'jam' the radar in *Spaceballs*, we see a huge jar of strawberry jam being hurled toward the radar dish. In the same film, the scene of Colonel Sandurz ordering his men to comb the desert for the escaped prisoners is followed by a shot of men dragging huge hair combs through the desert sand. Upon realizing this, Sandurz self-reflexively asks Dark Helmet: 'Are we being too literal?'

Transformation can also occur as descriptive adjectives become literalized into actions. In *Airplane!*, the request for a 'smoking ticket' on the plane is rewarded with a

Fig. 17: *Airplane II: The Sequel*

ticket emitting smoke. Adjectives can also be transformed into objects. When the air traffic controller in *Airplane!* states that 'the shit is going to hit the fan', the age-old saying is visualized as a soft, brown substance is thrown toward a room fan. In *Airplane II: The Sequel*, the air traffic controller informs the shuttle that they are 'putting everyone in jeopardy!', followed by the next scene consisting of the plane's passengers on the set of the popular television game show, *Jeopardy* (see Figure 17). In *Silent Movie*, Mel Funn leaves the office of the studio boss after selling his idea of making a silent movie and states through a title card, 'Wait till I tell the guys... they'll *flip!*' This is followed by an exterior shot of his two fellow film-makers literally doing back flips after hearing the good news.

Objects that are expected to surface within that logonomic system can also be transformed into other extraneous objects that are not expected. When the airport tower announces that the crew of the plane is flying on instruments in *Airplane!*, the next scene shows the cockpit crew playing *musical* instruments.

Dialogue can also be taken literally by other characters in parodic films and seize the narrative flow. As Neale and Krutnik remind us, 'comedy and the comic have their own – generic – regimes of verisimilitude, their own – generic – decorum, their own – generic – norms, conventions, and rules. In comedy, we expect the unexpected' (1990, p. 91). In other words, parody can subvert expectations based on models of parody, irony or the comic by having characters deliver dialogue that 'might' be expected in a literal (non-comical) sense. For example, in *Dracula: Dead and Loving It*, an usher is hypnotized by Dracula and instructed to deliver a message to a theatre patron. Just before departing, Dracula tells her that she will 'remember nothing of what I tell you'. The usher then proceeds to find the patron and literally forgets the message.

Literalization also occurs in the form of the parody self-reflexively exposing its material and extra-textual nature. For example, a scene in *Repossessed* features Nancy boasting of super powers in her attempt to frighten Father Brophy. Unimpressed, Brophy tells her to prove her great powers. She replies, 'Well, how about if I ... make the film break!' At that point, the film image becomes unsteady (as if it has slipped the loop in the projector) and then begins the dreaded 'centre melt'. The illusion that the film itself is literally disintegrating due to the actions of a fictional character disrupts the typical boundary drawn between the fictional narrative world and the world of the projected film.

The larger institution of Hollywood film-making and the related ancillary activities of tie-ins and merchandising are directly parodied by explicitly calling attention to their synergistic connections and literalizing them into the narrative. In *Spaceballs*, Yogurt informs the main characters that he is into a new area of interest – *merchandising*. He then takes them to his boutique where he peddles *Spaceballs* logo items, including T-shirts, lunch pails, toys and beach towels. *Amazon Women on the Moon* features a short spoof of pirate movies appropriately titled 'Video Pirates' which plays off of the notion of 'pirating' in the modern age by capturing a treasure of illegally-copied videotapes while sailing under the flag of 'MCA Home Video'.

The Hollywood institution of the Academy Awards is also parodied through the construction of syntaxes that self-reflexively comment on the revered status of the Academy in the film-making business by literalizing some of its associated scenarios. For example, the sacred religious artefact captured in *Raiders of the Lost Ark* becomes transformed in

UHF into another sacred artifact: the Academy Award-presented Oscar. In *Naked Gun 33 1/3*, the presentation of the prestigious Academy Lifetime Achievement Award is spoofed with the honoree (wheelchair-bound and IV bag attached) sitting in a virtually unconscious state as they celebrate his career making movies, including such classics as *Sandals and Loin Cloth, Sweaty Boat Men, The Leather-Clad Centurion* and *Big Shiny Spear*. Finally, in *Blazing Saddles*, Hedley Lamarr prepares to lead his bad guy gang into battle with the people of Rockridge. He garners the men's attention and announces: 'Now you will only be risking your lives, while I will be risking a most certain Academy Award nomination for best supporting actor!' Again, the actor's breaking out of character coupled with his reference to the cinematic institution works to unsettle the film's illusionary status and to highlight the film's situation in a larger, business enterprise.

Another form of literalization is the creation of visual puns within the syntax. This is achieved by taking verbal puns usually uttered by a character and then manifesting them as real objects. For example, *Airplane!* generates a clever metaphor when an air traffic controller states that he is going to 'talk him to the ground', and a big watermelon then falls immediately from above and crashes behind him. In *Love at First Bite*, Dracula goes to the municipal blood bank to make a 'withdrawal'. In *Young Frankenstein*, Igor tries to steal a designated brain, drops it, and instead steals the brain of another man named 'Abbie Normal'. During a tense moment during the courtroom scene in *Fatal Instinct*, a man runs to a door marked 'Press Room' and yells the clichéd line found in so many courtroom dramas, 'The jury's back!' At that moment, the reporters inside of the room stop operating the *shirt* presses and run back to the courtroom.

Yet probably the most narratively-motivated visual pun occurs in *Closet Cases of the Nerd Kind*. Throughout the film, the conventionalized element of the flying saucer is replaced by flying cream pies. When the scientist finally makes contact with the aliens, he repeatedly gets the same reply: '3.14'. For those in the know, this is the number for 'pi', the mathematical symbol for the ratio of circumference of circle to diameter. At that point, the huge mother ship arrives – a big pie with a red cherry on top. These examples, therefore, operate by altering expected syntactic relations by taking certain words and logically punning them by way of transforming them into narrative objects.

Style

Probably one of the most evoked techniques to create parody using sound is through the literalization of both sound form and content. Take, for example, the use of the voice-over. The primary way the voice-over is used in parodic discourse is for the generation of a self-reflexive break between diegetic and non-diegetic sound. Conventionally, a voice-over is presented either as a non-diegetic narrator or meta-diegetically within the head of a character. In the film, *The Last Remake of Beau Geste*, this confusion over aural diegetic space is played out wonderfully. As Digby and Isabel both silently read a letter left by Beau before he departed, a voice-over of Beau reading the letter's contents is heard, evoking a highly conventionalized syntax of reading a departed's letter. In a typical non-parodic film, Beau's reading would either be an evocation of his own reading while writing the letter, or the imaginary replication of Beau's voice in the minds of the readers with neither having any diegetic quality within the story space. Yet in this film, Digby and Isabel stop reading the letter briefly and look for the source of Beau's voice. A humorous touch is added when, after searching a couple of times for the sound source, they put their ears closer to the letter in order to *hear* the reading clearer (see Figure 18).

A similar play with the literalization of non-diegetic sound occurs in *Dead Men Don't Wear Plaid*. Following a tradition often found in films noir, the lead character constantly talks to himself through an internal voice-over (e.g. 'I knew trouble was brewing ... '). In one specific scene, the lead character looks at the woman he loves and ponders their future together. Through an internal voice-over, he states: 'How could I tell her that a man in my business can't have kids?' This is quickly followed by the woman's reply within the diegetic space, 'We wouldn't *have to* have kids.' This jolts the lead character, surprised by her ability to 'hear' what he was 'thinking'. Both examples violate diegetic expectation by employing cinematic techniques anchored in specific syntactic structures and the characters' reactions to such intrusive techniques.

Music can also be parodied in terms of its diegetic sources through a form of literalization. Typically, musical scores are non-diegetic and function to engender specific emotive responses to the presented visuals. This is parodied in *High Anxiety* as the characters constantly react to non-diegetic scoring by looking for the source of that music playing from 'above'. At one point in the film, Dr Thorndyke and his driver are cruising along in the desert accompanied by an orchestral score. The spectator is misdirected into believing that the music is non-diegetic by its lack of visible source and conventional uses of non-diegetic scoring. Yet this illusion is immediately shattered as a bus with the Los Angeles Symphony Orchestra abroad passes their car playing the score music.

Literalization also plays with diegetic musical sources as seen in *I'm Gonna Git You, Sucka*. Echoing a scene from *Shaft*, the camera follows John Slade as he walks down the city street, accompanied by his signature theme music. As he continues to walk along, the camera picks up a group of playing musicians following Slade. His friend, Jack, asks 'Who are these guys?' Slade replies 'They're my theme music!' Similarly, in *Fatal Instinct*, the *femme fatale* character, Lola, is constantly shadowed by her own jazz saxophonist playing her signature theme music.

In *Blazing Saddles*, the sheriff character, Bart, is featured riding along the desert on his horse with an atypical jazz score accompanying his ride. As he rides along, the music

Fig. 18: *The Last Remake of Beau Geste*

becomes anchored to a literalized diegetic source – Count Basie and his orchestra playing in the middle of an open field. Such transformation operates on a variety of levels. Not only is it an application of music that does not belong to the logonomic system and violates rules of diegetic sourcing, it also uses a known musical source that was historically developed after the genre's historical period.

Non-diegetic scoring can also shift to a diegetic source which has unsuspectedly always been present within the diegesis. In *Repossessed*, one scene opens with the priest entering Nancy's room accompanied by increasingly suspenseful music. As he approaches her bed, the music grows louder to the point of becoming irritating. Reacting to this loud music, the priest stops his approach and clicks off the portable tape recorder he has in his hand, thus silencing the music.

As with voice-overs, sound is often used meta-diegetically by occurring in a character's head. The film *Rustler's Rhapsody* does an interesting parody of meta-diegetic musical sources. After eating a 'special root', Rex O'Herlihan begins strumming his guitar. After a bit of solo strumming, other instruments along with back-up singers begin to surface on the soundtrack. Rex reacts with a smile of acknowledgment, stating 'The roots are kicking in now!' Thus, typical non-diegetic source music is attributed to his increasing hallucinatory mental state by way of a literalized meta-diegetic presentation.

Visual elements of film can also be parodied by literalizing their usage. One such element is the Hollywood cliché of the 'spinning newspaper' found in a number of older films. This effect is typically created by a rapid spin of the camera with the connotation of 'hot off the press'. This convention is spoofed in an interesting scene from *The Last Remake of Beau Geste* in which the butler walks into a room and finds the newspaper spinning on the floor; yet here the object itself is literally spinning, rather than an illusion being created by tricky camera movements. Spinning too fast for its contents to be read, the newspaper prompts the butler to state, 'Oh, I think I've found another movie cliché!' Another element parodied in *The Last Remake of Beau Geste* is the use of the iris shot. As Digby talks to the camera, an iris begins to form and close in on his face. When the iris gets close to completely closing, Digby puts out his hand and physically stops the iris from getting smaller, allowing himself enough time to finish reciting his lines.

The conventions denoting the flashback are humorously parodied in *Johnny Dangerously* as Johnny begins telling a kid a story about his own youth. Just as Johnny starts saying, 'I started out like you, kid. It must have been ... what ... twenty-five years ago ...,' the image begins to get blurry accompanied by the sounds of harps. Reacting to these cinematic codes for a flashback, the kid self-reflexively asks, 'What's going on?' to which Johnny replies, 'Ah, don't worry. It will end in a couple of minutes. It always does this when I talk of the past.' Again, the tricks of the trade are exposed and ridiculed by the narrative while still serving some function within the story.

With all of these examples of literalization, we can see how they function parodically by the setting up of certain expectations (based on the lexicon or syntactic rules of the target texts) and then transforming them based on specific linguistic or sociological rules of shared meaning.

8
Extraneous Inclusion

Film parodies often disrupt expected conventional associations through the method of 'extraneous inclusion'. This parodic method operates by inserting 'foreign' lexical units into a conventionalized syntax or through the inclusion of narrative scenes that fall outside of the target text's general conventions.

Lexicon

In order to generate and subvert narrative expectation, film parodies occasionally introduce extraneous film sets into prototextually conventional syntactic planes to create difference. For example, in *Blazing Saddles*, the old West town of Rockridge looks consistent with other traditional sets found in the Western genre except for one noticeable item: a 'frontier version' of Howard Johnson's Ice Cream Parlor (complete with a sign advertising '1 flavor'). The inclusion of a modern restaurant chain violates the historical realism of the set and generates a certain amount of incongruity between the time periods. Similarly, in *Austin Powers: International Man of Mystery* (1997), the familiar statue of the 'big boy' from the US-based Big Boy chain of restaurants appears perched on top of a swanky London club and therefore violates the expected look of the London location. Yet soon after, we find out that the 'big boy' statue is actually the spaceship of Dr Evil as it blasts off into the Earth's stratosphere – therefore serving an even greater absurd function within the narrative. Extraneous settings are also presented through the use of inappropriate film footage which does not fit within the established time period or narratively-placed geographical setting. *The Silence of the Hams* (1994), for example, opens with a subtitle stating 'Los Angeles, California', yet the images being shown behind the title are clearly old, stock footage of tourists exploring the streets and canals of Venice, Italy.

The use of projected back-drops can also be parodied by using extraneous back-drops that clash with either the narrative syntax or the historical period of the film. In a scene from *Hot Shots!*, a pilot named 'Washout' deviates slightly from his planned flight course off the California coast and seems to have gotten lost. When the plane finally lands, he accidentally finds himself in Las Vegas, complete with an intentionally obvious fake projected back-drop of the Sin City that looks like it was culled from an outdated travelogue. Misplaced projected back-drops are also utilized during the opening credits of the *Naked Gun* films. Filmed from the perspective of a camera mounted on the roof of a speeding police car (complete with spinning red light), the shot begins by depicting the car manoeuvring through a busy street. The 'setting' then changes as the car races through increasingly absurd locations: a mansion's interior, a women's locker room, a roller coaster and even a bowling alley. The spinning red police car light motif is taken to even further extremes in *Naked Gun 33 1/3: The Final Insult* (1994) as the 'car' becomes a fighter space craft and enters classic footage of the climactic Death Star raid scene from *Star Wars*. In all of these examples, an extraneous setting is inserted within a syntax of similarity in order to create incongruous difference.

Similar to the parodic methods of inversion and literalization, the inclusion of extraneous character types also functions to create incongruity within the parodic text. As stated previously, each logonomic system's syntax contains a certain constellation of expected character types that occur throughout the narrative. The placing of characters that violate this expectation can be seen in a variety of parody films. For example, the inclusion of a medieval hangman in *Blazing Saddles* violates the geographical and historical character determinants of the Western genre. Another example from *Blazing Saddles* has Hedley Lamarr assembling a gang of the 'meanest people of the West'. As they stand in line to 'sign up', the camera pans across a line of worldly (and historically removed) renegades, including white-hooded KKK members, Nazi soldiers, motorcycle gang members and rifle-toting Middle-Eastern characters riding camels. Such inclusion violates the syntactic expectation of what characters populate the world of the Western film. A similar example occurs as a line of men attempt to sign up for the Foreign Legion in *The Last Remake of Beau Geste* with the inclusion of a Santa Claus character and a nun scattered among the various tattered ex-con characters. Lastly, a character looking quite similar to Igor in *Frankenstein* plays a Martian astrologer in *Lobster Man from Mars* (1989). From these examples, we can see how the construction of parodic characters operates by utilizing a number of lexical techniques.

The concept of lifting dialogue spoken by these characters can exhibit a variety of parodic uses by the insertion of extraneous or inappropriate phrases that are recognizable excerpts from other films. A particularly interesting example of this occurs in *Naked Gun 33 1/3*. As the main characters hide out in the country after escaping from prison, they test their top secret new form of explosive by blowing up a tower in the distance. After the explosion (represented visually by old footage of an atomic blast), Rocco (played by Fred Ward) begins to laugh in a familiar 'Beavis-sounding' manner: ' heh, heh, heh, heh, cool. Heh, heh, heh, heh, cool.' The choice of appropriating an identifiable dialogue pattern from an already parodic television programme, *Beavis and Butt-head*, creates a transtextual, ironic layer which functions as a parody of a parody.

The use of costumes that extraneously fall out of the target text's range is another particularly effective method utilized in generating distance from that target. Thus, not only does Dracula dress in his typical attire in *Love at First Bite*, we later are presented with an opportunity to see him dressed quite differently, in this case, sitting in his underwear! Similarly, Frankenfurter's initial costume in *The Rocky Horror Picture Show* is fairly predictable for his character (a lab coat), yet becomes completely incongruous as it is transformed into a kinky lingerie outfit with pearls. The Zorro character in *Zorro, The Gay Blade* opts for a costume that veers away from the caped, black-masked prototype; choosing instead to wear a plum-coloured suit trimmed with lace.

Furthering the goal of disruption, costumes from outside logonomic systems can 'invade' that of the target. As pilot Ted Striker prepares to step on to the disco dance floor in *Airplane!*, he pulls off his uniform to expose another identifiable costume: John Travolta's white-vested suit from the 1977 *Saturday Night Fever* (see Figure 19). Thus,

EXTRANEOUS INCLUSION

Fig. 19: *Airplane!*

the inclusion of extraneous costumes disrupts expectations of how that character should typically dress and creates a high level of parodic incongruity between conventionalized costumes and 'outside' outfits.

The inclusion of extraneous or absurd icons can also disrupt the inter-relationship between sets of icons and their assemblage into an expected syntax. A scene from *Blazing Saddles* clearly demonstrates this mode of parodic disruption. On their way to attack the town of Rockridge, the gang of bad guys are seen riding across the open plains. At one point, they encounter a toll booth gate in the middle of an open field. Rather than logically going around the absurdly-placed booth, the leader sends one of his men back for 'a whole shit load of dimes'. Thus, the inclusion of an extraneous element results in a shift of syntactic action (waiting for dimes and then individually going through the gate). As we have seen from the presented examples, the shifting of lexical elements through the parodic method of extraneous inclusion both confirms and disrupts viewer expectations based on the prototexts as well as functions to problematize lexical contributions to the syntactic chain.

Syntax

In an effort to generate incongruity, parodic discourse also utilizes scenes that are borrowed from unrelated logonomic systems. This creates a parody not only of the target texts (through the inclusion of an extraneous element), but also of the incorporated scene. Set in 1960s London, *Austin Powers: International Man of Mystery* incorporates an extraneous scene from *A Hard Day's Night* (1964) which has Austin being chased through the streets of London by a mob of fans. Although this particular narrative scenario does not fit within the larger logonomic system being targeted (James Bond films), it does follow a logical lexical shift based on both time period and setting. Another example is *Hot Shots!* which pulls scenes from a number of films, including *Raging Bull* (1980), *Gone With the Wind* (1939) and *Superman* (1978), while *Top Secret!* borrows from *The Blue Lagoon* (1980) and a number of Elvis vehicles. At times, the scenes themselves are full of parodic exaggeration. Used as a romantic flashback scene in *Airplane!*, the famous intide love scene found in *From Here to Eternity* (1953) is evoked, yet this time the scene is less than romantic as they become entangled with floating debris and seaweed. This is also a complex parody of Burt Lancaster who not only played one of the romantic pair in *From Here to Eternity* but also starred in one of the central targeted texts, *Airport*.

Some films seem more ripe than others to be used for extraneous incorporation. Often, these are films that were highly popular when released (thus ensuring spectatorial recognition), yet have 'aged poorly' – often due to their topicality or investment in temporary fads. One film that continuously serves this role is *Saturday Night Fever* with its plot centred on disco dancing. In *They Call Me Bruce?*, the scene of Travolta's character, Tony, walking down the street of the city is mimicked, with the camera focusing on his feet in stride and looks of people passing him by (accompanied, of course, by the canonical strains of 'Staying Alive'). Yet in this scene, the rock instruments have been transformed into Chinese instruments. *Airplane!* also features an incorporation of an extraneous scene. As a spoof of disaster films, the inclusion of a 1970s disco film reaches beyond the targeted logonomic system. As Ted Striker sits in a bar and gets drunk, disco lights come on and the recognizable beat of 'Staying Alive' can be heard. As he enters the floor, changing his clothes into a vest mimicking Travolta's signature costume, Striker begins to replicate many of the dance moves seen in *Saturday Night Fever*, yet often extending them beyond sheer physical capacity (for example his ability to perform a Russian kick-step dance with *no* feet on the ground).

Another method for generating parodic juxtaposition is through the incorporation of extraneous material that is already imbued with either a parodic impulse or can be read as parodic. For example, a scene in *Repossessed* features the family sitting in the living room and watching television as an infamously hideous commercial for an electrical device comes on. The accompanying soundtrack clues us in to the product as we hear a familiar cheesy slogan: 'Clap on, clap off'. Here, the mere presence of the kitschy television commercial produces an element of parody to the surrounding syntax.

Extraneous scenes employed to create difference also often transcend both historical and technical boundaries of the target text. For example, in *Blazing Saddles*, the sheriff attempts to subdue 'monster man' Mongo by re-enacting a scene found in many cartoons. Dressed up as a 'candy-gram' man, Bart delivers to Mongo a box of candy containing a bomb. As Bart quickly leaves the room, the signature Warner Bros. tune of 'That's All Folks' plays as the bomb detonates. Similarly, the narrative of *Frankenweenie* initially follows the basic syntax found in *Frankenstein* with a couple of lexical shifts: a monster (Sparky the dog) is chased up a tall building (a castle in a miniature golf course) by irate citizens who end up setting fire to the building and killing the monster. Yet the following scene completely strays from the original as the citizens attempt to revive Sparky by linking jumper cables between their cars and connecting them to the dog's electrodes. Thus, the films incorporate a scene that not only was conventionalized after the historical period targeted, but which also fits outside of the targeted logonomic system to create an incongruity of narrative patterning.

Style

In terms of stylistically-created parody, film titles and graphics can be 'inappropriately' employed to generate ironic distance. In a typical non-parodic film, titles are often used, especially at the end of movies, to convey specific production information to the audience. Film parody often disrupts this tradition by including information that is extraneous to production credits. For example, the end credits for *Hot Shots!* mixes recipes and various lists ('Things to do after the movie') with actual production credits. In line with its role as a 'rocumentary', *This Is Spinal Tap* ends with an advertisement pitching the band's greatest hits album (a fictitious product, of course). Looking quite convincing, the ad is immediately followed by titles reading: 'For anyone who thought the preceding Greatest Hits commercial was real ... IT WASN'T! The aforementioned record does not exist. Neither does Spinal Tap. And there's no Easter Bunny, either! Have a nice day.' Thus, the film finally overtly exposes its artifice and announces its parodic status (although this did not deter the many viewers who reportedly showed up to record stores requesting Spinal Tap's 'Greatest Hits' album).

Rather than manipulating expected musical styles and sound effects, extraneous sounds and music can be introduced to disrupt the logonomic system. One identifiable theme that appears in many parodies is the signature tune from *Jaws* (1975). This tune emerges in two particular parodies that make a metaphorical association between 'Jaws' (the shark) and their flying vehicles. *Airplane!* opens with a shot of the sky above a thick blanket of clouds. The *Jaws* theme appears as the 'fin' of the plane winds back and forth, circling beneath the clouds. *Spaceballs* also utilizes the *Jaws* theme by playing it each time we get an exterior shot of the space station floating through space. The narrative action thus mimics a scenario from another 'unrelated' film as well as uses its related theme music.

The voice-over is another source for the inclusion of extraneous material that is either irrelevant to the narrative itself or borrowed from another identifiable source. One particular technique found in classical cinema is the use of voice-overs during a character's remembrance of past narrative events, especially during highly emotive scenes. In *Hot Shots!*, the main character, Topper, begins to lose faith in his ability to fly while on a mission. As he begins to concentrate on his ability to fly the plane safely, voice-overs of past people's comments regarding his ability to fly can be heard, ranging from the positive to the negative. As this battle of remembered voices wages, another voice-over enters his head: George Bush uttering his famous campaign promise: 'Read my lips, No new taxes.' A similar example occurs in *Repossessed* as Father Mayi encourages Father Luke Brophy for his upcoming exorcism with a voice stating: 'Luke – It is your destiny.' In contrast to the *Hot Shots!* example, the actual voice here belongs to the Mayi character and is indeed narratively relevant, but the dialogue has been reappropriated from *Star Wars*.

Finally, incongruity is generated in parody by employing extraneous visual elements which typically fall outside of the expected logonomic system. For example, stock footage is often incorporated in parody films in order to point to their obvious inclusion within the text. During the flashback scene previously discussed from *Johnny Dangerously*, the images representing the 1910s are composed primarily of black-and-white stock footage from old newsreels, including one reporting on the activities of President Taft. Stock footage is also used in *Airplane!* as Ted Striker remembers his plane crash from earlier years – visualized using an assortment of stock footage depicting plane crashes from different time periods. In a scene from *Repossessed*, the segment begins with a shot of a college campus which looks suspiciously like it is from a college recruitment film. The subtitle gives its source away, stating 'Stock footage: University of California at Chicago, seventeen years later...'. Not only does the inclusion of obvious stock footage parody the many times when such footage is used in the hope that no one will notice, its overt announcement of such exposes the traditional practice. As all three of these sections have demonstrated, filmic lexicon, syntax and style can be manipulated in a parodic manner by the inclusion of extraneous elements that disrupt conventional expectations.

Let us next turn to the last parodic method of 'exaggeration' and look at the ways in which it takes established norms and alters them through the processes of excess and repetition.

9
Exaggeration

When people think of parody, they often equate it directly with exaggeration – recognizing one of parody's central methods of ironic transformation. Essentially, exaggeration functions by targeting lexical, syntactic and stylistic elements of the prototext and extending them beyond their conventionally expected limits.

Lexicon

As a lexical element, character names in film parodies can be transformed and exaggerated to comment on larger qualities found in prototextual logonomic systems. This exploits the typical containment of character names in referring to their own qualities. As Seymour Chatman mentions, the proper name in film and literature 'is a kind of ultimate residence of personality, not a quality but a locus of qualities, the narrative-noun that is endowed with but never exhausted by the qualities, the narrative-adjectives' (1978, p. 131). Thus, parody characters often exceed their narrative-noun status by taking on qualities that reflect larger narrative issues. For example, as a critique of the basic homogeneity found in characters playing the townsfolk in a typical Western film, *Blazing Saddles* exploits this convention metatextually by naming *everyone* in the town of Rockridge 'Johnson'. *The Last Remake of Beau Geste* also pokes fun at homogeneous character names. In the original *Beau Geste* (1939), one scene features the Gary Cooper character protecting his anonymity while joining the Foreign Legion by reporting his name as 'Smith'. In the parody, *all* of the enlistees report their name as 'Smith'. A similar form of homogeneity is critiqued by way of exaggerating Hollywood's reliance on conventionalized stock characters by *not* naming them. In *Rustler's Rhapsody*, Rex O'Herlihan stops into the saloon to get acquainted with the townsfolk. The town drunk strides over and stands next to him and offers to introduce him to all of the people who 'mattered' in the town. Eventually, he describes (in a stodgy, script-like fashion) all of the typical, conventionalized characters found in a Western (e.g. 'Over there is the homely schoolmarm, and over there the evil ranch owner ...').

The parodic method of exaggeration also exists outside of the realm of character naming and operates in terms of the manner in which actors perform, which in turn influences the flow of lexical units along the syntactic chain. Certain amounts of exaggerated under-playing or over-acting can stall the narrative progression and lead to a fetishization of performance at the expense of narrative continuity. Under-playing by actors can often be seen in parodies where the actors are known for the serious performances. For example, in *Airplane!*, Robert Stack underacts his role as all of the characters surrounding him go over the top. This sets up a telling contrast between the roles and functions to comment ironically on past 'serious' depictions as well as the parody's goofy performances by otherwise serious actors.

In contrast, many performances are over-exaggerated and create an incongruity by distancing their place in the syntax. In horror films, one typically expects characters to scream, but when they do so very excessively, such as in *Saturday the 14th* (1981) the effect of horror is supplanted by one of comicality due to the inappropriateness of the emotional level. Similarly, when the neighbours are assembled in *Frankenweenie* to meet the newly 're-animated' Sparky, they begin panicking by screaming hysterically and hiding behind pieces of furniture – all of which exceed the 'fright level' of the little dog. In *Silent Movie*, the acting is done in an exaggerated and emotive style which evokes the acting found in early silent film melodramas. Not only is this acting style highly clichéd, it is also incongruent with the acting styles we expect in a contemporary film.

Parodic disruption can also focus on manipulating dialogue from the target text itself through the method of exaggeration. As a parody of Luke Skywalker's bright-eyed dialogue (words such as 'Gosh') in *Star Wars*, Fluke Starbucker delivers a line consisting of 'Gosh, wow-wee, geepers, Golly willikers' in *Hardware Wars*. In Susan Sontag's fictitious interview in *Zelig*, she delivers lines that not only parody typical 'expert' responses found in historical compilation documentaries, but also parody her own style of critical assessment. Opening up the film, Sontag states: 'He was the phenomenon of the 1920s. We think that, at that time, he was as well known as Lindbergh – it's really quite astonishing.' These two examples are helpful in that they display two sides of exaggeration. Starbucker's repetition clues the viewer into its blatant exaggeration, while Sontag's more subtle delivery calls for greater familiarity with the target text.

The exaggeration of a genre's recognized and familiar speech pattern through poor grammatical usage can generate lexical units that fit uneasily in some syntactic systems. For example, film noir, taken as a logonomic system, is canonical in its use of smooth-talking characters and quick delivery of snappy one-liners. Yet this expectation is violated in *The Cheap Detective*, as Peter Falk's character accidentally rattles off: 'Throw the bed on the gun!'

A more subtle level of distance is created when costumes in film parodies are designed to follow the basic design of expected dress, but are exaggerated to the point of absurdity. Dark Helmet's helmet in *Spaceballs* is well over three times the size of the already large helmet worn by Darth Vader in *Star Wars* (see Figure 20). Due to its huge size, the helmet constantly gets in the way of Dark's movement around the space station. In one scene, the helmet obstructs his vision and he walks directly into the camera, creates a loud thud and is hurled to the ground; this acknowledges the camera's presence on the set. Another identifiable costuming element from *Star Wars* is the hair-bun style of hair worn by Princess Leia. In *Hardware Wars*, the hair-buns are transformed into, literally, baked sticky-buns glued to the side of her head. Another scene in *Spaceballs* pokes fun at Leia's hair. As Princess Vespa and Dot Matrix make a get-away in their space car, Vespa seems to be ignoring Matrix's verbal advice on how to handle the situation. It is then revealed that the hair-buns are actually headphones piping loud music into her ears. Similarly, in *I'm Gonna Git You, Sucka*, the standard outfit is exaggerated for the pimp character Fly Guy. Accenting many of the stereotypical elements of a pimp's costume, as found in such films as *Cleopatra Jones* (1973) and *Superfly* (1972), Fly Guy's outfit con-

Fig. 20: *Spaceballs* (Mel Brooks, 1987)

sists of huge bell bottom trousers, a giant oversized feathered hat and eight-inched heeled shoes each containing a mini-aquarium with fish and water.

In terms of iconography, elements can be exaggerated in order to create a sense of irony with regard to how they are conventionally depicted. In *Airplane!*, what begins as a typical pan of the plane's control panel turns into a long-running shot of countless controls that would spatially exceed the confines of the cockpit. A similar exaggeration occurs during the first shot of *Spaceballs*. We begin to see the nose of the space station enter at the right hand of the film's frame as it passes our situated position – a common establishing shot in science-fiction films. Yet, in the parody, the shot (which typically takes less than fifteen seconds to complete) takes over a hundred seconds for the mega-huge *Spaceballs* space station to completely pass the camera position. Such exaggeration violates temporal and spatial expectations and creates an ironic comment on the film's iconic scale.

Syntax

As with the exaggeration of lexical units, the syntax can be extended to exaggerated lengths through the combination of actions which exceed expected quantity or order. One of the means to create such exaggeration is by stringing together narrative elements which overly state a specific point. In the film, *Top Gun*, the narrative role of luck is highly important as the flyers will do anything to increase their odds. In *Hot Shots!*, this role of luck is over-extended by repeated references to it. In a moment of foreshadowing the character, 'Dead Meat's' eventual crash, the narrative places before him: his missing 'lucky' gum, a black cat crossing his path, his walking under a ladder, a shattering mirror, his deciding to sign his life insurance policy *after* he returns, and his informing his wife that he has undeniable proof regarding John F. Kennedy's assassination and will keep it in his pocket until he returns. Another indicative example of narrative exaggeration occurs in *Dead Men Don't Wear Plaid* as the film utilizes one of the key elements found in film noir: a piece of paper or a note that provides some clue to solving a mystery. Rather than using such an element only so as to heighten its value, the note appears excessively in the parody – enjoying over ten appearances as a valuable clue.

Character actions that make up the plot are often exaggerated in order to exceed general syntactic rules of how characters should behave and perform tasks. Often, these are centred on certain bodily functions. Echoing a gesture often seen in gangster-type films, a group of mobsters in *Johnny Dangerously* begin a series of nods to acknowledge their agreement on a subject. Yet the nodding becomes excessive as each character nods for five rounds until the leader finally cries out, 'No more nodding!' In *Blazing Saddles*, the Western cliché of a cowboy's heavy drinking is parodied by having the Waco Kid guzzle entire bottles of whisky. Another example is played out in *Airplane!* as it parodies a scene from the 1957 film, *Zero Hour*, which features pilots of a plane felled by ptomaine poisoning. This scenario is played out in the parody as all three pilots get sick from eating the fish. Whereas in the 1957 film their sickness was abrupt and less than graphic, the parody plays on this subtly by making the sickness quite explicit. As the doctor begins to explain to the stewardess the symptoms of the poisoning, the captain begins to immediately manifest these symptoms, including a fever, drooling, spasms, flatulence and eventual collapse. By making the sickness graphic, the parody exceeds the expected behaviour based on the target and creates an ironic distance between the earlier film and the parody.

Airplane!, in fact, is full of a variety of syntactic exaggerations that I can only briefly mention here. One canonical scene that is parodied is the uncontrollable outburst of the 'hysterical passenger' so often seen in disaster films and typically climaxed by a swift slap on the face and those infamous words 'get a hold of yourself!' In the parody, the woman is slapped by the doctor, followed by a procession of people lined up to slap her, including a nun, two men brandishing a baseball bat and a woman holding a gun. Another scene features the doctor telling the passengers not to worry and that all was under control. Borrowing from the beloved Pinocchio cartoon character, the doctor's nose begins to grow as he continues to tell the passengers not to panic.

Narrative exaggeration also occurs when the actions performed by the characters do not fit with the logic of the plot in an overly-understated manner. At times, this is centred on the appropriateness of etiquette during certain narrative moments. For example, as the plane finally crash lands in *Airplane!*, the narrative features a smiling stewardess slipping back into her stereotypical role and saying 'Thank you for flying Transglobal' and 'Have a nice day!' while the frightened passengers disembark down the emergency slide. Similarly, parodic narratives often take an understated approach when juxtaposed with overly-exaggerated syntactic elements. In *Silent Movie*, the film-makers are waiting in the lobby to see how the opening night audience reacts to their newly released 'silent' movie. As the film ends and the lights come up, the audience breaks into hysterical applause, complete with balloons, confetti and circus performers doing trapeze acts from the cinema's ceiling. Responding to the audience's reaction, director Mel Funn exclaims in a most understated fashion via a title card, 'They seem to like it.' *Austin Powers: International Man of Mystery* uses a similar exaggerated form of the understatement by directly commenting on a clichéd story line often seen in James Bond films: the ridiculously drawn out attempt by the villain to eliminate the captured hero. As Dr Evil orders the death of Austin and Vanessa (by way of immersion into a pool of mutated sea bass) he instructs his guard to 'start the unnecessarily slow dipping process'. In line with Dr Evil's order, the entire scene is played out in a deliberately slow manner to accentuate the narrative pace often exhibited in the prototexts.

The action of a dead person falling down is often parodied by having the characters perform non-customary and exaggerated deaths. The old cliché of someone clutching their heart as they slump to the ground has long been the source of previous criticism for filmic realism. In *Beau Geste*, one of the more memorable scenes is filled with propped-up dead soldiers on the wall of the fort, a clever trick to send the impression of alive soldiers prepared to shoot. In *The Last Remake of Beau Geste*, the evil sergeant complains when everyone who gets shot fails to fall down. In *The Cheap Detective*, the shooting victims get shot so fast they don't have time to fall down and thus remain standing and stiff. All of these examples demonstrate how syntactic action can be both reiterated (a shooting in a film noir) and exaggerated (not falling down) in order to create an incongruity between the expected inter-relation of the two actions.

Narrative exaggeration can also be achieved by manipulating the editing of a shot. In *The Exorcist*, Regan kills a man by hurling him out of a window and down a long flight of outside stairs. In its parody, *Repossessed*, this scene is recreated with Father Mayi tripping down the stairs leading to the second floor and falling for a period that is at least ten times as long as in the original. This effect is achieved by repeating the shots of his fall over and over through an editing trick that is easily discernible. In *Austin Powers: International Man of Mystery*, one scene features Austin and Vanessa jumping on to a steamroller to evade capture by Dr Evil's guards. As they begin to drive forward, one of the guards is seen (by way of a quick zoom shot) to be immediately in front of the steamroller screaming and preparing to be flattened. There is then a cut back to a long shot and we see that the guard is over fifty feet away from the slow-moving steamroller. Humorously, he remains motionless and screaming. Finally, the steamroller does indeed reach the guard and, as expected, completely flattens him. Through the use of editing, the syntactic progression is jilted in a manner which exaggerates the story itself.

Lastly, parodic syntax can be exaggerated through the repetition of scenes – repeating actions that are not narratively motivated through flashbacks or other temporal-altering devices. One method for generating intra-repetition is through the repetition of imported, quoted material. In *Dead Men Don't Wear Plaid*, a stock footage shot of a woman extracting a bullet from a wounded arm with her teeth is repeated three times in the film – each time Rigby gets shot in the arm. The recognition of the same action (and shot) being repeated creates a syntax full of ironic *déjà vu*.

Newly shot material in a parody can also be repeated in order to destabilize the integrity of a discrete syntax. The parody film, *Movie, Movie*, is composed of two separate films within a 'double feature'. In order to create parodic intertextuality through intra-repetition, both films begin with the exact opening shots of a city street. Due to their close proximity within a single film, both instances of the same scene create a juxtaposition that highlights both parody's intertextual quality as well as the cinema's reliance on re-using movie lot sets in multiple films. Again, the syntax of both shorts is disrupted by the violation of narrative discreteness. In *Spy Hard*, a similar example of repeating narrative material occurs which parodies temporal continuity in film. When Dick Steele runs into his previous partner, Steven Bishop, he recalls how 'we go back a long way' which initiates a flashback, complete with a blurred visuals transition. But in this instance, the flashback turns out to be merely the same scene we have just watched, yet this time in black and white to connote 'the past'. Such narrative disruption, then, functions to derail syntactic progression by repeating material which one expects to have very specific temporal anchorings.

Style

Another means for generating parodic incongruity is through the stylistic exaggeration of titles and graphics. *Blazing Saddles* opens with a clichéd, wooden-looking title graphic commonly found in Western films. As its size begins to increase from the middle of the screen in front of a panoramic open plains back-drop, it begins to overtake the screen space until it fills the screen entirely, with only small amounts of the background still visible. A similar exaggeration of graphic size can be seen in *Spaceballs* with its titles completely blocking out the scene behind. This disruption of conventionalized background/foreground relations produces some incongruity by using graphics often utilized in prototexual presentations in a manner that violates the style of past presentations.

Certain signature uses of titles have also been parodied to create an exaggerated effect of ironic incongruity. One such famous example begins in *Star Wars*, which opens with a scrolling title reading: 'A long time ago in a galaxy far, far away …'. Using the same scrolling technique, the title is exaggerated in *Spaceballs*, reading 'In a galaxy very, very, very, very far away …'. The parody thus operates narratively and technically in the same fashion, but excessively repeats the word 'very' in order to generate some lexical incongruity within the syntax of economic adjectives. The film *Hardware Wars* similarly parodies the scrolling text by poking fun at the original's seeming vagueness in description: 'Meanwhile. … In another part of the galaxy, later that same day…'. *Star Wars*' scrolling titles technique (and typeface) is evoked yet again in *Airplane II: The Sequel*, with a title reading: 'By the close of the twentieth century, construction of colonies on the lunar surface had begun …' Here, only the style is evoked with the actual content being transformed.

Exaggeration in terms of sound effects can also be used to engender parodic discourse. In the film, *Love at First Bite*, the soundtrack focuses on the typical horror convention of the lone wolf howling in the distance. This, of course, functions as an element of similarity in reproducing a horror cliché. The film's transformation of the cliché begins by the inclusion of other howling wolves, thereby destroying the notion of a lone wolf readying to become a wolfman. When the howling reaches a very loud level, Dracula yells out to them to be quiet, and they immediately obey. This also violates expectations of character relations, with the wolves understanding and obeying the command on cue.

Anyone who has watched the *Star Wars* trilogy is familiar with one of the films' most identifiable aural elements – Darth Vader's deep, heavy breathing through his black-masked helmet. This signature quality is utilized in the two *Star Wars* spoofs. First, in *Spaceballs*, the breathing is heard in the same fashion – deep and amplified through the mouth piece. Soon, though, this breathing gets more rapid and irregular with the character, Dark Helmet, pulling up the face shield and exclaiming: 'I can't breath in this thing!' Second, in *Hardware Wars*, every time the character, Darph Nader, attempts to speak, none of the characters can understand him through the helmet. In one particular scene, Darph begins to torture the princess and lists his commands, yet since his deep voice is so muffled, she must repeatedly say to him, 'I can't understand you! What are you saying?' A similar scene occurs in *National Lampoon's Loaded Weapon 1* (1993) as Sgt Jack Colt and Sgt Wes Luger enter the high-security prison to question famed serial killer, Harold Leacher (a clever parody of the Hannibal Lecter character in *Silence of the Lambs*). Asked a pointed question by Sgt Colt, Harold attempts to respond, yet is only able to speak in a garbled mess with his security face mask prohibiting any form of clear speech. Such exaggeration works not only to connote a source of identification with the original sound source, but also to transform it to the logical extreme of unintelligibility.

Narrator voice-overs can be over-exaggerated in order to create a mood that stands beyond the tone set by the narrative. In a pointed comment directed toward its proto-text, the voice-over narrator in *Closet Cases of the Nerd Kind* states: 'Don't miss the incredibly over-budget finale!' In *Lust in the Dust*, the voice-over narrator over-exaggerates the effects of the New Mexico sun by employing over twenty-five synonyms for the word 'hot' including 'toasting' and 'searing'. Such exaggeration, as evidenced in the over-use of adjectives in narrative titles, works to break the narrative out of its seamless flow of causality and into an overtly constructed text.

Music is also exaggerated in order to punctuate both its similarity and difference. At the end of *Airplane!*, the soundtrack fills with a conventional 'angelic' choir. This remains conventional until the singers begin to hit the higher notes, transforming a sweet sound into loudly pitched screams, thus disrupting the smooth contours of such music. *High Anxiety* also mimics Bernard Herrmann's scores from past Hitchcock films, it, however, over-embellishes their tensional quality with overly strained violin slashes and pounding timpani.

Exaggeration of visual style is often employed in parody film not only to create a level of ironic incongruity, but also to highlight film's constructed nature. For example, the use of special effects has long been found in science-fiction films where the unbelievable can be visualized. In *Hardware Wars*, the film constantly attempts to expose its 'special' effects. 'The spoof is capsulized when the announcer says "Thrill to the expensive spine-tingling special effects," and we are shown a dinky sparkler' (Fosselius and Fadiman, 1978, p. 2). A canonical scene from *Star Wars* that is often parodied is the Millennium Falcon's jump into hyper-space – often signalled by the cockpit view of passing stars becoming only light trails. In *Hardware Wars*, the ship's move into light speed is accompanied by light trails that transform into a wacky kaleidoscope of psychedelic patterns. The ship in *Spaceballs* moves beyond hyper-space and into 'hyper-active' by hitting 'ludicrous' speed, again resulting in psychedelic patterns. As the graphics fill the screen, the ship bypasses the battle cruiser, resulting in Barf's observation that they have 'gone to plaid'! All of these special effects either under-impress (an obvious sparkler) or exaggerate the ability to create fantastic images – both resulting in the exposure of a film's constructed nature.

Part Three
Watching Film Parody

10
Reading the Parodic

The 'watching of film parody' is a complex and multi-tiered affair with numerous textual, pragmatic and ideological factors interacting to create a 'moment of meaning'. After examining the various 'methods' of film parody, it might prove fruitful to examine just how these operate textually (in terms of lexicon, syntax and style) within a cohesive segment of narrative to bring about a textual opportunity for parodic meaning.

This chapter analyses three 'readings' of film parodies – each of which focuses on different levels of analysis. The first reading analyses the opening scene of *UHF* (1989) – a film which provides a fairly convincing spoof of the 1981 adventure film, *Raiders of the Lost Ark* – to see how the various forms of lexical shifts work to create both similarity to and difference from the target text. The second reading looks at the cult, short film, *Porklips Now* (1980) – a parody of Francis Ford Coppola's *Apocalypse Now* – to see how parodic texts function systematically in terms of both lexical and syntactic operations. This chapter ends with a detailed and combined analysis (looking at lexical, syntactic and stylistic levels) of the opening three-and-a-half minutes of *Naked Gun 33 1/3: The Final Insult* (1994). Taken together, these readings illustrate not only the systematic means by which film parody operates, but also demonstrates how such analyses can be conducted on a number of different textual levels.

Lexical Analysis of Opening Scene in *UHF*

As a brief cast study of parodic, lexical transformation, let us first turn to an analysis of the opening scene of *UHF* – again a parody of *Raiders of the Lost Ark* (1981). What is especially interesting and appropriate about this filmic example is its syntactical similarity, which leaves the transformation of lexical elements as the primary method by which it creates the requisite difference.

The opening scene of the sequence is set in a Mexican jungle – which creates an immediate connection to its prototext – and is populated by three identifiable and reiterated characters from the target text: two local guides and an unnamed Indiana Jones-type main character. One of the initial disruptions which sticks out is the recognition that the main character is played by 'Weird Al' Yankovic (an extraneous use of a known star to play a different role). Adding to the parody is the knowledge that 'Weird Al' is a comedian known primarily for his outrageous parodies of songs and music videos. He is also dressed in the expected archeological attire: leather jacket, trademark Acubra-like hat, and a whip by his side (reiterated costume and iconographic elements). As they proceed through the jungle, one of the guides attempts to kill the main character, but instead gets his entire arm 'whipped' off as he flees in pain (iconographic exaggeration). The music which plays on the soundtrack for the entire segment mimics the music heard in the target text with its adventurous, tension-creating sounds.

As they enter a cob-webbed covered cave, the remaining guide points out that it is forbidden to enter the cave, stating: 'Señor, you must not go any further. Look . . .!' as he points to an Inca god carved into the cave's wall. Yet this icon has been transformed to take on a different-looking expression than expected, with his fingers pulling each corner of his mouth wide open and his tongue sticking out (iconographic inversion). As the guide backs out of the cave, an extraneous object within a jungle setting – a train – goes by and sweeps him to his certain death (extraneous inclusion). Unfazed, the main character elects to press on. As he enters the next section of the cave, he encounters an exaggerated and extraneous number of literal warning signs which seem out of place inside of a cave, including yellow crime scene police tape and roadside signs stating 'Do Not Enter' and 'Wrong Way. Stop: Severe Tire Damage' (iconographic literalization).

As the main character finally enters the end of the cave, he sees the coveted religious artefact: an Oscar statuette (which is both an inversion and a misdirection for the viewer). Reiterating a scenario from the original text, the main character pulls out a bag of sand to swap for the statuette in order to avoid setting off any booby-traps. After weighing out the correct amount of sand in the bag, he decides to forgo the swap and quickly snatches the Oscar – triggering a trap which begins a massive cave-in. As he runs through the cave avoiding falling rocks, he passes another extraneous and literal road-side sign: an orange 'Watch for Falling Rocks' sign (iconographic literalization).

Staying in accordance with the original narrative, the next scene features a huge, rolling boulder chasing the main character through the cave. It is an obvious matte shot with slightly off-matching colours and lighting that misdirects the viewer with its overt misplacement within the film's 'realism'. As he leaps out of the cave into expected safety, the boulder continues to chase him through a drastic change of locations, represented by various segments of extraneous stock footage: a sphinx in Egypt, a German village, a snow-covered mountainside and finally down a city street (misdirected and extraneous settings). The segment ends with the main character falling down in the middle of the street and the boulder literally flattening him completely, a probable misdirection of how we expect the hero to end up within the narrative.

As this brief sequence demonstrates, such lexical transformations operate to effectively produce both ironic distance and narrative incongruity by shifting not only the paradigmatic elements which are commonly placed within a particular logonomic system, but also their associated syntactic expectations.

Analysis of *Porklips Now*

Let us next turn to examining how both lexical and syntactic planes inter-relate in a single film text. Through an analysis of *Porklips Now* (a parody of Francis Ford Coppola's *Apocalypse Now*), we will see how parodic texts function systematically in generating both similarity to and difference from a variety of target texts.

Porklips Now opens with a voice-over by the director who introduces the film by making reference to the extra-textual production history of *Apocalypse Now* (one full of cost

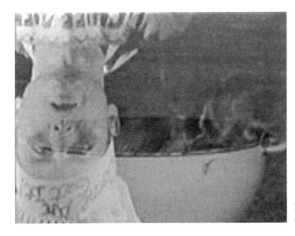

Fig. 21: *Porklips Now*
(Ernie Fosselius, 1980)

over-runs and excessive film footage), stating (and reiterating), 'While you are watching the film, I don't want you thinking about the forty million dollars that was spent and the millions and millions of feet of film that were shot over a period of four agonizing years.'

While the opening scene of *Apocalypse Now* consists of helicopters and lush palm trees bursting into flames from napalm charges (accompanied by the sound of helicopters and The Doors singing, 'The End'), *Porklips Now* opens with a lush backyard full of bushes, the huge flames of a BBQ, the sounds of a lawnmower and a similar-sounding Door's tune. Thus, the parody operates by transforming the lexical units of Vietnam warfare into backyard living, while reiterating the basic target syntax.

We next find out that Willard's name has been transmuted into 'Dullard', embodying both a phonetic shift and a play with the notion that a character's inner qualities can be read by his or her name (literalization through a pun). The actor playing Dullard not only physically resembles the original film's lead actor, Martin Sheen (creating a strand of similarity), he is, in fact, Billy Gray, better known as the son in the 1950s television programme, *Father Knows Best*. Thus, the casting of Gray simultaneously creates a sense of similarity (his resemblance to Sheen) and difference (his own self-parody).

The scene ends by echoing the original's image of Willard's face being superimposed, upside down, over a shot of a rotating ceiling fan by superimposing Dullard's face (with backyard chef's cap) over a shot of a flaming BBQ and a rotating lawn sprinkler (see Figure 21). Again, the syntactic graphic composition and elemental movement are reiterated but with different lexical items.

Dullard is then asked to join some men for a bite to eat in their mobile home trailer (repeating Willard's summons into a mobile military trailer). The main narrative begins at this point in *Apocalypse Now* as Willard receives orders to seek out and terminate a colonel named Kurtz who Willard's superiors believe has gone completely insane, likening him to a 'mad butcher'. In order to provide evidence of this, they play a recorded transmission of Kurtz speaking in Cambodia: 'I watched a snail crawling on an edge of a straight razor . . .'. In *Porklips Now*, many of the same syntactic elements are replicated, but the actual constituents are transformed. Dullard must seek out and terminate a mad butcher named Fred Mertz who is under-selling his competition by offering prime meat at only seven cents a pound. Again, the name Mertz represents a phonetic shift through literalization as well as parodying the name of the William Frawley character from the *I Love Lucy* television show. The men offer evidence to Dullard through a recorded transmission monitored from a local radio station ad: 'We're slashing prices with a straight razor!' Thus, the dialogue is altered (through logical misdirection) to reflect the transformed notion of a 'butcher' in the parody.

As the target film progresses, the action shifts to a military boat going up river to drop off Willard deep into enemy territory. He describes the boat's crew in a voice-over as 'rock n' rollers with one foot in their graves' and details each of the members: a mechanic named 'Chef', a surfer Lance, a ghetto boy 'Clean' and skipper Phillips. In *Porklips Now*, an inverted lexical shift has him picked up by a '63 Pontiac and driven to 'Chinatown'. Again, through a voice-over, he describes the other passengers: 'Rip' the skateboarder (a logical shift from water surfer to sidewalk skateboarder) and 'Slick', also called 'Cook' (a play with 'Chef') whom he describes as a 'rock n' roller with one foot on the gas and the other on the brake' (literalization). This segment of dialogue also thwarts established expectation by generating narrative misdirection, although still narratively motivated (he *is* the car's driver). As they move up the river, Willard pulls out the confidential dossier on Kurtz and begins to read. He describes Kurtz's credentials in a voice-over: 'third generation West Point, head of his class, Korea Airborne, etc., etc.'. In the parody, the dossier has been transformed through inversion into a scrapbook, in which he reads about Mertz's accomplishments: 'Head of the Rotary Club, Jaycees, Little League coach of the year, etc., etc.' (further inversion of Willard's distinguished military honours).

This scene is followed in *Apocalypse Now* with Willard meeting up with Colonel Kilgore played by Robert Duval. As Willard surveys the battle scene, he walks by a film director and crew (played by Coppola himself) who keep encouraging the soldiers to keep walking by and not to look into the camera. They all load into helicopters and lead an invasion, accompanied by the blasting sounds of Wagner's 'Ride of the Valkyrie'. As the soldiers on board prepare for battle, they all remove their helmets and sit on them so they 'don't get their balls blown off'. After they land, Kilgore announces his satisfaction of the raid, stating, 'I love the smell of napalm in the morning!'

Much of this scenario is reiterated in *Porklips Now*, yet with both lexical and syntactic transformation. Driving down the street, they are joined by a character based on Kilgore who is riding a moped instead of a helicopter (lexical inversion). After they talk for a while, complete with the declaration: 'I love the smell of carbon monoxide in the morning,' the gang rides on, accompanied by another version of the 'Ride of the Valkyrie' (complete with a disco beat and over-exaggerated singing). As they drive away, two riders sit on their helmets, mimicking the soldier's actions (narrative reiteration with the lexical revolving around type of helmet). Soon after, they pass a Coppola-looking director who coaches them to 'look at the camera, smile, smile, like you were acting!' – offering directions that invert the original's syntax.

Back in the target text, as Willard continues to examine Kurtz's file, he wonders how anyone could get charged with murder during a war, likening it to the absurdity of issuing a speeding ticket at the Indy 500. In *Porklips Now*, this scenario is repeated, yet in a transformed manner through a grammatical error in quoting the original dialogue, thus generating misdirection and subverting expectation. He states in a voice-over: 'But what did they really want with Mertz anyway? Accusing a guy like that of unfair pricing was like handing out parking tickets at the Indy Speedway, wait a minute, that's speeding ticket to the parkway, no wait a minute, let's see ...'

In *Apocalypse Now*, Willard's arrival at Kurtz's compound is accompanied by his voice-over stating that, 'I could feel his presence and knew he was nearby.' In an exaggeration of dialogue and narrative progression, Dullard's arrival to Chinatown is accompanied by a series of comments relating to Mertz's near presence: 'He was close, real close,' 'I couldn't see him yet, but he was real close,' 'He was almost too close for comfort,' and finally 'Boy, was he close now, way closer than earlier' (misdirection and exaggeration).

As Dullard finally arrives at Mertz's meat shop, he is greeted by a photographer closely resembling Dennis Hopper's character in the original, complete with philosophical quips such as 'Mertz, he's my main man, my chow mein man!' (reiteration and exaggeration). Dullard enters the shop and finds it dark and cavernous (almost identical to the setting in *Apocalypse Now*). We then get a glimpse of Mertz, half lit and acting in the same exaggerated style performed by Marlon Brando in the original. As Mertz quotes passages from various books, he then breaks out of character and delivers the lines, 'I coulda had class, I coulda been a contender,' dialogue lifted from Brando's famous film, *On the Waterfront* (1954). This serves not only to disrupt the syntax of the target text but also to parody Brando's previous film roles by mimicking them out of context and in an extraneous manner.

Immediately after this confrontation in *Porklips Now*, the actual film strip appears to break in a moment of overt self-reflexivity. A silhouette resembling Coppola appears as he announces that the film's ending has not yet been determined and that there will be multiple choice endings. This is a direct reference to the production history of *Apocalypse Now* in which Coppola had difficulty in determining an ending and filmed a number of possible endings. A title card appears to announce that the following segment is 'Ending A'. In the original, Kurtz asks Willard, 'Are my methods unsound?' to which Willard replies, 'I don't see any method, at all, sir.' *Porklips Now* alters this exchange, directly referring to Brando's acting style. Mertz states, 'Do you find my method acting unsound?' followed by Dullard, 'I saw no acting at all' (inversion and misdirection). As one of the endings in the original, Willard takes a machete to Kurtz, intercut metaphorically with graphic shots of a ritual cow slaughter. As Kurtz lay dying, a close-up of his face captures him uttering 'the horror, the horror'. In the parody, the killing is intercut with extraneous, instructional, stock footage of an electrical bologna slicing machine at work. Thus, there is the incorporation of quoted material that is unrelated to the original film which further extends the metaphor of cutting meat.

Ending B begins with Mertz reciting poor poetry and Dullard snoring in the background. Recognizing that Dullard is asleep, Mertz takes the machete to him, again intercut with the repeated bologna footage (exaggeration and misdirection). Ending C begins in an extraneous fashion with Mertz eating an orange, standing up and then having a heart attack (accompanied by the theme music of the 1972 Brando film, *The Godfather*). Yet, as the camera moves in on his face, he transforms the dying words from the original: 'the horror, the horror movies' (inversion).

Apocalypse Now ends with a superimposed still shot of Willard's face – his mouth open in extreme shock – as if caught in the midst of a scream. The Door's song, 'The End' is reprised as the film closes. In the parody, the same superimposition occurs, yet the still shot is put into motion and we find out that Dullard's mouth was not open in shock but was caught in the middle of a yawn. Again, we are drawn into the image based on its similarity to the original, but are misdirected by its allowed continuance and eventual inverted connotation. Just as it began, *Porklips Now* functions parodically by both lexical and syntactic elements from the original film and either reiterating them for an effect of similarity (and familiarity) or transforming them through inversion, exaggeration, literalization, misdirection and extraneous inclusion to create the difference needed to generate critical distance from the targeted logonomic system.

Analysis of *Naked Gun 33⅓*

In order to illustrate how all three textual planes (lexicon, syntax and style) function systematically to create parodic discourse, I will now turn to a detailed analysis of the opening three-and-a-half minutes of *Naked Gun 33½: The Final Insult* which effectively fleshes out these interacting processes.

The film opens by directly evoking an entire narrative scene from *The Untouchables* (1987) that also generally refers to a standard detective film scenario: the stake-out. The setting of this particular stake-out follows yet another cliché of the detective genre: the lobby of a train station. There are three central characters here: Lt Frank Drebin (played by parody veteran, Leslie Nielsen) sits at the base of a huge stairway in the station reading a newspaper (with a headline proclaiming 'Dyslexia For Cure Found'); Nordberg (played by O. J. Simpson) works undercover at a nearby hot dog stand; and Ed Hocken (played by George Kennedy) is stationed at the top of the stairway posing as a porter. They each exchange glances as the soundtrack builds with the type of tense chords one might expect to hear in a detective film (music which, ironically, is absent in *The Untouchables*). For the most part, each of the elements (lexical, syntactic and stylistic) up to this point has functioned to create a stable connection to the scene in *The Untouchables* while additionally evoking a fairly conventional scenario with a good deal of effort being placed on generating similarity to the prototext of the detective genre.

It is at this point in the film that certain exaggerations and syntactic shifts begin to occur. As in *The Untouchables*, Lt Drebin notices a woman attempting to pull her baby buggy up the steep stairway (and right into the apparent 'strike zone' of their planned ambush) and leaves his post to assist her. Immediately following this in an exaggerated manner, another woman appears with two baby buggies and tries to pull each of them up the stairway. Lt Drebin motions to Nordberg to help the woman as well. Stretching the scene even further, a third woman with a baby buggy appears at the top of the stairway and begins to go down – aided by a helping Ed Hocken. At the very moment when all three men reach the midway point of the stairs, the targeted organized crime boss and his men appear at the top of the stairs and begin their descent.

After a rapid exchange of glances between Drebin and the boss (complete with overly-rapid and exaggerated editing and zooming perspectives), the other criminals pull out their guns and begin shooting. As the detectives draw their guns, they each let go of the baby buggies which begin their unattended trip down the stairs. This initiates a sequence shot in slow motion as the rapid fire of the guns is juxtaposed with the buggies heading down the stairs (not only a parody of *The Untouchables*, but also a parody of Sergei Eisenstein's famous 'Odessa Steps' sequence in the 1925 *Battleship Potemkin*). Using the parodic method of literalization which evokes a sense of hyper-realism, the film focuses on Ed Hocken's frantic and unsuccessful attempt to unhook the holster strap of his gun. The camera again turns to the baby buggies and their prolonged slow motion descent down the stairway which creates a heightened sense of incongruity through the exaggerated stretching of narrative time. Realizing the babies and their buggies are accelerating down the stairway, Nordberg begins to run down the stairs to save the babies, accompanied by the muted yell of one of the mothers, 'My baby!' Keeping within the narrative flow, an extraneous iconographic element is introduced as a descending lawn mower begins to fall down the stairs, trailed by a gardener yelling, 'My lawn mower!'

With the guns still firing and the buggies still going down the stairs, we cut back to Hocken as he continues to unfasten his gun holster. The scene then cuts back to a gun-firing Lt Drebin who spots a shiny quarter on a step as one of the baby buggies passes by in the foreground. In a moment of narrative misdirection, he ignores the buggy and continues to fire his gun, pausing only briefly to pick up the quarter with a satisfied grin painted across his face. In yet another moment of narrative misdirection and extraneous character inclusion, a woman's voice yells out: 'Look, it's the President!' as a Bill Clinton look-alike and accompanying Secret Service agents quickly move down the stairs amidst the shooting. The next shot returns to Hocken's continued effort to draw his gun (which by now has not only become an example of literalization, but has also become an exaggerated moment through its repetition). This is followed by a Pope look-alike and guards descending the stairs that add to a sense of narrative exaggeration built around two world figures who probably should not be passing through this particular stairway at this moment.

At this point in the film, we cut to the bottom of the stairs where the baby buggies have finally arrived and simultaneously catapulted each baby into the air. Breaking narrative continuity once again, Nordberg stops shooting and rushes to save the babies. In order to push this scene even further into the logically absurd, another woman's voice yells out, 'Oh my God, look, it's the disgruntled postal workers!' as six men and women donning official US postal uniforms burst on to the stairway firing Uzis. The scene then cuts back to Lt Drebin who is now shooting a semi-automatic toward the postal workers. In the background, we see Nordberg catching each of the babies as they fall from the air. Creating an effective parody based on the casting of former professional football player O. J. Simpson in the role (lexical literalization), Nordberg then begins to celebrate his amazing 'catches' and does an end zone celebration dance with one of the babies (which looks overtly like a doll) palmed in one hand. Just as he begins to spike the baby on to the ground, one of the mothers yells out, 'Wait a minute! Give me my baby back!'

Overwhelmed by the still-firing postal workers running down the stairway, Lt Drebin begins to yell out loud. The scene quickly cuts to him continuing the yell, but now from the safety of his own bed. Just like a classic sequence from a war or action film, it was only a continuing nightmare.

As this analysis demonstrates, the lexicon, syntax and style of a parodic text operate by way of a complex pattern of shifting in which one or two of the planes work to anchor the parody to its prototext while the other functions to create ironic difference from the targeted text. Even though this process can be charted out to demonstrate a fairly systematic operation in place, one must not forget that all of these transtextual transactions occur within a realm of 'watching the parody' and are nestled in an array of pragmatic contexts. It is this activity of parodic spectatorship that we now turn to in Chapter 11.

11
Parodic Pragmatics

How does one even begin to tackle the difficult and complex issues associated with the pragmatic functionings of film parody with its multi-voiced discourse constantly tripping any effort to 'capture' the meanings produced? A method I would *not* advocate is to reduce the pragmatic activity of watching film parody into the often reiterated dichotomy of 'those who get it' and 'those who don't'. Rather, I suggest a more productive effort of examining the complex interaction of various pragmatic levels of parodic discourse by looking at a spectrum of production choices, spectatorial competencies, viewing strategies and contextual determinants.

Recall the response my young student had while watching *Airport* and his insightful reversing of target text. Others may view the film and have no familiarity with its subsequent parody, while my own viewing (infused with the constant pausing and rewinding of the videotape) is one inscribed with possibly knowing the genre, the target and the parody in too much detail. Such varied individual and contextual elements constitute markedly different spectatorial responses and need to be considered when attempting to characterize and analyse any form of standardized discourse. In a way, I want to avoid valorizing any specific (or privileged) way of viewing film parodies and would rather like to analyse the various modes and means which create parodic spectatorship.

Once again, I find social semiotics helpful for both dissecting and linking numerous pragmatic levels. At its core, social semiotics is grounded on the realization that signification is always a process; always the activity of producing and interpreting signs. In short, it is the functioning of discourse, or what Hodge and Kress describe as 'the process of semiosis rather than the product (i.e. text). It is always realized through texts and is inseparable from them' (1988, p. 264).

Such a focus is also similar to the concerns voiced in reader-response theory, yet strives to avoid the temptation to lunge into the associated and unproductive debates that revolve around the concretizing of 'correct' or 'incorrect' meanings. Social semiotics assumes that people read texts in different ways while also acknowledging that certain 'horizons of expectation' can develop through textual activity that constrict and guide (although never totally) the spectatorial response.

At the centre of any act of signification is the process of meaning production. All texts have meaning, but it becomes unclear exactly what meanings they possess. Social semiotics is more interested in the terms of understanding rather than any specific understanding of a text. Meanings are therefore seen as potential within their textual embodiments. In this manner, as Wolfgang Iser correctly asserts, 'the interpreter's task should be to elucidate the potential meanings of a text, and not to restrict himself to just one' (1978, p. 22).

Obviously, an important influence on the generation of meaning is the placement of the viewer within certain signifying contexts. Potential meanings are by no means solidly anchored and are therefore heavily susceptible to various, constant shifts in context. No matter how hard Mel Brooks tries to reference *Star Wars* in *Spaceballs*, a viewer who has not seen *Star Wars* will not pick up on many of the transtextual meanings. By recognizing the importance of reading strategies within various contextual placements on the generation of textual meaning, the spectator has been elevated from a passive recipient to an active contributor. The spectator works with the text by actively decoding and creating meaning. Yet by conceptualizing the spectator as active, we should avoid concluding that all viewers engage with parodic texts in an 'optimal' way by elucidating the various potential meanings. By working with the text, the actions of the spectator are characterized by the double process of taking textual cues and interpreting them through their contextual positioning. As Jonathan Culler sets out 'on the one hand, the responses of readers are not random but are significantly determined by the constituents of texts, yet on the other hand the interpretive orientation of a response is what gives certain elements significance within a work' (1981, p. 59). This double process of semiosis underscores how many spectators can 'pick up' on certain parodic references while others read the text in an entirely different way (often even picking up on many 'unintended' parodic jibes).

The double process of idiosyncratic readings and textually-produced positions is typically bridged through the spectator's employment of certain 'logics of reading'. Thus the contextual placement of knowing that one is engaging with a parodic text produces the potential logic of parodic discourse. This is exactly how one might 'know' that parody is occurring without specifically knowing the parodic references. Such a focus can thus contribute to generalized models of parodic spectatorship based on both the employment of various logical viewing strategies as well as the contextual placements that influence such viewings.

Hodge and Kress propose four interlocking regimes of analysis that function around and within textual systems that capture the complex interactions of any semiotic encounter. These revolve around:

> (i) producers, through production regimes, rules oriented to producers, specifying what meanings they can produce, how and to whom; (ii) receivers, through reception regimes, rules oriented to constrain the semiosic potential of receivers; (iii) texts, through genre regimes, which use categorizations of texts to enforce constraints on the possibilities of meaning, and production and reception relationships; (iv) referents, through regimes of knowledge, or categorizations of possible topics of semiosis in terms of specific versions of reality and social constraints concerning who can properly claim to know or understand them. (Hodge and Kress, 1988, p. 266)

Such regimes of analysis function as effective tools for identifying and examining the intricate semiotic clusters that form around parodic discourse. Since I have previously discussed the regime of genre, especially in terms of the spectator's active contribution to the process of transtextual reading, I will now analyse the functionings of parodic spectatorship by concentrating on the remaining three regimes of production, reception and knowledge.

The Production Regime

The production regime is concerned with the rules that influence the production of texts. In other words, it considers which 'preferred' meanings can be offered, what textual rules 'should' be followed, or even who is sanctioned to construct such discourse. All of these factors funnel into the construction of potential meanings and the generation of the textual embodiment of those meanings. One of the problems with analysing original production contexts (as well as reception contexts) is the fact that we are historically removed from the actual context of the textual performance. Thus, one can really only speculate on production contexts in a generalized form by analysing strategies of production.

Although we have no direct reference to specific production contexts, we can speculate the various constituents of such contexts. One of the central components in the context of production is the decision process revolving around what to include in the text – much of which is based on the availability of various choices. For example, we can examine who produces parody films and how they are institutionally situated. While many early parody films were relegated to fairly 'marginal' modes of film-making such as shorts or cartoons, parody features became more bankable in the 1970s and began to be produced by large, Hollywood studios capitalizing on shifting cultural sensibilities and generic exhaustion. Yet it is interesting to note that studios often do not select as parodic targets texts that have a history with that studio. For instance, while Paramount produced *The Big Bus*, its competitors produced nearly every disaster film parodied therein. While 20th Century-Fox released the Mel Brooks' films, *Young Frankenstein* and *High Anxiety*, their targets (*Frankenstein* and a host of Hitchcock films) were produced by Universal Pictures. Arguably the most transgressive parodies are the independently-produced parody shorts, such as those released by Pyramid Films (*Hardware Wars*, *Porklips Now* and *Bambi Meets Godzilla*) that are produced on shoe-string budgets and garner few ticket receipts. These initial institutional decisions centre on what targets to parody and greatly influence the film's eventual realization, thus constructing a basis for conceptualizing the production context.

On a textual level, the elements available for inclusion as well as those included in the text (what Iser (1978) refers to as 'schematized aspects') serve as potential meaning indicators that offer the possibility of certain meanings. This notion of textual potentiality correctly points to the importance of textual cues (or 'triggering signals') for guiding (or influencing) the spectator's encounter with a text. Meaning production is therefore seen as initiated by textual cues, yet completed by reading strategies. In this way, 'texts initiate "performances" of meaning rather than actually formulating meanings themselves. ... [and that] without the participation of the individual reader there can be no performance' (Iser, 1978, p. 26). In tandem with a social semiotic approach, the spectator (the performer) becomes an integral component in the signification process by 'concretizing' meanings offered by the text.

While textual elements have certain signified meanings associated with them, it is unclear how much power the text has in engendering those meanings. Manfred Naumann (1976) argues that textual meaning is highly conditioned by the 'structured prefigurement' of a text and that the role of the spectator is to realize such prefigurements. Although few would argue against the notion that 'structural prefigurements' influence how one reads a text, one should be wary of Naumann's insistence of 'realizing' prefigured (or could we say 'correct') meanings. Instead, one can think of prefigured readings as not definitive since spectators may read a text in a multitude of ways, including certain normatively-prescribed ways. In a sense, a text is complete in its assemblage of signs, yet the interpretation of those signs is always fluid and contextually bound.

At the nexus of textual production and reception is the logonomic system (such as film genre or mode) which helps to guide the viewer by evoking particular textual norms and conventions. It must be noted, though, that certain logonomic systems seem to function better than others in anchoring the spectator into a target–parodic text dialectic. In an expected parodic encounter, the target logonomic system must first be easily recognizable by the spectator. Thus, well-known film genres such as the Western or horror are typically used as parodic models. When a specific film is used as a target text, it is usually one that has had a wide audience as well as some sort of canonical status, such as *Star Wars*, *Apocalypse Now* or *The Maltese Falcon*. By employing logonomic systems that are highly codified through previous exhibition (and therefore probably well known), parodic discourse is more likely to generate recognition and identification which in turn establish a strong foundation in regard to which similarity and difference can be explored.

Increasing the number of targets in any one parodic text is another strategy that can ensure at least some parodic firing and intertextual recognition. An example of this is the variety of sets used in the parody film *The Big Bus* in order to make sure some recognition is made by the spectators. As the film's set designer Joel Schiller points out

> it's very hard to parody the tastes of the audience the film is aimed at.... That's why I decided each area should be distinctly different so that at least one of the decors stands a chance of registering as a joke with someone somewhere. (Byrne, 1975, p. E-4)

The parody, then, presents many intertextual clues in order to generate a number of possible recognition points.

Logonomic systems function in terms of generating viewer modality (or the spectator's stance toward the text) through both intertextual and extra-textual operations. In many ways, spectators engage specific viewing strategies based on textual and contextual 'appropriateness' that are signalled by various modality markers. As Hodge and Kress state, different logonomic systems

> establish sets of specific modality markers, and an overall modality value which acts as a base-line for the [logonomic system]. This base-line can be different for different kinds of viewer/reader, and for different texts or moments within texts, but these differences themselves acquire significance from their relationship to the [logonomic system's] basic modality value. (1988, p. 142)

In terms of rules of production, those making a parody film must employ and reiterate conventions from the target logonomic system in a manner that encourages the spectator to generate expectations based on both the target texts and the parody. In a way, the producer must have, at the very least, an 'implied' or potential viewer in mind at the moment of production in order to construct a text which effectively parodies the targeted logonomic system.

At the heart of the production context is the establishment of an implicit 'contract' that spectators are 'expected' to follow in comprehending the narrative. Again, this contract is based on a presupposed range of spectators' past experiences with the logonomic system and serves as the basis for generating narrative expectation. Thus, production rules revolving around the employment of specific systems function to provoke and to constrict viewer perception within a limited range of readings. Though it is by no means guaranteed, such constriction functions by evoking a specific logonomic system over another. If a viewer who is familiar with the science-fiction genre watches a clip from *Lobster Man from Mars*, chances are good that he or she will settle into a science-fiction genre paradigm, even though he or she will probably be knocked in and out of it throughout the course of the film by way of such parodic methods as misdirection, exaggeration and literalization.

In his discussion of the facetious text (another ironic discourse that parallels many of the semiotic conditions of parody), F. J. Ruiz Collantes indicates the necessity for the producer to frame the text in a manner that will ensure (or at least promote) a recognition of facetious, multiple signifieds during the reading of the text. Thus the producer 'introduces certain textual marks in his utterance that enable him to indicate, in a more or less clear manner, the medium to which the text he is producing should be assigned' (Ruiz Collantes, 1990, p. 315). Thus, one might preface the telling of a joke by actually stating, 'I'm going to tell you a joke.' This generates a modality that connects the text (a verbal joke) to the performative situation (the telling of a joke). In the same manner, contextual positioning exists within parody so that various modality markers are offered both extra-textually (a newspaper review or a promotional poster) and intra-textually to indicate that parodic discourse is indeed occurring.

Again, there is a correlation between the producer of a text and a spectator in which they are both drawn together through the textual object, though not always in tandem or at complete odds. How, then, do we productively discuss this relationship between parodist and reader? Julio Pinto suggests that this relationship is a snug one, with both agents possessing 'matching' competencies. He asserts that 'the linguistic competence of the writer is essentially the same as that of the reader' (Pinto, 1989, p. 23). Yet when one actually analyses the tremendous range of possible readings produced from a host of parodic encounters, one must conclude that such consistent matching is rarely (if ever) achieved.

This brings us to the often debated relevance of intention to the construction and reception of discursive meaning. At one level, all texts connote some intention identifiable by spectators. One could argue that the mere creation of a text (an act of communication) is indicative of an intention by the producer. A productive means for analysing parodic intention is to focus on the manner in which parodies are motivated as social texts, i.e. efforts to communicate 'something'. In fact, with parody, the motivation is even more heightened due to its status as a disrupter of logonomic systems and normative patterns. Such transgressive activity is typically motivated to create some reaction, although this does not have to be tied to a specific intention beyond the intention to create parody itself. Beyond an understanding that parody is motivated first as an initiation of a communicative act and second as an attempt to create a parody of an established logonomic system, one might ask what influence does 'producer intention' have on the construction of spectatorial meaning?

As a form of ironic discourse, film parody shares certain modalities with irony in terms of intended meaning. One of the ways for understanding the multiple signifieds of an ironic sign or text is through a realization of the text's modality as an ironic text. Marike Finlay writes that 'irony may be the impossibility of the identity of intended and received messages due to a corresponding impossibility of identity of competencies and/or representational identity between sign and meaning' (1988, p. 46). In line with the notion that signs present only potential signifieds to be read, one might agree with Eco in determining that there is no true assurance that an ironic response will occur. Thus

> in order to guarantee the communicative success of an ironic statement p, the Sender must assume that the Addressee knows that p is not the case. This is a typical instance of a communicative phenomenon that no semantic theory can keep under control. (Eco, 1990, p. 218)

In fact, such an 'ideal' communicative situation rarely occurs, although producers do operate under some basic assumption of what the spectator might do, i.e. that the spectator might be familiar with a specific logonomic system. Of course, ironic 'intention' can also be realized almost completely from the perspective of the viewer rather than the producer (e.g. unintentional irony). As Linda Hutcheon reminds us, 'all irony happens intentionally, whether the attribution be made by the encoder or the decoder' (1994, p. 118).

On the other hand, many theorists maintain that authorial intention is highly important in the theorization of parodic discourse. Owen Miller argues that

> we can of course seek to redefine such terms as parody in a more neutral manner, but we cannot deprive them entirely of all associations of intentionality and thereby avoid weakening the definition of intertextual identity as a purely reader-oriented concept. (1985, p. 22)

As ironic discourse, parody would possibly need to be decoded as having some authorial intention, especially in regards to the action of combining texts, but this does not necessarily rule out the potential for reading no intention into a text. This authorial intention might simply be the attempt to transcontextualize a previously established logonomic system. With such refashioning, the parodic text is viewed as being intended as a 'reformulated', multi-voiced text.

Linda Hutcheon also stresses the importance of recognizing the intention to parody in parodic texts. She writes that

> when we speak of parody, we do not just mean two texts that interrelate in a certain way. We also imply an intention to parody another work (or set of conventions) and

both a recognition of that intent and an ability to find and interpret the backgrounded text in its relation to the parody. (Hutcheon, 1985, p. 22)

Thus, one might need to recover only the intended mode of the texts and not the actual potential meanings of the text's content. In fact, one of the interesting aspects of parodic discourse is that a spectator can generate meaning out of the text's significance without any consideration of how the parody was intended by its producer. In other words, a spectator can watch a film such as *High Anxiety* and generate meanings based on a recognition of it as merely a comedy with no transtextual referencing to the many Hitchcock films it parodies.

I think Eco probably puts it best when he states that we typically perform two central activities in decoding parodic discourse – attempting to capture an original intention while also exercising our ability to generate new meanings out of the text. He writes that

> in the interpretive reading a dialectic between fidelity and inventive freedom is established. One the one hand the addressee seeks to draw excitement from the ambiguity of the message and to fill out an ambiguous text with suitable codes; on the other, he is induced by contextual relationships to see the message exactly as it was intended, in an act of fidelity to the author and to the historical environment in which the message was emitted. (Eco, 1976, p. 276)

This formulation of parodic spectatorship then leaves some leeway on the part of the spectator in decoding any form of producer intention. And of course, this includes viewing a text as parodic even when there was probably no producer intention to create parody, such as the viewing context built around the B-movies shown on *Mystery Science Theater 3000*. Indeed, Bakhtin also recognizes that not only do authors have intentions, but that readers do as well and that their meanings are just as valid as the authors. He writes that 'language is not a neutral medium that passes freely and easily into the private property of the speaker's intentions; it is populated – over populated – with the intentions of others. Expropriating it, forcing it to submit to one's own intentions and accents ...' (Bakhtin, 1981, p. 294). As we will see in the next section, such viewer intentions and responses vary widely.

The Reception Regime
Linda Hutcheon argues in *A Theory of Parody* that 'readers are active co-creators of the parodic text in a more explicit and perhaps more complex way than reader-response critics argue that they are in the reading of all texts' (1985, p. 93). Due to its heightened polysemic nature, parodic discourse's generation of meaning relies heavily on the spectator's familiarity with the prototexts and thus on their response to the text.[1] Without totally disregarding the functions of textual embodiments for the offering of potential meaning cues, one can argue that the signification process of parody cannot occur (or be completed) until the spectator engages with the text. Therefore, the parodic function can only be completed by *a* viewer.

Wolfgang Iser (1978) outlines three central components of the reading process I find productive: a text (the constructed potential used for the production of meaning); the spectator's activity of reading the text (the concretization of textually-induced potential meaning); and the conditions or contexts of the reading moment (which give rise to and govern the text–spectator interaction). As stated previously, the means for intermeshing these components is the existence of an implicit contract that regulates the viewing experience by providing an 'anticipated sense of the whole'. The idea of a shared contract is individualized in reader-response theory as the spectator's 'horizon of expectation' that mediates between the private inception and the public reception of a text. In other words, an individual's viewing is influenced by certain 'public' expectations that have been formulated prior to the viewing through established logonomic systems and traditions. The spectator moves through the text with a range of expectations of how the narrative will unfold.

At the heart of the 'horizon of expectation' is the action of hypothesis formation. As the viewer watches a film, he or she will posit a series of hypotheses of how the narrative will progress and continuously readjust these hypotheses according to if the expectations were met or not. At one end of this process, spectators often enjoy the recognition and the satisfying of their expectations. Yet, while spectators may find some pleasure in generating narrative hypotheses that are 'correct', much of the pleasure from parodic discourse is in the transgression of such expectations and the relishing of the disruption of a normative pattern.

Guided by rules of expectation and hypothesis formation, various types or levels of parodic spectatorship emerge that expand the simplistic categories of 'those who get it' and 'those who don't' towards one based on a spectrum of various viewings. Rose proposes four basic spectatorial responses to parody that consider such variation. These include 1) a spectator who does not notice or cannot identify the targeted text being parodied and thereby reads the film literally; 2) a spectator who recognizes the text's intertextual nature but not the relationship between the two (i.e. recognizes the parodic mode, but not the targeted text); 3) a spectator who notices the parodic mode and can identify the targeted text, but does not see the irony of the intertextual juxtaposition; and 4) the 'ideal reader reaction' – one who recognizes the parody and enjoys the irony created (Rose, 1979, p. 119). In order to analyse the range of parodic response, let us turn to the range of spectatorial competencies (or familiarity) involved in the reading of parodic discourse.

Due to its transtextual nature, parody is closely linked to notions of spectatorial competence or familiarity with the targeted logonomic system. The viewing moment of the parodic text therefore becomes the junction between the textual evocation of the target and the spectator's memory of that target. In other words, one's previous experience with the targeted logonomic system is typically needed in order both to sufficiently generate expectations based on that system and to notice the discrepancies generated from the target. For example, many viewers might recognize that *Rustler's Rhapsody* is a parody of the Western genre, but few may notice its spoofing of a particular sub-genre of the Western – the 'singing cowboy' Western. Such generic experience or contextual placement can be productively described by one's membership in what Stanley Fish (1980) calls 'interpretive communities' – the social realm that influences how we interpret texts through prescribed (and learned) grammars, rules and instructions. In this case, relevant 'interpretive communities' could include film buffs, teenagers, scholars or

German-speaking viewers – all of whom might view a particular film parody in drastically different ways.

Linda Hutcheon posits that the reading of any ironic discourse requires a triple competence. First, there is a linguistic competence in which 'the reader has to comprehend what is implied, as well as what is actually said' (Hutcheon, 1985, p. 94). Thus, the spectator must recognize the doubly-coded signifiers and understand their juxtaposition. Second, the reader must possess a generic competence in order to understand what logonomic system is being parodied or ironically played with. Finally, the spectator must also exhibit an ideological competence in understanding that norm violation is occurring and its implications. Hutcheon writes that

> Parody, like irony, can therefore be said to require a certain institutionalized set of values – both aesthetic (generic) and social (ideological) – in order to be understood, or even to exist. The interpretive or hermeneutic situation is one based upon accepted norms, even if those norms only exist to be transgressed.... (1985, p. 95)

Such competencies range from a knowledge of the discursive language to the parodied logonomic systems. Yet one should not conclude that such characterizations of model or ideal readers represent actual, historical spectators, but rather that they represent potential levels of readership and engagement with the text.[2] In other words, at a basic level, an English-language film implies an ideal viewer who understands English.

Linda Hutcheon, on the other hand, goes even further with the positing of a 'sophisticated subject'. She suggests that

> In the optimal situation, the sophisticated subject would know the backgrounded work(s) well and would bring about the superimposition of texts by the mediation of that parodied work upon the act of viewing or reading. This act would parallel the parodists' own synthesis and would complete the circuit of meaning. (Hutcheon, 1985, p. 94)

With her concept of the 'sophisticated subject', Hutcheon hints at a bit of cultural elitism with her suggestion that some spectators of parody are more preferable than others in the creation of parodic meaning. And there are no shortage of critics who share Hutcheon's implied elitism, including Andrew Sarris who reiterates this division of spectators in a review of *Zelig* by stating: 'though I wouldn't want to jinx it commercially, I believe that *Zelig* will flourish primarily as a comedy for the cognoscenti. It is really too good and too imaginative for the pabulum-craving masses' (1983, p. 39).

I am quick to critique the notion of any 'ideal' reader or the valorization of the 'sophisticated' spectator. Recognizing that interpretive strategies are always contextually and historically bound, I suggest that emphasis should be placed on contextually-based readers rather than any ahistorical reader positioned within the text. Putting it simply, different viewing contexts will produce different readings.

In contrast to the valorized 'ideal' reader, Derrida goes in the other direction by suggesting that parodic discourse essentially involves a necessary amount of naivety. He states that 'somewhere parody always supposes a naivety withdrawing into an unconscious, a vertiginous non-mastery' (Derrida, 1979, p. 101). An important element of the parodic process of watching a film parody is the constant manoeuvring through textually-constructed expectations and the spectatorial adjustment of expectations. Part of the pleasures from parodic viewing, then, are the moments when we do make hypothesis errors and the resulting confusion that pops up during the viewing experience. As spectators, we err in the generation of certain expectations, yet are able to subsequently adjust to compensate for parodic transformation.

For example, as I watch *The Big Bus*, I hear stereotypical 'background' music playing as the bus drives along. My expectation is that the music is non-diegetic and post-dubbed. This expectation is up-ended when the bus passes a car load of musicians producing the soundtrack music diegetically. I chuckle, adjust my expectations, and relish the pleasure I received from this moment of 'paradigmatic crisis'. Douglas Benson even suggests that every first-time reading is naive and that one obtains a level of competency with text at hand through second readings. He asserts that 'the second reading is in fact not a review of the text itself; it is an interpretation of his first reading, of where he "went wrong"' (Benson, 1982, p. 151). This may also help explain why many parody films such as *Airplane!* and *Young Frankenstein* are watched multiple times by some spectators and often take on cult status.

Returning to the concept of the 'naive spectator', I turn to the reading process for those whose familiarity with the target is low. In his review of *Rustler's Rhapsody*, Duane Byrge describes the film as 'a send-up of the B western, it should prove baffling to the teenage viewers who've probably never seen a western on the big screen much less a B' (1985, p. 3). As with any ironic text, there is always the risk of being taken literally. Such spectators then 'naturalize' the text as they watch the film literally with no means for making the transtextual associations. Texts are, therefore, detached from any parodic impulse. Linda Hutcheon describes this process further, stating

> if the reader does not notice, or cannot identify, an allusion (or even a quotation), he will merely naturalize it, adapting it into the context of the work as a whole. In the more extended form of parody, such naturalization would eliminate the form itself, in that the work would not be read as a parody of a backgrounded text at all. (1978, p. 203)

If the viewer sees a Western parody film as only a comedy, the bitextual nature of the discourse is reduced to univocality as the text is interpreted as simply a comedy. Again, if a viewer is familiar with the Western genre but not the specific sub-genre of the 'singing cowboy Western', he or she will probably interpret a film such as *Rustler's Rhapsody* as only a Western film and not the specific sub-genre. Yet some viewers might also 'learn the genre' as they watch the parody. For example, Andreas Böhn makes the telling point that 'one has to have a certain knowledge of the pre-text (even if it stems only from the parody itself . . .' (1997, p. 48). In other words, 'naive' spectators might glean enough about the targeted logonomic system from the parody itself by either implementing a 'quick lesson' on the parameters of the targeted text or by enacting a sort of logonomic 'reconstruction' by inverting the parodic signs into their pre-parodic signifiers. The presence of such spectatorial activity might better characterize the spectator as a fairly 'sophisticated naive' viewer.

In between the extreme poles of the naive and informed reader probably lies the position of most spectators – those who get some and miss other elements in the parody – what Pinto (1989) terms the 'ordinary reader'. While most people might pick up on a number of the spoofs of James Bond films in *Spy Hard*, few would probably catch the joke of using an executive Disney building as the spy headquarters. Still others can watch and understand parody film from an infinite amount of perspectives which resist categorization.[3] Although such viewings do not inform us much on the broader strategies employed in parodic discourse, these still must be acknowledged and held to be equally as valid as any other viewing.

Not only does the spectator need to have a familiarity with the targeted logonomic system, he or she also often needs to know other contextual factors that enrich a transtextual understanding of the parodic text. For example, a sub-plot in *Silent Movie* revolves around the threat of a huge multi-national conglomerate called 'Engulf & Devour' taking over the studio. This joke is quite funny if one possesses the extratextual knowledge of Gulf+Western's acquisition of Paramount Pictures in 1967. Parodic 'competency' can also involve some foreknowledge of a film's production history. The pointed joke stated at the beginning of *Porklips Now* that refers to Francis Ford Coppola's struggle to make *Apocalypse Now* under various unfavourable circumstances including an expanded budget is a perfect example. Often, filmic competency is groomed outside of the actual film text through the mass media or personal discussion without actually seeing the movie. As Chris Willman points out in his review of *Top Secret!*, 'despite the fact that most of those ideas came from old movies, I think people can appreciate the spoof of the clichés – even if they don't recognize the specific movies they're taken from – because they're repeated so frequently' (1984, p. 18). Thus, the competency required to 'get' the intertextual references in parodic discourse comes not only from previous experience with the target texts, but also from certain extra-textual discourses surrounding the film experience.

Realizing that spectators engage with texts at different levels and for different reasons, it is important to consider what a viewer's interpretive goals are for engaging in the textual moment. Hirsch acknowledges individual goals and separates them from the text itself in the generation of meaning. He states that 'any normative concept in interpretation implies a choice that is required not by the nature of written texts but rather by the goal that the interpreter sets himself' (Hirsch, 1967, p. 24). Thus, any engagement in a textual moment is framed by the spectator's goals, which in parody could vary from gaining pleasure through seeing and deciphering intertextual references, to viewing a film for its humour, to watching a movie simply to get out of the rain.

Along with these levels of competencies based on textual and extra-textual experience, one can also simultaneously relate to parody films' non-parodic membership in the targeted logonomic system in what has been termed an 'unnaturalized' manner. As previously argued, parody films typically function as comedy films in their own right. Therefore, parody films often include a large amount of jokes and humour that are not directly based on parodic borrowing or irony. In this sense, the humour of parody films might partially be attained through an appreciation of a number of jokes that are not within the realm of double coding. As Neale and Krutnik remind us, 'many gags, jokes, and wisecracks also share the property of being potentially, or actually, self-contained'

(1990, p. 43). This inclusion of non-parodic humour serves several functions, including providing material to secure the discourse's non-parodic, comical dimension as well as presenting material that could appeal to a viewer who is not familiar with the parodied texts. As film critic Vincent Canby mentions, 'the best film parodies ... are not only knowing and fond but, in addition, so self-contained that their humor will not escape people who haven't a clue about the subject being sent up' (1985, p. Y-22).

Other parody films narratively function in a manner similar to their target texts. Parodies of the disaster cycle not only spoof the narrative qualities of suspense and terror found in the target texts, they also embody those same qualities. Henry Jenkins describes how

> a film like *Airplane*, which displays the most extreme displacement of the conventions of an already un-realistic genre, reserves some potential to emotionally involve us in its narrative simply by the re-inscription of certain generic elements. We do often experience suspense as the battered plane approaches the landing field. (1986, p. 44)

Thus, films such as *The Big Bus*, *Fatal Instinct* and *High Anxiety* employ narrative strategies themselves that encourage highly suspenseful responses. Relatedly, other parodies evoke elements of mystery with their narratives. Discussing *Young Frankenstein*, Vieira writes that 'the film also demonstrates the hermeneutic caution characteristic of the genre, by which each step in the unwrapping of the mystery is accompanied by explanation, in a double process of clarification and the generation of new enigmas' (1984, p. 194). Now that I have analysed some of the dimensions involved in the response processes of making meaning from parodic texts, I would like to turn to discussing the regime of knowledge and how the parodic context in general is created through both textual and extra-textual means.

The Regime of Knowledge

Recalling Hodge and Kress's description of the regime of knowledge as one that includes the 'categorization of possible topics of semiosis in terms of specific versions of reality and social constraints concerning who can properly claim to know or understand them', we can also examine the means for constructing such realities that function to construct the parodic context (1988, p. 266). One of the central prerequisites for generating a parody-viewing context is the mere *recognition* that the parodic mode is being employed in the film. As Hutcheon argues,

> in order for parody to be recognized and interpreted, there must be certain codes shared between encoder and decoder. The most basic of these is that of parody itself, for, if the receiver does not recognize that the text is a parody, he or she will neutralize both its pragmatic ethos and its double structure. (1985, p. 26)

As stated previously, parody films generate certain modalities to define the viewing situation as parodic. Yet creating this modality is often difficult in film parodies because one cannot signal ironic moments through the literary use of quotation marks and therefore must employ other means to announce their status. One means for providing information about how to interpret the parodic text is simply to announce its parodic status.[4] This is achieved by clustering certain messages in the text to signify that the process of parody is occurring. 'Messages are normally organized in relation to the conditions of semiosis by a class of signs called metasigns. Metasigns signal different aspects of the semiosic plane in order to constrain the semiotic behaviour of participants' (Hodge and Kress, 1988, p. 262). In this manner, parodic texts themselves function as metasigns in their attempt to announce and constrict the generation of meaning and operate to construct the contextual base from which spectators will create meaning.

As a metasign, parody functions by offering certain modality markers within the text to signal the occurrence of parodic activity. As Margaret Rose mentions, 'the reception of the parody by the reader will depend on his reading of the "signals" in the text for the parodistic relationship between the parodist's imitation and the original text' (1979, p. 27). Often, these markers are even overtly presented, such as the opening titles of *The Big Bus* that announce its connection to other disaster cycle films, yet also indicate its humorous tone through musical and graphical representations. Other parodies open in the form of a coming attraction trailer (such as *Hardware Wars* and *Closet Cases of the Nerd Kind*), which, in effect, signal their departure from the normalized cinematic form and announce their parodic discourse.

An additional, yet less overt marker is the mere recognition that established norms of a targeted logonomic system are being disrupted, causing the film's 'grammar' to appear uncontrolled and out of place. Margaret Rose states how 'apparently meaningless, absurd changes to the message or subject matter of the original' can lead to signal that parody is occuring (1993, p. 37). As Michael Riffaterre further explains, the noticing of such intertextual disruption can indicate a change in the text's modality. Such markers include,

> intertextual anomalies – obscure wordings, phrasings that the context alone will not suffice to explain – in short, ungrammaticalities within the idiolectic norm ... which are traces left by the absent intertext, signs of an incompleteness to be completed elsewhere. (Riffaterre, 1980, p. 627)

Thus, the mere noticing that certain norms are being violated can signal the occurrence of parodic discourse. One might know very little about the Western genre, but probably few would fail to see the placing of Count Basie and his band in the middle of the open plains in *Blazing Saddles* as a violated generic norm.

Beyond the textual efforts to define the parodic situation, various extra-textual factors contribute to the securing of parodic viewing strategies and the framing of the parodic discourse. Conscious of extra-textual elements that go into creating a viewing context, Barbara Klinger argues that

> the single film does not enter the world or circulate through it without the active intervention of external forces, such as those which characterize the industry's commercialization of the film. These external forces in turn oblige the production of forms to accompany the film to its various destinies and situations of viewing. (1986, p. 2)

Some of these extra-textual factors include

> trailers, posters, billboard advertising, special 'How "X" Film Was Made' mini-films, TV commercials, music videos from its soundtrack, star interviews in magazines, ... TV review shows and in the print media and product creations derived from it, such as clothes and 'action figures'. (Klinger, 1986, p. 27)

Together, these factors contribute to the marketing and contextualization of the filmic text, or what John Ellis (1982) calls the film's 'narrative image'. Such narrative images function not only to promote the fact that the film *is a parody*, but also typically highlight what genre or logonomic system is being parodied.

One of the central factors in both announcing parodic discourse and identifying the target text is the title of the film itself. A relatively simple parodic signal found in titles is the use of exclamation marks to literally designate the film's 'over-the-top' nature. Thus, films such as *Airplane!*, *Top Secret!*, *Hot Shots!* and *Attack of the Killer Tomatoes!* all point to their ironic mode through the overt signalling of 'exciting' punctuation marks. Titles are also often constructed through parodic shifts that phonetically alter either the title of the target text or of a familiar motif. These transformations are also usually in accordance with the parody's new narrative. The title, *Apocalypse Now*, a film about eliminating a 'butcher' colonel, is transformed into *Porklips Now*, a film about eliminating a 'meat butcher' in Chinatown. Creating a lexical shift from the word 'sight' to 'bite', a parody of Dracula films becomes *Love at First Bite* while *Pulp Fiction* becomes *Plump Fiction* (1996).

Film titles also denote parodic discourse through shifts of emphasis from the target text. As a parody of the various *Airport* films, *Airplane!* not only resembles the original title linguistically, it also trivializes the emphasis on airport politics found in the original films by focusing on *an* airplane. At times, though, the linguistic similarity between titles becomes problematic. For example, when *Airplane!* was released in 1980, Universal Pictures (producer of the *Airport* films) filed a complaint with the MPAA charging that the parody's title was too similar to their films' titles. They argued that since the film *Airport – Concorde '79* was still being shown in Europe, the parody's similar title might confuse patrons and draw business away from the *Airport* film. Initially, the MPAA agreed and the title was changed to *Kentucky Fried Theatre's Airplane*. After further arbitration, the original title was restored.

Parody film titles also spoof certain motifs and elements found in the targeted texts. *I'm Gonna Git You, Sucka*'s title parodies the African-American jargon often found in the original 'blaxploitation' films. Marketing forces also help shape film titles by insisting that titles appeal to a broad enough audience to draw in the crowds. Originally, the title was to be *I Mo Git U Sucka*, but United Artists felt that the title would not be understood by a large enough audience, echoing the aspect of familiarity needed for the understanding of parodic discourse. In a similar fashion, the original title for *Mafia!* was *Jane Austen's Mafia!* (the title still used in the film, but dropped from all promotional materials) until early marketing research demonstrated that virtually no audience members 'got the joke'.

As a technique found in parody, some titles also originate as literalizations of the target text's title. For example, *The Maltese Falcon* becomes literally *The Black Bird* and spoofs the narrative's coveted black-bird statuette. Another parodic technique employed in the use of titles is through condensation by parodying more than one target film title. Although not eventually released as such, *Airplane II: The Sequel* was shot with the working title of *Airplane 2002* – a parody of the *Airport* films and *2001 – A Space Odyssey* (1968). Similarly, *They Call Me Bruce?* was originally released as *A Fistful of Chopsticks*, which takes its basic syntax from the Clint Eastwood film, *A Fistful of Dollars* (1964), and adds an Asian touch (based on Bruce Lee). Another example is the parodic compound generated for the title of *Fatal Instinct* by borrowing from two classic suspense thrillers, *Fatal Attraction* (1987) and *Basic Instinct* (1992). Parody films also announce their parodic status by taking aim at the production strategy of sequalization through the creation of titles that invert the standardized method for serial identification: *Airplane II: The Sequel*, *National Lampoon's Loaded Weapon 1*, *Naked Gun 2 1/2* (1991) and *Naked Gun 33 1/3*.

As previously argued, one of the important aspects of parodic spectatorship is the recognition of and familiarity with the target logonomic system. Accordingly, beyond the implicit references explained above, parody films often explicitly announce their targets within the titles themselves. While the working title of *The Black Bird* was originally *The Maltese Falcon Flies Again!*, other films retain their references, such as *Young Frankenstein* and *They Call Me Bruce?* Parody films also derive their titles from extra-textual references to the target texts. For example, *Lust in the Dust*'s title was lifted from a film review of the 1946 Western, *Duel in the Sun*, in which the critic described the love affair in the film as 'more lust in the dust than duel in the sun'.[5]

Titles of parodies can also be misleading in regards to their target texts. The horror spoof *Saturday the 14th* is not a parody of the slasher series, *Friday the 13th* (1980), as one might expect from its lexical shifting, but rather is a parody of *The Amityville Horror* (1979). Because parody is such 'risky business' in terms of hooking up with an audience that has a past experience with the targeted texts, some titles are changed in order to secure a broader audience based on the film's comedic rather than parodic elements. For example, *Airplane II: The Sequel*'s title was changed for exhibition in non-English speaking territories to *Flying High* – a title that alters the parodic indicators into primarily comedy signals. Finally, titles often exhibit a form of self-reflexivity evident in parodic discourse. Some films point to their status as either sequels of the target texts or of other parodies, such as *The Last Remake of Beau Geste* and *Airplane II: The Sequel*. Other films self-reflexively indicate their status as films themselves, such as the original, complete title of *Hot Shots! An Important Movie*. From each of these examples of titles, we can clearly see that the generation of a parodic viewing context begins well before the spectator enters the cinema through the employment of parodic film titles.

Another means for evoking parodic reading contexts is through the creation of 'tag lines' that are used in media advertising. *Attack of the Killer Tomatoes!* was billed as the 'world's first comedy disaster film' and clearly signals the ironic discrepancies which the film promises to deliver. Similarly, *Saturday the 14th* used an ad campaign that featured a tiny tombstone inscribed with 'The Year's #1 Horror-Comedy Spoof'. The Hitchcock spoof, *High Anxiety*, featured ads that made direct reference to one of the parodied texts, calling the film a 'Psycho-Comedy' in text superimposed over a photo of director, Mel Brooks, with his out-stretched arms on a 'vertigo' pattern.

Fig. 22: *Dead Men Don't Wear Plaid*

Advertising efforts for parody films also utilize parodic associations that exist extra-cinematically. Ads for both *The Adventures of Sherlock Holmes' Smarter Brother* and *Hot Shots!* feature art work by artists, Steve Miller and Aragones, whose work is associated with the parodic *Mad* magazine. Advertising campaigns are also used to broaden the film's audience by highlighting non-parodic elements, such as their comedy. For example, in a *Variety* article detailing the promotional efforts by distributor New World to sell *Lust in the Dust*, Richard Klein reports that 'believing that the entry is capable of appealing to a wide audience, [a New World executive] said advertising efforts will focus on its broad comedic aspects in a similar vein to the Mel Brooks comedy, "Blazing Saddles"' (1984, p. 28). Often, part of the advertising campaign is centred around the creation of a distinctive logo for the film. As discussed in previous chapters, films such as *This Is Spinal Tap* and *Hot Shots!* utilize logos which help market the film as a product, yet also play with the conventions of previously established logos, such as the highly marketed *Top Gun* military patch.

As an important element in the film's advertising campaign, posters are used to identify both parodic discourse and the target texts. Some posters create their parodic discourse through linguistic shifts in the tag lines. Taking the famous W. C. Fields line, 'never give a sucker an even break,' the poster for *Blazing Saddles* makes direct reference to its parodic 'attitude' with the tag line 'or never give a saga an even break'! In *Dead Men Don't Wear*

Plaid, the poster depicts the Steve Martin character pointing a gun accompanied with the words, 'Laugh, or I'll blow your lips off ...' (see Figure 22). In *Schlock* (1973), the poster sarcastically announces that this is 'the first musical monster movie in years'.

Posters are also used to make direct reference to the parodied source. For example, the poster for *They Call Me Bruce?* features a battered Bruce Lee look-alike with the words 'with a little practice ... anyone can be as good as Bruce Lee!' Some parody film posters utilize lexical transformations to engender a parodic response. The poster for *Young Frankenstein* features Gene Wilder and Peter Boyle as the monster. While the lettering is done in conventional horror script – letters formed out of a cracked castle wall – there are also elements of parody on the poster. Through parodic transformations of alien inclusion and exaggeration, the image of the 'monster' includes a zipper-stitch on his neck, a happy face button and a bracelet donning the name, 'Monster' (see Figure 23). Finally, film posters often announce their parodic mode by parodying other parody film posters. For example, the poster designed to promote *This Is Spinal Tap* takes the general graphics of the *Airplane!* poster – a cartoon of a plane with 'knotted' wings flying through the sky – and replaces the plane with a knotted guitar neck flying through the air.

An additional important extra-textual aspect in the pre-generation of parodic context includes the entire network of publicity that surrounds the release of a film. As Henry Jenkins suggests

Fig. 23: *Young Frankenstein*

pre-filmic publicity, among other things, activates the proper schemata to be applied in making sense of the film and, in many cases, presents enough concrete information that our processes of schema adjustment may begin before we settle into our seats. (1986, p. 39)

Press releases often directly identify the film as a parody and thus frame publicity discourse around its status as parody. In a press release issued by Paramount Pictures for their film, *The Big Bus*, the text mentions that Ruth Gordon's role is a spoof of her 'good friend' Helen Hayes, who had a role in the targeted *Airport*. In Orion's press release material for *Haunted Honeymoon*, the production information mentions that director Gene Wilder has 'created both a spoof and hommages [sic] to the chillers – on screen and radio – which gave him some of his happiest young nightmares'. Other press releases attempt to encourage certain attitudes toward the film such as Warner Bros.' press release for *Movie, Movie* which quotes director Stanley Donen stating that 'we hope that people will not laugh at the film but will laugh with it, as we did while making it.'

Yet not all press releases and publicity material announce a film's parodic discourse. Some play into the deception of the parodic 'hoax' by presenting the film as singly-coded and non-ironic. The press material that accompanied the release of *This Is Spinal Tap* describes the film's focus, the band Spinal Tap, with no tongue-in-cheek and makes no reference to the film's parodic mode. In fact, the distribution company, Embassy Pictures, even released a 'fictional' discography listing of the band, Spinal Tap.

Another important component in the publicity efforts of a film is the TV advertising campaign. One particularly interesting example was that for *Hot Shots!* The commercial itself is a spoof of the often used 'testimonial' ads in which people leaving the movie theatre are asked their opinions of the film. As Anita Busch describes it:

The commercial opens with Fox executive VP marketing, Smitty, handing out money to a line of moviegoers, with the voice-over: 'audiences across America are being paid to talk about Hot Shots!' ... One redheaded boy exiting a theater says in disappointment, 'It was OK,' and then after being handed a stack of $20 bills, smiles widely and proclaims: 'It's the best movie of the summer!' (1991, p. 7)

Thus, the television ad self-reflexively points to its marketed quality and highlights the film's ironic mode.

Equally important are the marketing efforts which occur indirectly through film reviews and articles in newspapers, magazines and television, as well as everyday conversation about film. Often, reviews function to position the viewer for a parodic experience by 'instructing' the viewer on how to watch the film. At the end of her review of *I'm Gonna Git You, Sucka*, Julie Salamon suggests that 'before you go, you can brush up on the blaxploitation heritage. "Shaft," "Superfly" and "Cleopatra Jones" are all available on videotape' (1989, p. A-16).

Another means for extra-textually defining the situation is the use of star images to sell the film in advertising, trailers and other promotional media that build certain expectations and guide the viewing experience. Parodic star images are often based on both the parodied stars and the stars within the parody films. For example, films that contain a large degree of star self-parody, such as Linda Blair in *Repossessed*, will use her image not only to connect the parody to its target, but also to build certain expectations based on her previous performance. Part of the pleasure one gets from *Airplane!* is generated prior to the viewing experience by knowing that Robert Stack is one of the featured actors. Knowing the star persona of Divine surely guides how one is going to approach a film such as *Lust in the Dust*. Thus, foreknowledge of a film's cast helps construct the narrative image by both announcing the film's parodic mode and identifying the film's target texts. Together, these extra-textual elements function to set up and frame the viewing experience and work in tandem with the textual elements that signal the occurrence of parodic discourse.

One of the consequences of recognizing parody's status as a metasign is that its own textual patternings become normalized and create some predictability of how the narrative will transform the parodied text. Linda Hutcheon describes a situation of parodic viewership in which 'the parodist establishes a rhythm of "counter-expectation" which ends by "denuding" the structural principles of the work' (1978, p. 206). Thus, the spectator becomes attuned to the parodic discourse which itself becomes normative in its patterned transformations of target elements. In a way, the parody becomes self-parodic as it pokes fun of itself within the narrative.

By examining the dimensions of parodic spectatorship through the analytic regimes of production, reception and knowledge, it should be clear that parody exists not only as a textual category, but also as a mode of spectatorship. Based on numerable levels of previous textual experience, viewing goals and access to extra-textual elements, parodic spectatorship involves a complex negotiation between the parodic text and its prototexts. Far from privileging any type of 'ideal viewer' of parody, I am more concerned with the many factors which cue and influence the way we make parodic meaning and how these operate in a fairly standardized fashion.

As a process couched in ironic semiotics, I believe that parody's normalized manner of doubling-back must have some effect beyond the recuperating dimensions of hegemonic maintenance. The spectator, shedding that particular contextual jacket, moves along, awaiting their next entrance into cinematic irony or the moment in which they pop into the cinema to get out of the rain.

Notes

1. Some critics even go erroneously as far as to place *total* emphasis on the reading process, such as Joseph Dane's declaration that 'parody and satire ... are created by readers and critics, not by the literary texts themselves ...' (1980, p. 145).
2. Jonathan Culler reminds us, 'the ideal reader is, of course, a theoretical construct, perhaps best thought of as a representation of the central notion of acceptability' (1975, p. 124).
3. As Umberto Eco correctly asserts, 'naturally, a text can also be read as an uncommitted stimulus for a personal hallucinatory experience, cutting out levels of meaning, placing upon the expression "aberrant" codes' (1979, p. 40).
4. Or as Roland Barthes asks, 'What could a parody be that did not advertise itself as such?' (1974, p. 45).
5. See Sheila Benson (1985).

12
Conservative Transgressions and Canonical Conclusions

Often championed as a staunch partisan for the transgressive properties of parody, Bakhtin paradoxically argues that 'in modern times the functions of parody are narrow and unproductive. Parody has grown sickly, its place in modern literature is insignificant' (1981, p. 71). In contrast, Ella Shohat describes how parodic discourse can be effectively harnessed for addressing (and expressing) issues of marginality, arguing how

> parody is especially appropriate for the discussion of 'center' and 'margins' since – due to its historical critical marginalization, as well as its capacity for appropriating and critically transforming existing discourses – parody becomes a means of renewal and demystification, a way of laughing away outmoded forms of thinking. (1991, p. 238)

Both writers are correctly remarking on the constricted tension of current day parody and highlight its status as, what I term, a form of 'conservative transgression'. In other words, I suggest that parody does have *some* effect through its unsettling of established normative systems, yet ends up losing most of its radical verve by becoming a normative system itself. In order to examine this process, I will draw attention to the growing influence film parodies (particularly from the 1970s onward) have had on the generic landscape by looking at how parodies affect subsequent developments of certain genres as well as reposition canonical films. Next, I will focus on how these textual effects are transposed to a larger sociological arena by looking at how the juggling of normative frames alter spectatorial engagement both within the film-viewing situation as well as in a broader, cognitive context. I will conclude by reasserting the normative and canonical status of film parody and spectatorship as well as query how long film parody can indulge in this ironic activity in an ever-consuming age of irony.

In order to examine how parody affects the historical, diachronic development of logonomic systems, a charting of parody's influence on ending, regenerating and adding to such systems should be considered. In other words, I want to look at how the release of a film such as *Frankenweenie* threatens to end certain aspects of the horror genre, or re-establishes the classical horror film, or even simply adds to the genre as a constituent film. My approach acknowledges the way in which film parody embodies a pointed realization of historical process by critiquing established traditions while simultaneously adding to such traditions. These actions, therefore, are lodged within a constant effort to redefine normative boundaries. Linda Hutcheon highlights this realization when she writes that 'modern artists seem to have recognized that change entails continuity, and have offered us a model for the process of transfer and reorganization of that past. Their double-voiced parodic forms play on the tensions created by this historical awareness' (1985, p. 4). These tensions, centred on the diachronic relationship between parodic discourse and the precedent texts, provide a potential impulse for transgressive positionings.

A productive means for tracing this diachronic relationship is by examining the emergence of parody within the developmental path of a particular genre (the primary logonomic system evoked in film parody) through four basic stages: 1) an experimental stage of conventional formulation; 2) a 'classical' stage of conventional stabilization; 3) the 'refinement' stage, or what Barry Grant (1980: 39a) terms, the 'intellectualization' stage (the expansion of the genre in terms of increased variation); and 4) the self-reflexive stage in which parody typically arises. Although by no means a fixed sequence, these stages follow a rough pattern of increased canonization with the continual addition of novel elements. As the canon becomes increasingly saturated in terms of viewer expectations, new twists and alterations are added within the canon's basic structure.[1]

This movement through stages in film genre is usually propelled by the need to secure profit by providing audiences with a standardized (and recognizable) form that has enough novelty value to 'add something new' to the genre experience. Although the general notion that logonomic systems develop in a pattern of increased self-reflexivity and variation is probably less debatable, the idea that this development is a linear process of increased refinement definitely is. Instead, I suggest that a more productive way to conceptualize the development of logonomic systems is in terms of its cyclicism rather than linear evolution.[2] In other words, the appearance of parody in a logonomic system not only signals the possible end of an established tradition, it also marks the possible regeneration and continuation of that tradition. For example, a parody of the science-fiction genre such as *Lobster Man from Mars* not only takes the wind out of certain worn-out conventions of the genre, it also introduces new lexical elements and plays out new narrative scenarios (no matter how outlandish – especially in an already outlandish genre).

As a logonomic system becomes increasingly self-reflexive (noted by its novelty beginning to exceed its standardization), an increasing amount of critical attention begins to turn upon its own developmental history as parodic discourse emerges. At this point, conventional saturation begins, followed by supersaturation when certain identifiable devices and motifs become over-used and lose their novelty value from repeated employment. Many film genres (such as horror and gangster) experienced this stage in the 1950s after twenty years of conventional development. This, in turn, often leads to an even higher level of spectatorial predictability. Audiences raised on Western films in the 1930s and 1940s (as well as those raised on television's re-screening of such films in the 1950s and 1960s) were prime spectators for Western parodies in the 1970s since they knew the conventions of the Western all too well. Clearly put, parodic discourse repeats worn-out conventions that have been transcontextualized in order to highlight their dislodged status. Yet parody is not, as Hutcheon asserts, the mere 'hurry[ing] up what is a natural procedure: the changing of aesthetic forms through time' (1985, p. 35). Rather, it is a purposive activity (especially in the realm of commercial cinema) of altering traditions in order to maintain a certain level of popularity and profitability. As parody emerges, it concurrently critiques its own status through repetition with difference and demonstrates the mutable qualities of any established canon.

Typically, these later stages of development are marked not only by an increase in formal and thematic self-reflexivity, but also by fewer films in that canon being produced. This signals a period of relative dormancy in the tradition's output and a period that has some effect on the 'timing' of when a film parody will emerge. Anton Popovic argues that there usually exists a temporal gap between the later products of a tradition and parodic texts. He writes that 'one important factor here is the time interval between the rise of a work of art and its primary communication on the one hand, and its meta-communication, i.e. the rise of its metatexts, on the other hand' (Popovic, 1976, p. 232). If we examine the later stages of Hollywood film genres, a similar pattern is evident: a dramatic decrease in classical genre films in the early sixties followed by a period of relative dormancy until the early seventies with the marked appearance of parodic films. In a way, such dormancy may actually serve as a 'digestive' period in which spectators can possibly distance themselves from the targeted logonomic system. Some parodies, though, require far less of a dormancy period as they capitalize on the fairly recent success of the popular targets they are spoofing. For example, the cartoon classic *Bonanza Bunny*, released in 1959, ran concurrently with the hit television programme it was parodying, *Bonanza*, while *Silence of the Hams* came out only three years after its prototext, *Silence of the Lambs*, was released.

The timing of parodies is especially important in terms of securing both a saturation of conventional recognizability as well as a remembrance of such conventions. Some logonomic systems, such as the major film genres, typically develop over a relatively long period while other logonomic systems, such as sub-genres and cycles, take less time and thus have less of a dormancy period. As previously discussed, one of the primary features of the film cycle is its topicality with a limited time-frame of production ranging from two to six years. Discussing the emergence of a disaster cycle parody in 1976, Thomas Schatz, in essence, describes how the period of dormancy was not adequate enough for people to conceive and internalize the cycle's conventions. He writes that

> the disaster genre, whose classic stage was launched with *The Poseidon Adventure* and *Airport*, has evolved so rapidly that a parody of the genre, *The Big Bus* (1976), appeared within only a few years of the form's standardization. Interestingly, the audience didn't seem to know what to make of *The Big Bus*, and the film died at the box office. Apparently, the genre hadn't sufficiently saturated the audience to the point where a parody could be appreciated. (Schatz, 1981, p. 40)

What Schatz is highlighting here is probably less of a case of insufficient saturation and rather one of insufficient dormancy (or, perhaps, merely a poor film to which people did not flock). This factor is made clearer by pointing out that just four years later, *Airplane!* (one of the most successful parody films of all time), was released without the benefit of any additional significant disaster cycle film being released. In this case, it is not a question of adequate developmental time, but possibly of dormancy time, again that time necessary for generating a certain level of ironic distance from the targeted tradition.

In contrast to a clipped dormancy period where insufficient ironic distance is fostered, some dormancy periods last too long and people literally 'forget' the conventions of the tradition. One reason many people may not 'pick up' on the specific references to the 'singing cowboy' sub-genre of the Western in *Rustler's Rhapsody* might be due to its long period of dormancy – almost fifty years since the cycle's hey-day. In fact, a majority of the viewers of this film have probably never even seen a 'singing cowboy' Western and thus naturalize it as a general Western parody. One might also attribute the low box-office figures of *I'm Gonna Git You, Sucka* to the fact that many viewers had simply 'forgotten' the 'blaxploitation' films of the 1970s when it was released in 1989.

As parodies arrive to scavenge worn-out conventions and their accompanying overpredictability, some critics argue that this signals the end of the tradition and its approaching moment of extinction.[3] In his discussion of *Young Frankenstein*, Harold Watts describes how the parody seems to have virtually destroyed a narrative tradition. He writes that 'in truth, by the film's end, often enough, some tradition of narrative and the sensations it once stirred are no longer just moth-eaten; all that is left is disparate tatters fluttering in the breeze' (1978, p. 146). Stephen Schiff adds that 'with *Blazing Saddles*, ... the genre spoof became an entrenched form – and a death knell. No one could take, say, the detective genre seriously after it had been turned on its head for so many years' (1982, p. 35).

Does film parody actually *kill* the canon, or does it merely maim with a smile? Bakhtin argues that 'everything has its parody, that is, its laughing aspect, for everything is reborn and renewed through death' (1984, p. 127). Yet more often than not, parodic discourse seems to signal the end of a particular phase of a canon rather than an entire tradition through regenerating that tradition by working with the established system. In other words, parody's reworking of predictable traits might simply shift certain aesthetic conventions to one side as new or hybrid ones become increasingly popular with film audiences. This was obviously evident with the resurgence of the Western genre in the mid-1980s with such successful films as *Silverado* and *Pale Rider*, both released in 1985. Although both films possess a certain level of ironic self-consciousness, they still primarily conform to the conventions of the Western genre. In this manner, film parody can be seen as a source of renewal by breathing new life into worn-out canons without specifically burying that tradition.

Such attention to film parody's ability to renew or revitalize a canon might also contribute to one of parody's more conservative functions, namely its ability to reaffirm a tradition's entrenched status. Gary Saul Morson acknowledges this when he notes that 'even a true parody cannot help paying one compliment to its original, namely, that the original is important enough to be worth discrediting' (1989, p. 73). Film parody, therefore, serves the function of 'weeding-out' clichéd conventions in order to allow for the canon's continued healthy growth.

Not only does parodic discourse seem to regenerate some logonomic systems, it also adds to their existing corpus.[4] One of the ways in which parody has directly added to a logonomic system's corpus is through the narrative property of the sequel with parodies serving as new additions to their targeted texts. Films such as *Young Frankenstein*, *The Adventures of Sherlock Holmes' Smarter Brother*, *Zorro, the Gay Blade*, *The Cheap Detective* and *Repossessed* all directly continue the narratives of the originals and thus add to the targeted canons.[5] Film parody, therefore, becomes a constituent of that tradition, no matter how much criticism it has heaped upon the target.

Yet there seems to be more at stake here other than whether or not film parodies actually end or perpetuate established genres. Contrary to Bakhtin's contention that parody has grown 'sickly' and no longer possesses the potency to affect the larger cultural situation, Hutcheon argues that parody has become critically vibrant by harnessing the social 'sanctionness' of established canons. Hutcheon points out that 'many parodies today do not ridicule the backgrounded text but use them as standards by which to place the contemporary under scrutiny' (1985, p. 57). Parody is therefore seen as implemented as a technique to pry open the insularity of canons and to expose their 'constructedness'. Film parody's inherent satiric impulse critiques the unity of normative structures and unsettles fixed distinctions; therefore questioning the legitimacy of established norms. And it is this somewhat overt positioning of textual practice with social praxis that invests film parody with its potentially radical verve.

Sociologically speaking, parody, in general, can be seen to serve as a 'working example' of transcontextualization by functioning as a meta-critical device in an ever-increasing ironic world. Such transcontextual activity is akin to Bakhtin's valorization of carnival culture as a means for critical expression. Not surprisingly, parody is viewed as a form invested with counter-cultural energies along with the ritual spectacle and the act of cursing. According to Bakhtin, parody achieves this potentially political vitality from two central attributes: its critique of normative systems and its proposal of alternative ideologies.

One of the central means proposed in the carnivalesque for critiquing normative systems is the breaking down of imposed hierarchies in both textual and social practice. Such debasing is seen as effectively highlighting the active maintenance of hierarchical systems and, therefore, their mutability. A central means for disturbing normative hierarchies is achieved in parody through the joining and juxtaposing of dissimilar conventions by bringing together elements that are usually segregated on cognitive and physical levels. Bakhtin writes that 'carnival brings together, unifies, weds and combines the sacred with the profane, the lofty with the low, the great with insignificant, the wise with the stupid' (1984, p. 123). As we have seen in the previous chapters, a good deal of the transgressive energy generated in film parodies is created through the juxtaposition of traditional genre conventions with completely 'unrelated' elements, such as the use of jumper cables to 'revitalize' sparky the dog in *Frankenweenie* or the repeated action of characters giving each other 'high-fives' in medieval-based *Robin Hood: Men in Tights*. It is this act of juxtaposition that transgressively disrupts not only fixed structures, but also the hierarchical positions within that structure by troubling the perceived 'unity' of cultural products.

An additional means for generating an exposé of constructedness is through parody's over-stylization by pointing toward its own artifice. Peter Wollen explains that

> on the one hand, parody implies the possibility of detaching style from subject-matter; a style can be displaced and transferred from one thematic 'location' to another. On the other hand, the forms of parody can be used to inflect social or personal criticism towards comedy or mockery. (1985, p. 44)

Thus, 'the obsolete device is not thrown overboard, but repeated in a new, incongruous context, and thus either rendered absurd through the agency of mechanization or made "perceptible" again' (Erlich, 1981, p. 258). Film parody's disturbance of hierarchical structures and stylistic unities therefore fosters a demonstration of the constructed nature of any cultural product. And by constantly demonstrating its own constructedness, parody disturbs its hegemonic placement as a 'contained' creation of art.

As previously discussed, one must not focus solely on textual configurations in order to examine discursive processes. One should also address the textual–spectatorial matrix in analysing the 'effects' of film parody with particular attention being paid toward how film parodies problematize various viewing strategies. By virtue of their social construction, texts are always contextually and ideologically charged and read by contextually and ideologically charged readers. With this conceptualization, texts serve as a crucial nexus of subject and ideology – a vehicle for ideological articulation. In terms of parody films, they 'demystify their parodic targets in order not only to deny or revise them, but more important, to awaken the spectator to the ambiguity of cinematic discourse and its powers of concealment and distraction' (Vieira, 1984, p. 182). While watching a unique parody film such as *Silent Movie*, one is constantly aware of the overt deconstructive activity occurring within the text with its lack of dialogue and use of title cards. And this leads to a certain jarring of expectations encased and nurtured through classic Hollywood cinema.

Not surprisingly, such aesthetic fragmentation is evident in a variety of contemporary cultural products. One may argue that it also functions to disrupt the general act of perception itself. In this vein, the activity of disrupting any viewing strategy may lead to a transference of viewing strategies into other realms of life. This, then, recognizes the effect parodic texts possibly have on our perceptual framing of the world as well as our cognizance of those perceptual frames. Again, by demonstrating the plurality and multiplicity of any act of signification, parodic discourse critiques traditional notions of fixed, unified and 'natural' meaning in textual interpretation.

Due to its ironic posturing and hierarchical debasing, much of film parody's subversive potential can be tied to its status as comical. Through its creation of incongruities in the text, parodic discourse presents the possibility of laughter and comic appreciation as seen in virtually every film parody, from *Sherlock Jr.* to *Austin Powers: International Man of Mystery*. Some theorists attempt to minimize this crucial element in parody by championing a non-comical form of parody. Linda Hutcheon, Gary Saul Morson, and others argue for a form of 'serious' parody that is devoid of any comical element. Morson writes that 'parody recontextualizes its object so as to make it serve tasks contrary to its original tasks, but this functional shift need not be in the direction of humor' (1989, p. 69). In a way, Morson is arguing that the textual cues of parody can foster a reading which is essentially non-humorous. Yet, as discussed in the previous chapter, it is very difficult to predict *any* direction of reading in terms of humour. It might be more productive to propose that, at the very least, the generation of textual incongruency and the recognition of it may lead to the potential of comic effect. In fact, the 'seriousness' of parody is indeed its comical dimension and should be closely linked to the serious pleasures of humorous transgression and subversive play. In this manner, parody (as well as other modes of carnival culture) opens up spaces to think out alternatives and 'play' with established conventions and norms.

Much of parody's humour arises out of its choice of target – the taking of 'serious' logonomic systems and creating incongruency. Henri Bergson writes that parody creates a humorous effect from the 'reframing' of past models not usually tied to the comic. He states that

> transpose the solemn into the familiar and the result is parody. The effect of parody, thus defined, extends to instances in which the idea expressed in familiar terms is one that, if only in deference to custom, ought to be pitched in another way. (Bergson, 1956, p. 140)

This might help to explain why more 'serious' genres, such as the Western or horror, serve as particularly vulnerable parodic targets while other 'less serious' genres such as the screwball comedy seem to be already imbued with a sense of irony and humour and therefore, less prime for spoofing.

Another means for creating a potential comic effect is by engaging with the elements of similarity found in parody. Such connection to familiar elements, then, provides a base for creating socially different cognitions. Thus, one source of pleasure and laughter arises out of a film parody's degree of similarity to its target logonomic system. This is surely the reaction I have while watching films such as *Medusa: Dare to Be Truthful* or *The Brady Bunch Movie* in which the parody, on at least a few levels, is so faithful to its prototext. I also find pleasure at how 'real' *Zelig* looks as a documentary or by knowing that the lab equipment used in *Young Frankenstein* is from the original classic film.

Although some of our pleasure from parody arises from the similarity and faithfulness to the target logonomic system, I would argue that most of the pleasure potentially comes from the joy of watching somewhat rigid norms being violated and relishing such transgressions of boundaries. Spectators laugh aloud as they watch tried and true genre conventions literally being thrown out of the window by film parodies. One such method of transgression is the perception that devices or techniques are being 'misused' and utilized in a fashion that violates normal usage. Thus, we begin to watch a film based on an established logonomic system and become 'surprised' by moments that look like accidental violations of norms. As discussed in Chapter 6, one of the prevalent methods for transforming syntax in film parodies is through narrative misdirection which uses generic codes to 'lure' the viewer into a particularly narrative expectation and then to surprise the spectator with an unexpected turn of events.[6]

Bergson also argues that the illumination of a mechanical arrangement is another form that encourages comic responses. He writes that 'any arrangement of acts and events is comic which gives us, in a single combination, the illusion of life and the distinct impression of a mechanical arrangement' (Bergson, 1956, p. 105). As such, the recognition of illusion in parody is very crucial in the generation of a comic response – i.e. recognizing the illusion that a certain element introduced into a logonomic system does not belong (the Howard Johnson's Ice Cream Parlor in the Western *Blazing Saddles*) or of the film-making process itself (Nancy making the actual film strip break in *Repossessed*). In fact, we could conclude that *any* incongruency can be potentially funny and therefore, all parodies must be considered to at least have the potential to be comical.

This parodic laughter, then, symbolically represents a break from official decorum and becomes a signal of transgression. While some theorists describe parodic laughter as 'harmless' or 'aesthetic',[7] others postulate a more direct, political function of laughter. Bergson believes that 'laughter is, above all, a corrective' (1956, p. 187). Thus, parodic laughter may be a cultural signal for the wish or need to make changes; to alter the ruling hegemonic structures we live in. Probably a better way to characterize the potentially subversive effect of parodic discourse is to describe it as corrosive – a gradual, but steady shaking of normative standards. As Robert Stam writes, parody film 'mocks the official seriousness of all these formulaic procedures, subjecting them to corrosive laughter to the point that it becomes retrospectively difficult to take them seriously again' (1989, p. 201). Once again, it might be increasingly difficult to watch an old detective film with complete seriousness after it has been shown in a parodic manner on the screen of *Mystery Science Theater 3000*.

Along with its function as a critique of normative systems, parodic discourse also posits alternative visions of social order in a postmodern fashion. Ana López argues that parody is 'special because it is a critical practice, a form that by challenging an antecedent text or a prevailing mode of thought, can disturb preconceptions and prejudices and can give rise to new forms of consciousness' (1990, p. 63). In this fashion, parody is envisioned as serving an almost emancipatory function by jolting people out of their normatively-constructed compliance with social rules and norms. And of course, the argument for film parody's potentially 'radical' nature is not one centred on any type of direct effect (i.e. go watch *Bugsy Malone* and change the world), but rather is based on a form of cognitive 'exercise' – a reminder that no normative system is absolutely stable and immutable.

If parody, then, is potentially a comedic discourse, who laughs? On the one hand, some posit that one of the basic competencies required in order to enjoy parodic discourse is an extensive cultural 'literacy'. This suggests that only an elite few can actually engage with the ironic workings of parodic texts; therefore excluding many from the dialogic manoeuvres operating in the parody. These exclusionary practices of parodic discourse are clearly explained by Eco when he discusses the 'imaginary' quotation marks found in any intertextual text. He writes that:

> these imperceptible quotation marks, more than an aesthetic device, are a social artifice; they select the happy few (and the mass media usually hope to produce millions of the happy few). To the naive spectator of the first level the film has already given almost too much; that secret pleasure is reserved, for that time, for the critical spectator of the second level. (Eco, 1990, p. 94)

And because many spectators have limited access to cultural forms, they also have limited opportunities to become 'genre-literate'. Thus, in many ways, film parody's reliance on spectatorial competency actually impedes mass viewer participation and functions conservatively to exclude the margins from participating.

On the other hand, many critics argue that parodic discourse can productively serve the function of clearing space for marginalized groups to explore alternative social orders, with such groups effectively gaining the needed 'competency' to utilize parody as a critical mode. As stated in Ella Shohat's quote at the beginning of this chapter, parody and various social groups share this marginalized quality and therefore have proven to be a perfect match in their discursive efforts to 'clear some space'. Thus, many marginalized groups have found the mode to be particularly effective in critiquing American cultural norms. Hutcheon writes that

> parody has certainly become a most popular and effective strategy of the other ex-centrics – of black, ethnic, gay, and feminist artists – trying to come to terms with and to respond, critically and creatively, to the still predominantly white, heterosexual, male culture in which they find themselves. (1988, p. 35)

In agreement with Hutcheon, Ella Shohat adds that

> parody's capacity to appropriate different genres – most associated with hegemonic ethnic discourses – allows for a broad interweaving of different texts, defamiliarized from their original context, especially through associating them with 'ethnic' discourses, in order to forge a satiric palimpsest of synchretic identities. (1991, p. 239)

Providing an example of such defamiliarization, Shohat points to the ironic inclusion of an African-American character in the role of the Western sheriff in *Blazing Saddles*. She writes that the

> provocative articulation of previous discursive silence concerning American historiographical representation is also seen in the carnivalesque inversion of an exploited black laborer who is transformed into a sheriff, as well as in the criss-crossing of identifications and displacements among the marginalized. (Shohat, 1991, p. 246)

As this example demonstrates, film parody cannot be totally dismissed as conservative by virtue of its ability to problematize social roles based on race and class and explore alternative worlds where such distinctions are unnecessary.

Although I am arguing that there exists a correlation between textual transgression and potential social subversion, one must remember that they are still not the same thing. Parodic discourse is obviously first and foremost a *textual* transgression. Its displacement and transformation of logonomic systems are characterized as a disruption of textual normative unity. As Michel Foucault writes,

> transgression is an action which involves the limit, that narrow zone of a line where it displays the flash of its passage, but perhaps also its entire trajectory, even its origin; it is likely that transgression has its entire space in the line it crosses. (1977, p. 34)

Transgression therefore straddles the boundary, but does not move beyond it. Transgression is the act of violating rules, yet only barely crossing the limits of the prescribed boundaries. To move beyond such limits (and to totally violate the macro-codes of the social structure) is to subvert. Yet far too often in cultural critique, transgression is erroneously collapsed with notions of subversion, although the two are indeed connected. Subversion, I would suggest, is more directly tied to the attempt to weaken authority.

One can transgress without the motivation to weaken authority (although it may have this effect). Figures of authority can transgress – bend rules or step outside of assigned regulation – without any subversive tendency. In other words, texts transgress while people subvert. Transgressive actions merely serve as a potential instigating agency. Subversiveness, therefore, lies within how it is used by spectators (e.g. how meaning from the encounter is constructed, how it is interpreted, or what actions proceed from such an interaction). Thus, when discussing aesthetic properties in film parodies, we can only discuss the potential offering of transgressive concepts within a specific arena of social interaction. The link between the two is in what people *do* with transgressive texts in certain contexts.

Thus we must pose the question, how does transgressive action lead to potential subversive action? Parody, in many ways, posits potential subversive thought by its extra-textual reference with its satiric impulse to critique the larger social order. In this fashion, parodic transgression is used to comment on larger cultural issues and might lead to cognitive realizations that change *is* possible. As Terry Caesar argues, 'if we see parody not as living off popular culture but hosting it, then may we not also see parody as a route to the leading edge?' (1979, p. 211).

On one level, the engagement with any logonomic system is a hegemonic engagement by way of the contractual nature of production and reception of texts. Part of parody's conservative functionings revolve around an unavoidable acknowledgment of the structure it is critiquing. Hodge and Kress warn that

> an excessive concentration on normative systems (logonomic systems, genres, ideology) contains an inbuilt distortion and reinforces the ideas of their dominance. These systems only constrain the behaviour and beliefs of the non-dominant in so far as they have been effectively imposed and have not been effectively resisted. (1988, p. 7)

Such violations almost always suffer from acknowledging the structure being transgressed and therefore end up being authorized by those very norms. As Patricia Waugh (1984) points out, any attempt to 'break a frame' immediately suffers from a reacknowledgment of that frame – thus reasserting its position. Yet as a disruption of 'typical' hegemonic response, parodic discourse encourages a plurality of responses with some of them counter-hegemonic. Not only are such responses pluralistic, they also run in tandem with various alternative or counter-hegemonic structures. In this film manner, parody's conservative tendency to grasp hegemonic structures is simultaneously undercut by its transgression of those structures.

I would hesitate, though, to conclude that film parody has no transgressive effects outside of its authorized arena of exhibition. Within a film, the suspension of norms may remain temporary, but the residual effects of the inversion leave memory traces of resistance to the established order and therefore have a far more lasting effect than the temporary transgressions viewed during a film's screening. As stated at the beginning of this chapter, parodies have a major influence on how subsequent films of the targeted logonomic system are viewed. Thus, the viewing of a Western parody such as *Blazing Saddles* will probably have at least some lasting effect on later viewings of non-parodic Westerns. This in turn may have some cumulative effect in the restructuring of consciousness and the re-imagining of alternative social orders. Again, it is what people do with such aesthetics that defines subversion.

Due to this status as a 'conservative transgression', film parody can be viewed as straddling the same ideological fence as many other forms of postmodern discourse. It questions normative orders and, while it does indeed include that norm in its critique, provides a lasting dislodging of conventional limits. In contrast to Bakhtin's shaming of contemporary parody for being unproductive, it can be said that film parody's amazing effectiveness in transgression within this ironic age has, in fact, made it a privileged and canonized mode of discourse; incorporated and valorized by the cultural configuration it sets out to critique.

Insightfully, Baudrillard quips that 'parody makes obedience and transgression equivalent, and that is the most serious crime, since it *cancels out the difference upon which the law is based*' (1983, p. 40). In other words, parody marks an epochal shift in cultural conceptualization by encasing an erasure of ironic distance. In contemporary culture, one might claim that parody now fronts us directly with little pretense of a mask or sheer duplicity.

Throughout this work, I have examined the contours and functionings of film parody by differentiating it as a distinct mode of discourse dripping in transtextuality. And while it does seem that film parody offers a potential platform for an ever-so-subtle shifting of social consciousness, its embodiment of authorized norms firmly keeps it within the hegemonic fold. Its discursive standardization has, in fact, contributed to its own canonization and secured a relatively easy co-option by a market economy oh-so-eager to capitalize on 'radical' iconicity.

Parody's demonstration of a contestatory political attitude exhibits both conservational and potentially progressive attributes. Parody not only includes its target norm within its text, but also highlights the mutable quality of that norm by showing how change to relatively rigid normative systems is possible. As proposed in Chapter 11, a consideration of spectatorial viewing goals may be necessary, in the long run, for determining parody's actual ideological effects. How a viewer *uses* a text remains paramount in the consideration of textual meaning. While some have found parody to be exclusionary, elitist and limiting, others have grasped parodic discourse as a well-spring for potentially progressive action.

Surveying our contemporary, media-drenched landscape, though, might convincingly suggest that this well-spring has all but dried up, or, more appropriately, has flooded our culture to the point of ironic supersaturation and christened this the 'ironic age' – an era where postmodern activity has become more the norm than any type of alternative practice.[8] As our culture becomes increasingly complex and diversified, some cultural forms may seem stable in comparison, with parody possibly being one mode that can bring a stabilizing influence in its activity of defining the limits of cultural traditions. While postmodernists attempt to transcontextualize past cultural practice, they are constantly reminded that they, too, are part of that cultural practice, and that any attempt to produce truly transgressive expression will eventually find itself folding back upon its target and embracing its very structures.

This shift from norm-breaker to norm-creator has clearly been fostered by the marketplace's ability to co-opt the 'fun' of parodic discourse into channels of commercialization. Radical ideas become co-opted by commercial interests, yet are also still allowed to be expressed as 'oppositional' (reminiscent of carnival's 'authorized nature'). In other words, parody's ability to seep into mainstream aesthetic practice may have left it effectively neutered in terms of its potential radicalness – well entrenched into a canonical state and easily co-opted by normalized discourse.

In terms of film parody, critic David Denby agrees, arguing that the increasing emergence of parodies is more of an economic move to secure greater profits than any co-ordinated effort to instigate socio-political change on the aesthetic front. He writes

> Why all the spoofing? I think the main reason is simple fear of putting new experiences on the screen. Along with remakes and sequels, parodies have become endemic in a panicky industry intent on endless replication of past successes as a safeguard against risk. (Denby, 1978, p. 115)

Denby therefore suggests that the film parody serves the stabilizing commercial function of securing modest profits while banking on past familiarity with established canons and an oscillation located at the very heart of parodic discourse.

A look at the financial success of past film parodies seems, to a certain extent, to support Denby's contention that, as a commercial product, film parodies make good financial sense. Prior to 1970, the few film parodies that were made usually failed to be strong box-office draws or were relegated to the cartoon and short film format. Then came a vigorous run of film parodies, some successful, others not. One of the most successful film parodies to date has been *Young Frankenstein* which, since its release in 1974, has generated over $130,000,000 at the domestic box office. In fact, the opening weekend for *Austin Powers: The Spy Who Shagged Me* (1999) on 3312 screens brought in a total of $54,917,000 in US receipts (and over $309,000,000 in world-wide box-office receipts) – clearly not a poor figure for 'oppositional' discourse. Additionally, film production companies like Troma Pictures have found their niche by specializing in film parodies, releasing such titles as *Chopper Chicks in Zombietown* (1992), *Sgt. Kabukiman N.Y.P.D.* (1996) and the *Toxic Avenger* series of films.

Another indication that parodies have slid into canonicity (and are also overtaking their models as norms) is evidenced by the fact that a film parody such as *Hot Shots! Part Deux* (1993's fourteenth top-grossing US film) can generate almost as much at the box office as the model it parodies.[9] Even within the Hollywood establishment, film parodies have been ushered into that category of 'respected' art.

When Harvey Korman makes the speech in *Blazing Saddles* about his risking of a possible Oscar nomination, we laugh at the absurd incongruency of such a statement. Yet, when the 1975 Academy Award nominations were announced, *Blazing Saddles* picked up no less than three nominations for 'Best Supporting Actress', 'Film Editing', and 'Best Song'.[10] Silly comedies? Yes, but serious business, no doubt.

Other film parodies have moved beyond their status as ironic commentators and have virtually become the model they originally parodied. An interesting example of this is the emergence of Spinal Tap as an actual, heavy-metal band whose life has transcended its 'fictional' depiction in the film, *This Is Spinal Tap*. In 1992, they even released an album, *Break Like the Wind*, and went on a world tour. In fact, some music magazines such as

Pulse! have covered the band with no reference to their parodic, fictive origins, thus contributing to a sense of the parody effectively replacing the object it originally spoofed.[11]

As a production and marketing tool, film parodies out of Hollywood have become lucrative business for an identifiable group of film-makers who return again and again to the parodic mode. Film-makers, such as Mel Brooks and the Abrahams/Zucker team, have virtually made their careers out of spoofing film traditions and have made money doing it to boot. This has been taken up in the marketing of subsequent film parodies, with such 'branded' tag lines as 'From the people who brought you …' accompanying new film parody releases.

Film parody has also become bankable with its role in fostering well-known parodic 'stars'. The champion of this category must be Leslie Nielsen, who has starred in a variety of film parodies, including: *Airplane!*, *Airplane II: The Sequel*, *Repossessed*, *Naked Gun*, *Naked Gun 2 1/2*, *Naked Gun 33 1/3*, *Spy Hard* and *Dracula: Dead and Loving It*. His star image is so intertwined with parodic discourse that it has been further co-opted as a marketing tool in television advertising. For example, a recent advertising campaign for Dollar Rent-A-Car features Nielsen walking in an airport terminal and avoiding a barrage of assaults that stand in the way of his renting a car. The ad is clearly making parodic references to the *Naked Gun* series of spoofs as well as to a similar television advertising campaign by major competitor, Hertz Rent-A-Car, that featured Nielsen's *Naked Gun* co-star, O. J. Simpson, hurdling through a busy airport lounge.

Finally, one must question the status of parodies when, through the process of their

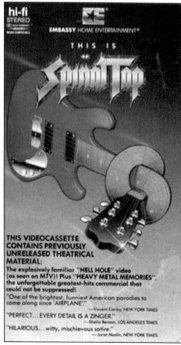

Figs 24 & 25: Poster for *Airplane!*; video cover for *This is Spinal Tap*

own canonization, they, themselves, become targets for further parodies.[12] With parody exhibiting such an explosive proliferation of meaning suggested by deconstructionist theory, one can't help but notice how it enters into that 'strange loop' of meaning that self-reflexively unfolds onto itself. As Adena Rosmarin argues, this 'strange loop, then, is not simply a suggestively incomplete series but one that explicitly turns back on itself, remarking on its own incompletion' (1985, p. 44). For example, *Robin Hood: Men in Tights* features an appropriately-placed medieval hangman character (played by Robert Ridgely) that recalls and parodies the lexically-alien hangman character in *Blazing Saddles* (also played by Ridgely). Obviously, it is an odd circumstance when a 'befitting' character type in a standardized genre can be viewed as parodic due to its previous ironic placing.

On a narrative level, parodies are compacting their sites of reference by evoking other parody films. A particular example occurs in *Bob Roberts*, with a scene centred on folk-singing politician Bob Roberts getting 'lost' back-stage at a beauty contest. This directly spoofs a scene in *This Is Spinal Tap* where the band is lost in the never-ending back-stage corridors of a concert hall (itself, a parody of Bob Dylan lost back-stage in *Don't Look Back*). In *Mafia!* (1998), one scene depicts an assassination attempt on Vincenzo Cortino (played by Lloyd Bridges in his last film) while he is dancing at his son's wedding. With each bullet that hits his writhing body, his dancing takes a new turn as the assembled guests applaud each 'new' dance move. Of course, this scene directly evokes the hilarious scene in *Airplane!* in which a man is stabbed in the back while dancing and his erratic attempts to draw attention to his wound are mimicked by Elaine Dickinson (played by Julie Hagerty) as new dance moves.

Marketing materials for film parodies also evoke previous parodies as they double-back upon themselves in creating the 'strange loop' of referencing. Take, for example, the promotional image for *This Is Spinal Tap* – a guitar flying through the air with its neck twisted into a knot. Not only does this generate a satiric comment on the state of contemporary rock music, it also parodies the film poster for *Airplane!* – a 'knotted' jet flying through the sky (see Figures 24 and 25).

As such, parody's postmodern impulse indicates its inability to arrive at any final meaning; reminding us quite overtly that meaning is always fluid and shifting. Such an acknowledgment, while theoretically radical in its abstract fashioning of indeterminate placings, is, in the long run, possibly too circular to engender any real, positive change. Parody's subversive pleasures subside and we are still left with social and cultural problems that are not shaken by utopian-inspired fantasies. And when parodies begin parodying parodies, we have moved beyond logonomic critique and into the 'strange loop' of ironic, self-referential signification. We are left wondering what sort of discourse can follow in parody's twice-removed footsteps.[13]

As we have seen throughout this book, the employment of parodic discourse in contemporary culture serves as a telling indicator of both the emerging and dissolving nature of postmodern transgressiveness. Fredric Jameson argues that postmodern elements 'no longer scandalize anyone and are not only received with the greatest complacency but have themselves become institutionalized and are at one with the official culture of Western society' (1984, p. 56). Or probably more appropriately, postmodern modes such as film parody scandalize *everyone*, which is exactly why the postmodern has become so popular (and profitable) in today's cultural life. Once compromised, parody slides quite easily into its own canonized status where it begins to cannibalize its own previous transformations.

Film parody, therefore, has developed into a mode which is both anti-canonical and canonical. Its discursive procedures (based on the parodic methods of reiteration, inversion, misdirection, literalization, extraneous inclusion and exaggeration) operate across the lexical, syntactical and stylistic planes to create a parodic text which simultaneously disrupts established logonomic systems while reaffirming its own standardized process. These textual patternings, then, have led to the development of viewing strategies which are in-sync with parodic discourse as viewers become 'ironically ironic' about the meanings they derive from cultural texts. In terms of ideological efficacy, 'parody, once considered a means of ridicule and irreverence, now represents postmodern discontinuity which must, ironically, also resist becoming normative through being canonized' (Berman, 1987, p. 21). And as this book has demonstrated, such resistance has long fled from the battle front as film parody continues its canonical excursion.

Notes

1. For more about these stages of genre development, see Barry Grant (1980, p. 139a) and Thomas Schatz (1981, p. 37).
2. This is profitably argued in Tag Gallagher (1986).
3. Robert Chambers argues that 'parody is the principle means of removing deadwood from art' (1974, p. 108).
4. Steve Neale and Frank Krutnik seem to think contrary to this when they state that '*Blazing Saddles* is not a comedy western, but a comedy, albeit one which relies upon a knowledge of the western to work' (1990, p. 19).
5. Linda Hutcheon concurs, writing that 'it is in this sense that parody is the custodian of the artistic legacy, defining not only where art is, but where it has come from' (1989b, p. 100).
6. Umberto Eco points out that 'the laughing response is the side-effect of a misuse of the code, or of a contradiction posited within the code' (1976, p. 64).
7. See, for example, J. G. Riewald (1966, p. 131).
8. In fact, as Linda Hutcheon suggests, 'irony may be the only way we can be serious today' (1988, p. 39).
9. *Hot Shots! Part Deux* grossed over $124,000,000 in world-wide-box office receipts during 1993 compared to *Top Gun*'s $176,000,000.
10. Other film parodies receiving Oscar nominations include *The Dove* (Best Short Subject–Live Action Subjects; *Bugsy Malone* (Best Music); *Young Frankenstein* (Best Sound, Best Writing–Screenplay Adapted from Other Material); and *Zelig* (Best Cinematography, Best Costume Design).
11. See Nebitt Bireley (1992).
12. A number of X-rated films seem to have taken to spoofing (in their own way) previous film parodies, including *Austin Prowler* (1999).
13. Or as Barry Day insightfully queries, 'What do you do for an encore?' (1987, p. 20).

Filmography

Abbott and Costello Go to Mars (1953, Universal Pictures, Charles Lamont).
Abbott and Costello Meet Frankenstein (1948, Universal Pictures, Charles Barton).
Abbott and Costello Meet Captain Kidd (1952, Warner Bros., Charles Lamont).
Adventures of Sherlock Holmes' Smarter Brother, The (1975, 20th Century-Fox, Gene Wilder).
Africa Screams (1949, United Artists, Charles Barton).
Airplane! (1980, Paramount Pictures, Jim Abrahams, David Zucker, Jerry Zucker).
Airplane II: The Sequel (1982, Paramount Pictures, Ken Finkleman).
All You Need Is Cash (1978, Above Average Productions, Eric Idle, Gary Weis).
Amazon Women on the Moon (1987, Universal Pictures, Joe Dante, Carl Gottlieb, Peter Horton, John Landis, Robert K. Weiss).
Attack of the Killer Tomatoes! (1979, NAI Entertainment/Four Square Prod., John De Bello).
Austin Powers: International Man of Mystery (1997, New Line Cinema, M. Jay Roach).
Austin Powers: The Spy Who Shagged Me (1999, New Line Cinema, M. Jay Roach).
Bambi Meets Godzilla (1969, Pyramid Films, Marv Newland).
Bear's Tale, The (1940, Warner Bros., Tex Avery).
Big Bus, The (1976, Paramount Pictures, James Frawley).
Big Moments from Little Pictures (1924, Pathé, Hal Roach).
Black Bird, The (1975, Columbia Pictures, Michael Levee, Lou Lombardo).
Blazing Saddles (1974, Warner Bros., Mel Brooks).
Boat, The (1921, First National, Buster Keaton, Eddie Cline).
Bob Roberts (1992, Live Entertainment/PolyGram, Tim Robbins).
Bonanza Bunny (1959, Warner Bros., Robert McKimson).
Bosko's Picture Show (1933, Warner Bros., Hugh Harman).
Brady Bunch Movie, The (1995, Paramount Pictures, Betty Thomas).
Bugsy Malone (1976, Paramount Pictures, Alan Parker).
Bunny and Claude (1968, Warner Bros., Robert McKimson).
Casino Royale (1967, Columbia Pictures, Val Guest, Ken Hughes, John Huston, Joseph McGrath, Robert Parrish).
Charcuterie mécanique (1895, Lumière, Auguste and Louis Lumière).
Cheap Detective, The (1978, Columbia Pictures, Robert Moore).
Chopper Chicks in Zombietown (1992, Troma Pictures, Dan Hoskins).
Citizen Kane (1941, RKO, Orson Welles).
Closet Cases of the Nerd Kind (1979, Pyramid Films, Rick Harper).
Coal Black and the Seben Dwarfs (1943, Warner Bros., Robert Clampett).

College (1927, United Artists, James W. Horne).
Coo Coo Nut Grove, The (1936, Warner Bros., Fritz Freleng).
Corny Concerto, A (1943, Warner Bros., Robert Clampett).
Cowboy Sheik, The (1924, Pathé, Hal Roach).
Curtain Pole, The (1909, Biograph, D. W. Griffith).
Dead Men Don't Wear Plaid (1982, Universal Pictures, Carl Reiner).
Débuts d'un patineur, Les (1906, Linder, Max Linder).
D' Fightin' Ones (1961, Warner Bros., Fritz Freleng).
Dove, The (1968, George Cole, Anthony Lover).
Dr. Pyckle and Mr. Pryde (1925, Standard Cinema/Selznick, Joe Rock).
Dracula: Dead and Loving It (1995, Columbia Pictures, Mel Brooks).
Drip Along Daffy (1951, Warner Bros., Chuck Jones).
Duck Amuck (1953, Warner Bros., Chuck Jones).
Duck Dodgers in the 24 1/2th Century (1953, Warner Bros., Chuck Jones).
Escamatage d'une dame chez Robert Houdin (1896, Méliès, Georges Méliès).
Everything You Always Wanted to Know About Sex* (*But Were Afraid to Ask) (1972, United Artists, Woody Allen).
Fatal Instinct (1993, MGM, Carl Reiner).
Fearless Vampire Killers (or Pardon Me, But Your Teeth Are in My Neck), The (1966, MGM, Roman Polanski).
Flintstones, The (1994, Universal Pictures, Brian Levant).
Frankenweenie (1984, Walt Disney Productions, Tim Burton).
Frozen North, The (1922, First National Pictures, Buster Keaton, Eddie Cline).

Garden Scene (1896, Edison Co., Thomas Edison).
Germany Calling (1944, Spectator Productions/US Ministry of Information).
Go West (1925, Metro-Goldwyn, Buster Keaton).
Go West (1940, MGM, Edward Buzzell).
Hardware Wars (1978, Pyramid Films, Ernie Fosselius).
Haunted Honeymoon (1986, Orion Pictures, Gene Wilder).
High Anxiety (1977, 20th Century-Fox, Mel Brooks).
High Sign, The (1920, Metro, Buster Keaton, Eddie Cline).
His Bitter Pill (1916, Keystone, Mack Sennett).
Hollywood Steps Out (1941, Warner Bros., Tex Avery).
Honolulu (1939, MGM, Edward Buzzell).
Honey-Mousers, The (1956, Warner Bros., Robert McKimson).
Hot Shots! (1991, 20th Century-Fox, Jim Abrahams).
Hot Shots! Part Deux (1993, 20th Century-Fox, Jim Abrahams).
I Haven't Got a Hat (1935, Warner Bros., Fritz Freleng).
I'm Gonna Git You, Sucka (1989, United Artists, Keenen Ivory Wayans).
Johnny Dangerously (1984, 20th Century-Fox, Amy Heckerling).
Kentucky Fried Movie (1977, KFM Films, John Landis).
Killer Klowns from Outer Space (1988, Trans World Entertainment, Stephen Chiodo).
L'arroseur arrosé (1895, Lumière, Auguste and Louis Lumière).
Last Remake of Beau Geste, The (1977, Universal Pictures, Marty Feldman).
Lobster Man from Mars (1989, Electric Pictures, Stanley Sheff).
Lone Stranger and Porky, The (1939, Warner Bros., Robert Clampett).

FILMOGRAPHY

Love and Death (1975, Jack Rollins & Charles H. Joffe Productions, Woody Allen).
Love at First Bite (1979, American International Pictures, Stan Dragoti).
Lust in the Dust (1984, Fox Run, Paul Bartel).
Mafia! (1998, Touchstone Pictures, Jim Abrahams).
Max médecin malgré lui (1918, Linder, Max Linder).
Medusa: Dare to Be Truthful (1992, Columbia Tristar, Julie Brown, John Fontenberry).
Mouse That Jack Built, The (1959, Warner Bros., Robert McKimson).
Movie, A (1958, Conner, Bruce Conner).
Movie, Movie (1978, Warner Bros., Stanley Donen).
Mud and Sand (1922, Quality-Metro, Stan Laurel).
Naked Gun: From the Files of Police Squad!, The (1988, Paramount Pictures, David Zucker).
Naked Gun 2 1/2: The Smell of Fear, The (1991, Paramount Pictures, David Zucker).
Naked Gun 33 1/3: The Final Insult, The (1994, Paramount Pictures, Peter Segal).
National Lampoon's Loaded Weapon 1 (1993, New Line Cinema, Gene Quintano).
Once upon a Horse (1958, Universal Pictures, Hal Kanter).
Paleface, The (1921, First National, Buster Keaton, Eddie Cline).
Paleface, The (1948, Paramount Pictures, Norman Z. McLeod).
Pardners (1956, Paramount Pictures, Norman Taurog).
Play It Again, Sam (1972, Paramount Pictures, Herbert Ross).
Plump Fiction (1996, Rhino, Gary Binkow).

Porklips Now (1980, Pyramid Films, Ernie Fosselius).
Porky's Movie Mystery (1939, Warner Bros., Robert Clampett).
Purple Rose of Cairo, The (1985, Orion Pictures, Woody Allen).
Repossessed (1990, Seven Arts, Bob Logan).
Ride Him, Bosko (1932, Warner Bros., Hugh Harman).
Robin Hood: Men in Tights (1993, 20th Century-Fox, Mel Brooks).
Rocky Horror Picture Show, The (1975, 20th Century-Fox, Jim Sharman).
Rustler's Rhapsody (1985, Paramount Pictures, Hugh Wilson).
Saps in Chaps (1942, Warner Bros., Fritz Freleng).
Saturday the 14th (1981, New World Pictures, Howard R. Cohen).
Schlock (1973, Jack H. Harris Enterprises, John Landis).
Sgt. Kabukiman N.Y.P.D. (1996, Troma Pictures, Michael Herz, Lloyd Kaufman).
Sherlock Jr. (1924, Metro, Buster Keaton).
Silence of the Hams, The (1994, Thirtieth Century Wolf, Ezio Greggio).
Silent Movie (1976, 20th Century-Fox, Mel Brooks).
Sleeper (1975, United Artists, Woody Allen).
Soapdish (1991, Paramount Pictures, Michael Hoffman).
Son of Paleface (1952, Paramount Pictures, Frank Tashlin).
Spaceballs (1987, MGM, Mel Brooks).
Spy Hard (1996, Hollywood Pictures, Rick Friedberg).
Star Is Hatched, A (1938, Warner Bros., Fritz Freleng).
Sunbonnet Blue, A (1937, Warner Bros., Tex Avery).
Take the Money and Run (1969, Palomar Pictures, Woody Allen).
Tale of Two Kitties, A (1942, Warner Bros., Robert Clampett).

This Is Spinal Tap (1984, Embassy, Rob Reiner).

They Call Me Bruce? (1982, Artists Releasing Corporation, Elliot Hong).

Three Ages, The (1923, Metro, Buster Keaton, Eddie Cline).

Three Must-Get-Theres, The (1922, Linder, Max Linder).

Top Secret! (1984, Paramount Pictures, Jim Abrahams, David Zucker, Jerry Zucker).

Transylvania 6-5000 (1963, Warner Bros., Chuck Jones).

Transylvania 6-5000 (1985, New World Pictures, Rudy DeLuca).

Tunnelvision (1976, Media Home Entertainment, Neal Israel).

UHF (1989, Orion Pictures, Jay Levey).

Uncensored Movies (1924, Pathé, Hal Roach).

Uncle Josh at the Moving Picture Show (1900, Edison Co., Edwin S. Porter).

Wacky Wildlife (1940, Warner Bros., Tex Avery).

Waiting For Guffman (1996, Castle Rock Entertainment, Christopher Guest).

Way Out West (1937, Hal Roach/MGM, James Horne).

Weakly Reporter (1944, Warner Bros., Chuck Jones).

What's Opera, Doc? (1957, Warner Bros., Chuck Jones).

What's Up, Tiger Lily? (1966, American International, Woody Allen).

Who Framed Roger Rabbit (1988, Touchstone Pictures, Richard Zemeckis).

Young Frankenstein (1974, 20th Century-Fox, Mel Brooks).

Zelig (1983, Orion Pictures, Woody Allen).

Zorro, the Gay Blade (1981, 20th Century-Fox, Peter Medak).

Bibliography

Altman, Rick, 'The Semantic/Syntactic Approach to Film Genre', in Barry Grant (ed.), *Film Genre Reader* (Austin: University of Texas Press, 1986).
Altman, Rick, *The American Film Musical* (Bloomington: Indiana University Press, 1987).
Altman, Rick, *Film/Genre* (London: BFI, 1999).
Andrasha, Mikhail, 'Can a Parodist Keep From Being Run Out of Town?', *Soviet Life* no. 292, 1981.
Andrew, J. Dudley, *Concepts in Film Theory* (New York: Oxford University Press, 1984).
Anonymous, 'Imaginative "Black Bird" Campaign Creates Awareness With Cleverly Designed Tie-ins', *Boxoffice Showmandiser*, 2 February 1976.
Antoine, Shannon, 'Melville and the Art of Satire: Perspective Through Parody and Caricature', unpublished PhD dissertation, Louisiana State University and Agricultural and Mechanical College, 1979.
Austin, Bruce A. and Thomas F. Gordon, 'Movie Genres: Toward a Conceptualized Model and Standardized Definitions', in Bruce A. Austin (ed.), *Current Research in Film: Audiences, Economics, and Law* Volume 3 (Norwood, NJ: Ablex Publishing, 1987).
Badley, Linda, 'The Aesthetics of Postmodern Parody: An Extended Definition', *The Comparatist: Journal of the Southern Comparative Literature Association* no. 7, 1983.
Bakhtin, Mikhail, *Rabelais and His World* (Cambridge, MA: M.I.T. Press, 1968).
Bakhtin, Mikhail, *The Dialogic Imagination: Four Essays*, ed. Michael Holquist (Austin: University of Texas Press, 1981).
Bakhtin, Mikhail, *Problems of Dostoevsky's Poetics* (Minneapolis: University of Minnesota Press, 1984).
Bakhtin, Mikhail, 'The Problem of the Text in Linguistics, Philology, and the Human Sciences: An Experiment in Philosophical Analysis', in Caryl Emerson and Michael Holquist (eds), *Speech Genres and Other Late Essays* (Austin: University of Texas Press, 1986).
Barthes, Roland, *Elements of Semiology* (New York: Hill and Wang, 1968).
Barthes, Roland, *S/Z* (New York: Hill and Wang, 1974).
Baudrillard, Jean, *Simulations* (New York: Semiotext(e), 1983).
Beck, Jerry and Will Friedwald, *Looney Tunes and Merrie Melodies: A Complete Illustrated Guide to the Warner Bros. Cartoons* (New York: Henry Holt and Co., 1989).
Ben-Porat, Ziva, 'Method in Madness: Notes on the Structure of Parody Based on MAD TV Satires', *Poetics Today* vol. 1 no. 1/2, 1979.
Ben-Porat, Ziva, 'Ideology, Genre and Serious Parody', in Anna Balakian (ed.), *Proceedings of the Xth Congress of the International Comparative Literature Association* (New York: Garland Publishing, 1985).

Bennett, David, 'Parody, Postmodernism, and the Politics of Reading', in David Roberts, Pavel Petr and Philip Thomson (eds), *Comic Relations: Studies in the Comic, Satire and Parody* (Frankfurt am Main: Verlag Peter Lang, 1985).
Bennett, Tony, *Formalism and Marxism* (London: Methuen & Co., 1979).
Bennett, Tony, 'Texts, Readers, Reading Formations', *The Bulletin of the Midwest Modern Language Association* vol. 16 no. 1, 1983.
Bennett, Tony, 'Texts in History: The Determinations of Readings and their Texts', *The Bulletin of the Midwest Modern Language Association* vol. 18 no.1, 1985.
Bennett, Tony and Janet Woollacott, *Bond and Beyond: The Political Career of a Popular Hero* (London: Macmillan Education, 1987).
Benson, Douglas K., 'Linguistic Parody and Reader Response in the Worlds of Angel González', *Anales De La Literatura Española Contemporanea* vol. 7 no. 1, 1982.
Benson, Sheila, ' "Lust" Gets Lost in its Own Dust', *Los Angeles Times*, 8 March 1985.
Berger, Carole, 'Viewing as Action: Film and Reader Response Criticism', *Literature/Film Quarterly* vol. 6 no. 2, 1978.
Bergson, Henri, 'Laughter', in Wylie Sypher (ed.), *Comedy* (Garden City, NY: Doubleday Anchor Books, 1956).
Berman, Jaye, 'Parody as Cultural Criticism in "The Dead Father" ', *Dutch Quarterly Review of Anglo-American Letters* vol. 17 no. 1, 1987.
Bireley, Nebitt, 'How Many Ümlauts Does it Take to Screw in a Light Bulb?' *Pulse!* no. 102, 1992.
Blesh, Rudi, *Keaton* (New York: Macmillan, 1967).
Böhn, Andreas, 'Parody and Quotation: A Case-Study of E. T. A. Hoffmann's *Kater Murr*', in Beate Müller (ed.), *Parody: Dimensions and Perspectives* (Amsterdam: Rodopi, 1997).
Bolton, Richard, 'The Modern Spectator and the Postmodern Participant', *Photo Communique* vol. 8 no. 2, 1986.
Booth, Wayne C., *A Rhetoric of Irony* (Chicago, IL: University of Chicago Press, 1974).
Bromwich, David, 'Parody, Pastiche, and Allusion', in Chaviva Hosek and Patricia Parker (eds), *Lyric Poetry: Beyond New Criticism* (Ithaca, NY: Cornell University Press, 1985).
Busch, Anita M., 'Fox Execs Get Their Goat With Spoof Ad for "Hot Shots!" ' *Advertising For Films*, 28 August 1991.
Byrge, Duane, 'Review of "Rustler's Rhapsody" ', *Hollywood Reporter*, 10 May 1985.
Byrne, Bridget, 'Star Sing-a-Long on "Big Bus" in Splashy Sea of Soda Pop', *Los Angeles Herald-Examiner*, 14 December 1975.
Byrne, Margaret, 'A Working Theory of Film Genre', unpublished PhD dissertation, University of Southern California, 1988.
Caesar, Terry, ' "Violating the Shrine": Parody Inside and Outside Literature', unpublished PhD dissertation, University of Washington, 1979.
Caesar, Terry, ' "Impervious to Criticism": Contemporary Parody and Trash', *Sub-Stance* no. 64, 1991.
Canby, Vincent, ' "Airplane!" – A Parody That Works', *New York Times*, 13 July 1980.
Canby, Vincent, 'Screen: "Rustler's Rhapsody" ', *New York Times*, 10 May 1985.
Cawelti, John G., *Adventure, Mystery, and Romance: Formula Stories as Art and Popular Culture* (Chicago, IL: University of Chicago Press, 1976).

Cawelti, John G., ' "Chinatown" and Generic Transformation in Recent American Films', in Barry K. Grant (ed.), *Film Genre Reader* (Austin: University of Texas Press, 1986).

Chambers, Robert, 'Parodic Perspectives – A Theory of Parody', unpublished PhD dissertation, Indiana University, 1974.

Chatman, Seymour, *Story and Discourse: Narrative Structure in Fiction and Film* (Ithaca, NY: Cornell University Press, 1978).

Cobley, Evelyn, 'Sameness and Difference in Literary Repetition', *Recherches Sémiotiques/ Semiotic Inquiry* vol. 3 no. 2, 1983.

Cohen, Ralph, 'Do Postmodern Genres Exist?', *Genre* vol. 20 no. 3/4, 1987.

Cooper, J., 'Contestability of the Image: Postmodernist Appropriation and Intellectual Property Rights', *Cinema Papers*, no. 127, 1998.

Crafton, Donald, 'The View From Termite Terrace: Caricature and Parody in Warner Bros. Animation', *Film History* no. 5, 1993.

Cripps, Thomas, *Black Film as Genre* (Bloomington: Indiana University Press, 1979).

Crosman, Inge, 'Reference and the Reader', *Poetics Today* vol. 4 no. 1, 1983.

Culler, Jonathan, *Structuralist Poetics: Structuralism, Linguistics, and the Study of Literature* (Ithaca, NY: Cornell University Press, 1975).

Culler, Jonathan, 'Presupposition and Intertextuality', *Modern Language Notes* vol. 9 no. 6, 1976.

Culler, Jonathan, *The Pursuit of Signs: Semiotics, Literature, Deconstruction* (Ithaca, NY: Cornell University Press, 1981).

Curran, Trisha, 'Review of "Movie, Movie"', *Films in Review*, March 1979.

Curry, Ramona, 'Madonna From Marilyn To Marlene – Pastiche and/or Parody?' *Journal of Popular Film and Video* vol. 42 no. 2, 1990.

Dane, Joseph, 'Parody and Satire: A Theoretical Model', *Genre* vol. 13, Summer 1980.

Dane, Joseph, *Parody: Critical Concepts Versus Literary Practices, Aristophanes to Sterne* (Norman: University of Oklahoma Press, 1988).

Dane, Joseph, 'An Overview of Directions in Contemporary Criticism of Literary Parody', *Quarterly Review of Film and Video* vol. 12 no. 1/2, 1990.

Dardis, Tom, *Keaton: The Man Who Wouldn't Lie Down* (New York: Penguin Books, 1980).

Davies, John and Michael Berrell, 'Australian Television Satire – A.S.I.O. and S.W.A.T', in David Roberts, Pavel Petr and Philip Thomson (eds), *Comic Relations: Studies in the Comic, Satire and Parody* (Frankfurt am Main: Verlag Peter Lang, 1985).

Davis, Joe, 'Criticism and Parody', *Thought: Fordham University Quarterly* vol. 26 no. 101, 1951.

Day, Barry, 'Split-Level Communication', *Advertising Age*, 23 March 1987.

de Man, Paul, 'The Rhetoric of Temporality', in Charles S. Singleton (ed.), *Interpretation: Theory and Practice* (Baltimore, MD: Johns Hopkins University Press, 1969).

Denby, David, 'Double Jeopardy', *New York*, 11 December 1978.

Denby, David, 'The Past Revisited', *New York*, 18 July 1983.

Derrida, Jacques, *Spurs: Nietzsche's Styles* (Chicago, IL: University of Chicago Press, 1979).

Derrida, Jacques, 'The Law of Genre', *Critical Inquiry*, vol. 7 no. 1, 1986.

Dienstfrey, Harris, 'Hitch Your Genre To a Star', *Film Culture*, vol. 34, Fall 1964.

Doane, Mary Anne, 'The Dialogical Text: Filmic Irony and the Spectator', unpublished PhD dissertation, University of Iowa, 1979.

Dolezel, Lubomir, 'A Scheme of Narrative Time', in Ladislav Matejka and Irwin R. Titunik (eds), *Semiotics of Art: Prague School Contributions* (Cambridge, MA: The M.I.T. Press, 1976).

Douglas, Mary, 'The Social Control of Cognition: Some Factors in Joke Perception', *Man: The Journal of the Royal Anthropological Institute* vol. 3 no. 3, 1968.

Dyer, Richard, *Stars* (London: BFI, 1986).

Easthorpe, Antony, 'Notes on Genre', *Screen Education* vol. 32 no. 3, 1979/80.

Eco, Umberto, *A Theory of Semiotics* (Bloomington: Indiana University Press, 1976).

Eco, Umberto, *The Role of the Reader: Explorations in the Semiotics of Texts* (Bloomington: Indiana University Press, 1979).

Eco, Umberto, *Semiotics and the Philosophy of Language* (Bloomington: Indiana University Press, 1984).

Eco, Umberto, 'Casablanca: Cult Movies and Intertextual Collage', *Sub-Stance* vol. 14 no. 2, 1985.

Eco, Umberto, *The Limits of Interpretation* (Bloomington: Indiana University Press, 1990).

Eden, Rick Anthony, 'The Rhetoric of Hypocrisy: Five Studies in Parody With a Pedagogical Postscript', unpublished PhD dissertation, University of California, Los Angeles, 1980.

Edenbaum, Seth, 'Parody and Privacy', *Arts Magazine*, vol. 62 no. 2, 1987.

Eidsvik, Charles, *Cineliteracy: Film Among the Arts* (New York: Horizon Press, 1978).

Elam, Kier, *The Semiotics of Theatre and Drama* (London: Methuen, 1980).

Elley, Derek, 'Review of The Black Bird', *Films and Filming*, May 1976.

Ellis, John, *Visible Fictions* (London: Routledge & Kegan Paul, 1982).

Erlich, Victor, *Russian Formalism: History – Doctrine*, 3rd edn (New Haven, CT: Yale University Press, 1981).

Feinberg, Leonard, *Introduction to Satire* (Ames: Iowa State University Press, 1967).

Fineman, Daniel, 'Parody and Production: Criticism and Labor', *Minnesota Review* no. 18, 1992.

Finlay, Marike, *The Romantic Irony of Semiotics: Friedrich Schlegel and the Crisis of Representation* (Berlin: Mouton de Gruyter, 1988).

Finlay-Pelinski, Marike, 'Semiotics or History: From Content Analysis to Contextualized Discursive Praxis', *Semiotica* vol. 40 no. 3/4, 1982.

Fish, Stanley, *Is There a Text in This Class? The Authority of Interpretive Communities* (Cambridge: Harvard University Press, 1980).

Fish, Stanley, 'Short People Got No Reason to Live: Reading Irony', *Daedalus* vol. 112 no. 1, 1983.

Fokkema, Douwe, 'The Semantic and Syntactic Organization of Postmodernist Texts', in Douwe Fokkema and Hans Bertens (eds), *Approaching Postmodernism* (Amsterdam: John Benjamins Publishing, 1986).

Fosselius, Ernie and Dorothy Fadiman, *Hardware Wars Study Guide* (Los Angeles, CA: Pyramid Films, 1978).

Foster, Hal, 'Wild Signs: The Breakup of the Sign in Seventies' Art', in Andrew Ross (ed.), *Universal Abandon? The Politics of Postmodernism* (Edinburgh: Edinburgh University Press, 1989).

Foucault, Michel, 'A Preface to Transgression', in Donald F. Bouchard (ed.), *Language,*

Counter-Memory, Practice: Selected Essays and Interviews (Ithaca, NY: Cornell University Press, 1977).

Foucault, Michel, *This is Not a Pipe* (Berkeley: University of California Press, 1983).

Fowler, Roger and Gunther Kress, 'Critical Linguistics', in Roger Fowler, Bob Hodge, Gunther Kress and Tony Trew (eds), *Language and Control* (London: Routledge & Kegan Paul, 1979).

Freud, Sigmund, *Jokes and Their Relation to the Unconscious* (London: Routledge & Kegan Paul, 1960).

Freud, Sigmund, 'Humour', in Philip Rieff (ed.), *Character and Culture* (New York: Collier Books, 1963).

Freund, Elizabeth, *The Return of the Reader: Reader-Response Criticism* (New York: Methuen, 1987).

Gallagher, Tag, 'Shoot-out at the Genre Corral: Problems in the "Evolution" of the Western', in Barry K. Grant (ed.), *Film Genre Reader* (Austin: University of Texas Press, 1986).

Garfinkel, Harold, *Studies in Ethnomethodology* (Englewood Cliffs, NJ: Prentice-Hall, 1967).

Geltrich-Ludgate, Brigitta, 'Teenage Jokesters and Riddlers: Profile in Parody', *Maledicta: The International Journal of Verbal Aggression* no. 7, 1983.

Genette, Gérard, 'Boundaries of Narrative', *New Literary History* vol. 8 no. 1, 1976.

Genette, Gérard, *Narrative Discourse: An Essay in Method* (Ithaca, NY: Cornell University Press, 1980).

Genette, Gérard, *Palimpsestes: la litterature au second degre* (Paris: Seuil, 1982).

Gitlin, Todd, 'Television's Screen: Hegemony in Transition', in Donald Lazere (ed.), *American Media and Mass Culture: Left Perspectives* (Berkeley: University of California Press, 1987).

Goffman, Erving, *Frame Analysis* (Philadelphia: University of Pennsylvania Press, 1974).

Goodheart, Eugene, 'The Text and the Interpretive Community', *Daedalis* vol. 112 no. 1, 1983.

Grant, Barry K., 'Prolegomena to Contextualistic Genre Criticism', *Paunch* nos 53–4, 1980.

Grant, Barry K., 'Experience and Meaning in Genre Films', in Barry K. Grant (ed.), *Film Genre Reader* (Austin: University of Texas Press, 1986).

Grant, Barry K., 'Science Fiction Double Feature: Ideology in the Cult Film', in J. P. Telotte (ed.), *The Cult Film: Beyond All Reason* (Austin: University of Texas Press, 1991).

Greenstone, Richard J., 'Protection of Obscene Parody as Fair Use', *The Entertainment and Sports Lawyer* vol. 4 no. 3, 1986.

Gross, Harvey, 'Parody, Reminiscence, Critique: Aspects of Modernist Style', in Monique Chefdor, Ricardo Quinones and Albert Wachtel (eds), *Modernism: Challenges and Perspectives* (Urbana: University of Illinois Press, 1986).

Guilhamet, Leon, *Satire and the Transformation of Genre* (Philadelphia: University of Pennsylvania Press, 1987).

Hall, Stuart, 'The Narrative Construction of Reality', *Southern Review* no. 17, 1984.

Hall, Stuart, 'Encoding/Decoding', in Stuart Hall, Dorothy Hobson, Andrew Lowe and Paul Willis (eds), *Culture, Media, Language* (London: Hutchinson, 1980).

Halliday, M. A. K., *Language as Social Semiotic: The Social Interpretation of Language and Meaning* (Baltimore, MD: University Park Press, 1978).

Halliday, M. A. K. and Ruqaiya Hasan, *Language, Context, and Texts: Aspects of Language and Meaning* (Victoria: Deakin University Press, 1985).

Handwerk, Gary, *Irony and Ethics in Narrative: From Schlegel to Lacan* (New Haven, CT: Yale University Press, 1985).

Hannoosh, Michelle, 'The Reflexive Function of Parody', *Comparative Literature* vol. 41 no. 2, 1989.

Harrell, Wade, 'When the Parody Parodies Itself: The Problem With Michael Frayn's *Noises Off*', in Karelisa V. Hartigan (ed.), *From the Bard to Broadway* (Lanham, MD: University Press of America, 1987).

Harries, Dan, 'Camping With Lady Divine: Star Persona and Parody', *Quarterly Review of Film and Video* vol. 12 no. 1/2, 1990.

Harries, Dan, 'Semiotics, Discourse and Parodic Spectatorship', *Semiotica* vol. 113 no. 3/4, 1997.

Hassan, Ihab, 'The Culture of Postmodernism', in Monique Chefdor, Ricardo Quinones and Albert Wachtel (eds), *Modernism: Challenges and Perspectives* (Urbana: University of Illinois Press, 1986).

Hawkes, Terence, *Metaphor* (London: Methuen, 1972).

Hausman, Carl R., *Metaphor and Art: Interactionism and Reference in the Verbal and Nonverbal Arts* (Cambridge: Cambridge University Press, 1989).

Hebdige, Dick, *Subculture: The Meaning of Style* (London: Methuen, 1979).

Herman-Sekulic, Maja, 'Towards a New Understanding of Parody', *European Studies Journal* vol. 2 no. 2, 1985.

Hernadi, Paul, *Beyond Genre: New Directions in Literary Classification* (Ithaca, NY: Cornell University Press, 1972).

Herrnstein Smith, Barbara, 'Narrative Versions, Narrative Theories', *Critical Inquiry* vol. 7 no. 1, 1980.

Hirsch, E. D., *Validity in Interpretation* (New Haven, CT: Yale University Press, 1967).

Hodge, Robert and Gunther Kress, *Social Semiotics* (Ithaca, NY: Cornell University Press, 1988).

Hope, Edward, *The Language of Parody: A Study in the Diction of Aristophanes* (Baltimore, MD: J. H. Furst, 1906).

Horányi, Özséb, 'Culture and Metasemiotics in Film', *Semiotica* vol. 15 no. 3, 1975.

Horton, Andrew, 'Bakhtin, Carnival Triumph, and Cinema: Beyond Barreto's *Dona Flor and Her Two Husbands* and Dusan Makavejev's *Innocence Unprotected Reconsidered*', *Quarterly Review of Film and Video* vol. 12 no. 1/2, 1990.

Howes, Craig, 'Rhetorics of Attack: Bakhtin and the Aesthetics of Satire', *Genre* vol. 20 no. 3/4, 1987.

Hutcheon, Linda, 'Parody Without Ridicule: Observations on Modern Literary Parody', *Canadian Review of Comparative Literature* vol. 5 no. 2, 1978.

Hutcheon, Linda, *A Theory of Parody: The Teachings of Twentieth-Century Art Forms* (New York: Methuen, 1985).

Hutcheon, Linda, *A Poetics of Postmodernism: History, Theory, Fiction* (New York: Routledge, 1988).

Hutcheon, Linda, *The Politics of Postmodernism* (New York: Routledge, 1989a).

Hutcheon, Linda, 'Modern Parody and Bakhtin', in Gary Saul Morson and Caryl Emerson (eds), *Rethinking Bakhtin: Extensions and Challenges* (Evanston, IL: Northwestern University Press, 1989b).

Hutcheon, Linda, 'An Epilogue: Postmodern Parody: History, Subjectivity, and Ideology', *Quarterly Review of Film and Video* vol. 12 no. 1/2, 1990.

Hutcheon, Linda, *Irony's Edge – The Theory and Politics of Irony* (New York: Routledge, 1994).

Hutchings, Patrick, 'Bergson's Laughter – A Master-Code?' in Pavel Petr, David Roberts and Philip Thomson (eds), *Comic Relations: Studies in the Comic, Satire and Parody* (Frankfurt am Main: Verlag Peter Lang, 1985).

Huyssen, Andreas, *After the Great Divide: Modernism, Mass Culture, Postmodernism* (Bloomington: Indiana University Press, 1986).

Iser, Wolfgang, *The Act of Reading: A Theory of Aesthetic Reception* (Baltimore, MD: Johns Hopkins University Press, 1978).

Iser, Wolfgang, 'Interaction Between Text and Reader', in Susan R. Suleiman and Inge Crosman (eds), *The Reader in the Text: Essays on Audience and Interpretation* (Princeton, NJ: Princeton University Press, 1980).

Issacharoff, Michael, 'Parody, Satire and Ideology, or the Labyrinth of Reference', *Rivista di Letterature Moderne e Comparate* vol. 42 no. 3, 1989.

Jameson, Fredric, *The Political Unconscious: Narrative as a Socially Symbolic Act* (Ithaca, NY: Cornell University Press, 1981).

Jameson, Fredric, 'Postmodernism and Consumer Society', in Hal Foster (ed.), *The Anti-Aesthetic: Essays on Postmodern Culture* (Port Townsend, Washington, DC: Bay Press, 1983).

Jameson, Fredric, 'Postmodernism, or the Cultural Logic of Late Capitalism', *New Left Review* no. 146, 1984.

Jauss, Hans Robert, *Toward an Aesthetic of Reception* (Brighton: The Harvester Press, 1982).

Jayyusi, Lena, 'Toward a Socio-Logic of the Film Text', *Semiotica* vol. 68 no. 3/4, 1988.

Jencks, Charles, *What is Post-Modernism?* (New York: St Martin's Press, 1989).

Jenkins, Henry, III, 'The Amazing Push-Me/Pull-You Text: Cognitive Processing, Narrational Play and the Comic Film', *Wide Angle* vol. 8 no. 3/4, 1986.

Jerrold, Walter and R. M. Leonard (eds), *A Century of Parody and Imitation* (London: Oxford University Press, 1913).

Johnson, Emmette B., III, 'The Mode of Parody: A Theoretical Inquiry', unpublished PhD dissertation, University of California, Los Angeles, 1971.

Kaufer, David S., 'Irony, Interpretive Form, and the Theory of Meaning', *Poetics Today* vol. 4 no. 3, 1983.

Kawin, Bruce F., *Telling it Again and Again: Repetition in Literature and Film* (Ithaca, NY: Cornell University Press, 1972).

Kent, Thomas, *Interpretation and Genre: The Role of Generic Perception in the Study of Narrative Texts* (Lewisburg, PA: Bucknell University Press, 1986).

Kiremidjian, Garabed, 'A Study of Parody: James Joyce's *Ulysses*, Thomas Mann's *Doktor Faustus*', unpublished PhD dissertation, Yale University, 1964.

Kiremidjian, Garabed, 'The Aesthetics of Parody', *Journal of Aesthetics and Criticism* vol. 28 no. 2, 1969.

Klein, Richard, 'New World Gets Rights to "Dust" ', *Variety*, 20 December 1984.

Klinger, Barbara, 'Cinema and Social Process: A Contextual Theory of the Cinema and Its Spectators', unpublished PhD dissertation, University of Iowa, 1986.

Kress, Gunther and Robert Hodge, *Language as Ideology* (London: Routledge & Kegan Paul, 1979).

La Capra, Dominick, *Rethinking Intellectual History: Texts, Contexts, Language* (Ithaca, NY: Cornell University Press, 1983).

Lachman, Renate, 'Bakhtin and Carnival: Culture as Counter-Culture', *Cultural Critique* vol. 11, Winter 1988–9.

Lang, Candace, *Irony/Humor: Critical Paradigms* (Baltimore, MD: Johns Hopkins University Press, 1988).

Lemert, Charles C. and Garth Gillan, *Michel Foucault: Social Theory and Transgression* (New York: Columbia University Press, 1982).

Lemon, Lee T. and Marion J. Reis, *Russian Formalist Criticism: Four Essays* (Lincoln: University of Nebraska Press, 1965).

Levine, Jacob, *Motivation in Humor* (New York: Atherton Press, 1969).

Lodge, David, *After Bakhtin: Essays on Fiction and Criticism* (London: Routledge, 1990).

López, Ana, 'Parody, Underdevelopment, and the New Latin American Cinema', *Quarterly Review of Film and Video* vol. 12 no. 1/2, 1990.

Lotman, Jurij, *The Structure of the Artistic Text* (Ann Arbor: Department of Slavic Languages and Literature, University of Michigan, 1977).

Louvre, Alf, 'Notes on a Theory of Genre', *Working Papers in Cultural Studies* vol. 4, Spring 1973.

Lukow, Gregory and Steven Ricci, 'The "Audience" Goes "Public": Intertextuality, Genre, and the Responsibilities of Film Literacy', *On Film* vol. 12, Spring 1984.

Macdonald, Dwight (ed.), *Parodies: An Anthology From Chaucer to Beerbohn – and After* (New York: Random House, 1960).

Maltin, Leonard, *The Great Movie Comedians* (New York: Harmony Books, 1982).

Mamber, Stephen, 'Parody, Intertextuality, Signature: Kubrick, DePalma, and Scorsese', *Quarterly Review of Film and Video* vol. 12 no. 1/2, 1990.

Markiewicz, Henryk, 'On the Definitions of Literary Parody', in *To Honor Roman Jakobson: Essays on the Occasion of His Seventieth Birthday* Volume 2 (The Hague: Mouton, 1967).

Mayer, Geoff, 'Formula and Genre: Myths and Patterns', *Australian Journal of Screen Theory* no. 4, 1978.

McLuhan, Marshall and Wilfred Watson, *From Cliché To Archetype* (New York: Viking Press, 1970).

Medvedev, P. N. and M. M. Bakhtin, *The Formal Method in Literary Scholarship: A Critical Introduction to Sociological Poetics* (Baltimore, MD: Johns Hopkins University Press, 1978).

Metzidakis, Stamos, *Repetition and Semiotics: Interpreting Prose Poems* (Birmingham, AL: Summa Publications, 1986).

Mihaies, Mircea, 'The Emblem as a Sign of Parody', *Degres – Revue de Synthese a Orientation Semiologique* vol. 28, Fall 1981.

Miller, Owen, 'Intertextual Identity', in Mario J. Valdés and Owen Miller (eds), *Identity of the Literary Text* (Toronto: University of Toronto Press, 1985).

Milner, G. B., 'Homo Ridens: Towards a Semiotic Theory of Humour and Laughter', *Semiotica* vol. 5 no. 1, 1972.
Morawski, Stefan, 'The Basic Functions of Quotation', in C. H. Van Schoonevelt (ed.), *Sign, Language, Culture* (The Hague: Mouton, 1970).
Morson, Gary Saul, 'Who Speaks for Bakhtin?: A Dialogic Introduction', *Critical Inquiry* vol. 10 no. 4, 1983.
Morson, Gary Saul, 'Parody, History, and Metaparody', in Gary Saul Morson and Caryl Emerson (eds), *Rethinking Bakhtin: Extensions and Challenges* (Evanston, IL: Northwestern University Press, 1989).
Muecke, D. C., *The Compass Of Irony* (London: Methuen, 1969).
Naumann, Manfred, 'Literary Production and Reception', *New Literary History* vol. 8 no. 1, 1976.
Neale, Stephen, *Genre* (London: BFI, 1980).
Neale, Steve and Frank Krutnik, *Popular Film and Television Comedy* (London: Routledge, 1990).
Nichols, Bill, *Ideology and the Image: Social Representation in the Cinema and Other Media* (Bloomington: Indiana University Press, 1981).
Oring, Elliot, 'Jokes and the Discourse on Disaster', *Journal of American Folklore* no. 100, 1987.
Papp, James Ralph, 'Parody: Cognition, Rhetoric and Social History', unpublished PhD dissertation, University of California, Los Angeles, 1993.
Paravisini, Lizabeth, 'Mumbo Jumbo and the Uses of Parody', *Obsidian II: Black Literature in Review* vol. 1 no. 1/2, 1986.
Pedersen, Bertel, 'The Theory and Practice of Parody in the Modern Novel: Mann, Joyce, and Nabokov', unpublished PhD dissertation, University of Illinois, Urbana-Champaign, 1972.
Petlewski, Paul, 'Complications of Narrative in the Genre Film', *Film Criticism* vol. 4 no. 1, 1979.
Petr, Pavel, 'Marxist Theories of the Comic', in Pavel Petr, David Roberts and Philip Thomson (eds), *Comic Relations: Studies in the Comic, Satire and Parody* (Frankfurt am Main: Verlag Peter Lang, 1985).
Pinto, Julio C. M., *The Reading of Time: A Semantico-Semiotico Approach* (Berlin: Mouton de Gruyter, 1989).
Poague, Leland, 'The Problem of Film Genre: A Mentalistic Approach', *Literature/Film Quarterly* vol. 6 no. 2, 1978.
Poirier, Richard, 'The Politics of Self-Parody', *Partisan Review* vol. 35 no. 3, 1968.
Popovic, Anton, 'Aspects of Metatext', *Canadian Review of Comparative Literature*, Fall 1976.
Pratt, Mary Louise, *Toward a Speech Act Theory of Literary Discourse* (Bloomington: Indiana University Press, 1977).
Price, J. B., 'Parody and Humour', *Contemporary Review* no. 180, 1951.
Rabinowitz, Peter, ' "What's Hecuba To Us?": The Audience's Experience of Literary Borrowing', in Susan R. Suleiman and Inge Crosman (eds), *Reader in the Text: Essays on Audience and Interpretation* (Princeton, NJ: Princeton University Press, 1980).
Ray, Robert B., *A Certain Tendency of the Hollywood Cinema, 1930–1980* (Princeton, NJ: Princeton University Press, 1985).

Redfern, Walter, *Puns* (London: Basil Blackwell, 1984).
Ricoeur, Paul, *The Rule of Metaphor: Multi-Disciplinary Studies of the Creation of Meaning* (Toronto: University of Toronto Press, 1977).
Ricoeur, Paul, 'The Metaphorical Process as Cognition, Imagination, and Feeling', in Sheldon Sacks (ed.), *On Metaphor* (Chicago, IL: University of Chicago Press, 1978).
Ricoeur, Paul, 'Narrative Time', *Critical Inquiry* vol. 7 no. 1, 1980.
Ricoeur, Paul, *Time and Narrative* Volume 1 (Chicago, IL: University of Chicago Press, 1984).
Riewald, J. G., 'Parody as Criticism', *Neophilologus* vol. 50 no. 1, 1966.
Riffaterre, Michael, 'The Poetic Functions of Intertextual Humor', *Romantic Review* vol. 65 no. 4, 1974.
Riffaterre, Michael, 'Syllepsis', *Critical Inquiry* vol. 6 no. 4, 1980.
Rimmon-Kenan, Shlomith, 'The Paradoxical Status of Repetition', *Poetics Today* vol. 1 no. 4, 1980.
Roberts, Matthew, 'Poetics Hermeneutics Dialogics: Bakhtin and Paul de Man', in Gary Saul Morson and Caryl Emerson (eds), *Rethinking Bakhtin: Extensions and Challenges* (Evanston, IL: Northwestern University Press, 1989).
Robinson, David, *Buster Keaton* (Bloomington: Indiana University Press, 1969).
Rose, Margaret A., *Parody/Metafiction: An Analysis of Parody as a Critical Mirror to the Writing and Reception of Fiction* (London: Croom Helm, 1979).
Rose, Margaret A., 'Defining Parody', *Southern Review* vol. 13 no. 1, 1980.
Rose, Margaret A., 'Parody Revisited', in Pavel Petr, David Roberts and Philip Thomson (eds), *Comic Relations: Studies in the Comic, Satire and Parody* (Frankfurt am Main: Verlag Peter Lang, 1985).
Rose, Margaret A., 'Parody and Post-Structuralist Criticism', *Jahrbuch Fur Internationale Germanistick* vol. 18 no. 1, 1986.
Rose, Margaret A., 'Post-Modern Pastiche', *British Journal of Aesthetics* vol. 31 no. 1, 1991.
Rose, Margaret A., *Parody: Ancient, Modern, and Post-Modern* (Cambridge: Cambridge University Press, 1993).
Rosmarin, Adena, *The Power of Genre* (Minneapolis: University of Minnesota Press, 1985).
Ruiz Collantes, F. J., 'The Pragmatics of Comico-Facetious Texts', *Semiotica* vol. 81 no. 3/4, 1990.
Rush, Jeffrey S., 'Who's in on the Joke: Parody as Hybridized Narrative Discourse', *Quarterly Review of Film and Video* vol. 12 no. 1/2, 1990.
Rutsky, R. L. and Justin Wyatt, 'Serious Pleasures: Cinematic Pleasure and the Notion of Fun', *Cinema Journal* vol. 30 no. 1, 1990.
Salamon, Julie, 'Review of "I'm Gonna Git You, Sucka" ', *Wall Street Journal*, 31 January 1989.
Salvaggio, Jerry L., 'Neglected Areas of Semiotic Criticism', *Quarterly Review of Film Studies* vol. 4 no. 1, 1979.
Sandro, Paul, 'Parodic Narration in "Entr'acte" ', *Film Criticism* vol. 4 no. 1, 1979.
Sarris, Andrew, 'Woody Allen at the Peak of Parody', *Village Voice*, 19 July 1983.
Schatz, Thomas, *Hollywood Genres: Formulas, Filmmaking, and the Studio System* (New York: Random House, 1981).
Schaubner, Ellen and Ellen Spolsky, *The Bounds of Interpretation: Linguistic Theory and Literary Text* (Stanford, CA: Stanford University Press, 1986).

Schiff, Stephen, 'The Repeatable Experience', *Film Comment* vol. 18 no. 2, 1982.
Schleusener, Jay, 'Convention and the Context of Reading', *Critical Inquiry* vol. 6 no. 7, 1980.
Schneider, Steve, *That's All Folks! The Art of Warner Bros. Animation* (New York: Holt and Co., 1988).
Sherzer, Joel, 'Oh! That's a Pun and I Didn't Mean It', *Semiotica* vol. 22 no. 3/4, 1978.
Shindler, Merrill, 'Coppertone Zorro', *Los Angeles Magazine*, August 1981.
Shlonsky, Tuvia, 'Literary Parody: Remarks on its Method and Function', in François Jost (ed.), *Proceedings of the IVth Congress of the International Comparative Literature Association* (The Hague: Mouton, 1966).
Shohat, Ella, 'Ethnicities-in-Relation: Toward a Multicultural Reading of American Cinema', in Lester D. Friedman (ed.), *Unspeakable Images: Ethnicity and the American Cinema* (Urbana: University of Illinois Press, 1991).
Siegal, Mark, 'Ozymandias Melancholia: The Nature of Parody in Woody Allen's *Stardust Memories*', *Literature/Film Quarterly* vol. 13 no. 2, 1985.
Simon, John, 'Review of "The Big Bus"', *New York*, 12 July 1976.
Simon, William G., 'Welles: Bakhtin: Parody', *Quarterly Review of Film and Video* vol. 12 no. 1/2, 1990.
Small, Edward S., 'Literary and Film Genres: Toward a Taxonomy of Film', *Literature/Film Quarterly* vol. 7 no. 4, 1979.
Sobchack, Vivian, 'Postmodern Modes of Ethnicity', in Lester D. Friedman (ed.), *Unspeakable Images: Ethnicity and the American Cinema* (Urbana: University of Illinois Press, 1991).
Stam, Robert, 'Film and Language: From Metz to Bakhtin', *Studies in the Literary Imagination* no. 1, 1986.
Stam, Robert, *Subversive Pleasures: Bakhtin, Cultural Criticism, and Film* (Baltimore, MD: Johns Hopkins University Press, 1989).
Stam, Robert, *Reflexivity in Film and Literature: From Don Quixote to Jean-Luc Godard* (New York: Columbia University Press, 1992).
Stam, Robert, Robert Burgoyne and Sandy Flitterman-Lewis, *New Vocabularies in Film Semiotics: Structuralism, Post-Structuralism and Beyond* (New York: Routledge, 1992).
Stevenson, Sheryl Anne, 'The Never-Last Word: Parody, Ideology, and the Open Work', unpublished PhD dissertation, University of Maryland, 1986.
Stewart, Susan, 'Shouts on the Street: Bakhtin's Anti-Linguistics', in Gary Saul Morson (ed.), *Bakhtin: Essays and Dialogues on His Work* (Chicago, IL: University of Chicago Press, 1986).
Suleiman, Susan, 'Interpreting Ironies', *Diacritics* vol. 6 no. 2, 1976.
Thompson, John B., *Studies in the Theory of Ideology* (Berkeley: University of California Press, 1984).
Threadgold, Terry, 'Semiotics–Ideology–Language', in Terry Threadgold, E. A. Grosz, Gunther Kress and M. A. K. Halliday (eds), *Semiotics, Ideology, Language* (Sydney: Sydney Association for Studies in Society and Culture, 1986).
Todorov, Tzvetan, 'Reading as Construction', in Susan R. Suleiman and Inge Crosman (eds), *The Reader in the Text: Essays on Audience and Interpretation* (Princeton, NJ: Princeton University Press, 1980).

Todorov, Tzvetan, *Theories of the Symbol* (Ithaca: Cornell University Press, 1982).
Todorov, Tzvetan, *Mikhail Bakhtin: The Dialogical Principle* (Minneapolis: University of Minnesota Press, 1984).
Tudor, Andrew, 'Genre: Theory and Mispractice in Film Criticism', *Screen* vol. 11 no. 6, 1970.
van Dijk, Teun A., *Text and Context: Explorations in the Semantics and Pragmatics of Discourse* (London: Longman Group, 1977).
Vernet, Marc, 'Genre', *Film Reader* no. 3, 1978.
Vieira, João Luiz, 'Hegemony and Resistance: Parody and Carnival in Brazilian Cinema', unpublished PhD dissertation, New York University, 1984.
Vieira, João Luiz and Robert Stam, 'Parody and Marginality: The Case of Brazilian Cinema', *Framework* no. 28, 1985.
Volosinov, V. N., *Marxism and the Philosophy of Language* (New York: Seminar Press, 1973).
Waller, Gregory A., 'Midnight Movies, 1980–1985: A Market Study', in J. P. Telotte (ed.), *The Cult Film Experience: Beyond All Reason* (Austin: University of Texas Press, 1991).
Warshow, Robert, *The Immediate Experience: Movies, Comics, Theatre, and Other Aspects of Popular Culture* (Garden City, NY: Doubleday, 1962).
Watts, Harold H., 'An Alternative Irony: Film on Film', *Journal of American Culture* vol. 1 no. 1, 1978.
Waugh, Patricia, *Metafiction: The Theory and Practice of Self-Conscious Fiction* (London: Methuen, 1984).
Wead, George, *Buster Keaton and the Dynamics of Visual Wit* (New York: Arno Press, 1976).
Weisstein, Ulrich, 'Parody, Travesty, and Burlesque: Imitations With a Vengeance', in François Jost (ed.), *Proceedings of the IVth Congress of the International Comparative Literature Association* (The Hague: Mouton, 1966).
White, Allon, 'Bakhtin, Sociolinguistics and Deconstruction', in Frank Gloversmith (ed.), *The Theory of Reading* (Brighton: The Harvester Press, 1984).
Wilde, Alan, *Horizons of Assent: Modernism, Postmodernism, and the Ironic Imagination* (Baltimore, MD: Johns Hopkins University Press, 1981).
Williams, Raymond, *Marxism and Literature* (Oxford: Oxford University Press, 1985).
Willman, Chris, 'Top Secret! Directors Tell All!', *Bam*, 27 July 1984.
Wollen, Peter, 'Komar & Melamid Exhibition Catalogue' (Edinburgh: Fruitmarket Gallery, 1985).
Wright, Will, *Sixguns and Society: A Structural Study of the Western* (Berkeley: University of California Press, 1976).
Yacowar, Maurice, 'Recent Popular Genre Movies: Awash and Aware', *Journal of Popular Film* vol. 4 no. 4, 1975.
Yacowar, Maurice, *The Comic Art of Mel Brooks* (London: W. H. Allen & Co., 1981).
Yacowar, Maurice, 'The Bug in the Rug: Notes on the Disaster Genre', in Barry K. Grant (ed.), *Film Genre Reader* (Austin: University of Texas Press, 1986).
Yacowar, Maurice, 'Beyond Parody: Woody Allen in the 80s', *Post Script* vol. 6 no. 2, 1987.
Yunck, John A., 'The Two Faces of Parody', *Iowa English Yearbook* no. 8, 1963.
Zima, Peter V., 'Text and Context: The Socio-Linguistic Nexus', in Peter Zima (ed.), *Semiotics and Dialectics: Ideology and the Text* (Amsterdam: John Benjamins, 1981).

Index

Abbott and Costello Go to Mars, 19
Abbott and Costello Meet Captain Kidd, 19
Abbott and Costello Meet Frankenstein, 19
Academy Awards, 74, 131
acting, 13, 14, 29, 46, 83, 84, 96, 97
Adventures of Sherlock Holmes' Smarter Brother, The, 46, 116, 123
Africa Screams, 19
Airplane II: The Sequel, 28, 45, 52, 69, 73, 88, 115, 132
Airplane!, 3, 28, 45, 52, 55, 57, 59, 63, 68, 69, 72-74, 80, 81, 83, 85, 86, 89, 110, 114, 117, 118, 122, 132, 133
All You Need is Cash, 32
Allen, Woody, 12, 20, 27, 29, 49
allusion, 26, 110
Altman, Rick, 8, 36, 37
Amazon Women on the Moon, 49, 53, 60, 73
Apocalypse Now, 34, 93-98, 104, 111, 114
Attack of the Killer Tomatoes!, 56, 114
Austin Powers: International Man of Mystery, 77, 80, 86, 87, 125;
Austin Powers: The Spy Who Shagged Me, 9, 131

Bakhtin, Mikhail, 4, 23, 35, 50, 55, 107, 120, 123, 124, 130
Bambi Meets Godzilla, 64, 103
Baudrillard, Jean, 22, 130
Bear's Tale, The, 16
Bergson, Henri, 126, 127
Big Bus, The, 6, 45, 48-50, 52, 53, 60, 72, 103, 104, 110, 112, 113, 118, 122
Black Bird, The, 27, 44, 52, 62, 115
'blaxploitation' films, 46, 69, 114, 118, 123
Blazing Saddles, 3, 9, 21, 29, 34, 45, 46, 48, 52, 56, 58, 60, 61, 63, 66, 67, 71, 74, 76, 77-80, 83, 86, 88, 113, 116, 123, 126, 128, 129, 131, 133
Boat, The, 13
Bob Roberts, 51, 133
Bonanza Bunny, 20, 122
Bosko's Picture Show, 17
box-office, 3, 15, 122, 123, 131
Brady Bunch Movie, The, 21, 25, 126
Brando, Marlon, 46, 97
Brooks, Mel, 3, 21, 26, 67, 71, 102, 103, 116, 132
Bugsy Malone, 23, 58, 60, 127
Bunny and Claude, 17

Caesar, Terry, 7, 34, 129
camera angle, 53, 70
camera movement, 29, 54, 70, 76
camp, 7
carnivalesque, 4, 124, 125, 128, 130
casting, 44-47, 56-58, 95, 99
characterization, 45, 46, 56
Charcuterie mécanique, 12
Cheap Detective, The, 45, 46, 59, 66, 68, 84, 87
Citizen Kane, 18, 28, 53
Closet Cases of the Nerd Kind, 60, 63, 69, 74, 89, 113
Coal Black and the Seben Dwarfs, 17
College, 15
competencies, 101, 105, 106, 108, 109, 111, 127
Coo Coo Nut Grove, The, 17
Corny Concerto, A, 17
costumes, 47, 63, 64, 78, 79, 80, 93

D' Fightin' Ones, 17
D. W. Griffith, 12, 13, 14, 58
Dane, Joseph, 4, 7, 32
Dead Men Don't Wear Plaid, 27, 44, 48, 52, 53, 67, 75, 85, 87, 116
Derrida, Jacques, 36, 110
detective genre, 33, 59, 98, 123, 127
dialogue, 49, 52, 58, 63, 65, 68, 73, 78, 81, 84, 96, 97, 125
Direct Cinema, 33, 52, 53, 54
disaster films, 3, 6, 19, 44, 48, 49, 50, 57, 80, 86, 103, 112, 113, 116, 122
Disney, 16, 17, 111
Divine, 58, 118
documentary, 21, 27, 29, 33, 45, 51, 52, 53, 54, 126
Dove, The, 6, 20, 29
Dr. Pyckle and Mr. Pryde, 15
Dracula: Dead and Loving It, 3, 73, 132
Drip Along Daffy, 17, 29
Duck Amuck, 3, 16, 27
Dyer, Richard, 44, 56, 71

Eco, Umberto, 106, 107, 127
Escamatage d'une dame chez Robert Houdin, 12

Fatal Instinct, 38, 59, 65, 68, 74, 75, 112, 115

Fearless Vampire Killers (or Pardon Me, But Your Teeth Are in My Neck), The, 61
film cycles 24, 33, 49, 50, 112, 113, 122, 123
film noir, 27, 44, 48, 68, 75, 84, 85, 87
Flintstones, The, 21
Frankenstein, 9, 19, 26, 37, 43, 47, 60, 63, 78, 80, 103
Frankenweenie, 37, 47, 53, 63, 80, 84, 120, 124
Frozen North, The, 11

gangster, 23, 33, 36, 58, 60, 86, 121
Garden Scene, 12
Genette, Gérard, 26, 27, 29, 52
genre, 6, 8, 9, 18, 19, 27, 29, 33, 34, 36, 37, 38, 47, 78, 84, 102, 104, 105, 108, 110, 112, 113, 114, 120-127
Germany Calling, 18, 32
Go West (1925), 18
Go West (1940), 14
Grant, Barry K., 121

hair styles, 64, 72, 84
Hardware Wars, 59, 60, 65, 66, 69, 71, 84, 88, 89, 103, 113
Haunted Honeymoon, 52, 58, 118
heteroglossia, 4, 20, 23, 24
High Anxiety, 29, 34, 43, 45, 49, 50, 57, 70, 75, 89, 103, 107, 112, 116
High Sign, The, 13
His Bitter Pill, 13
Hodge, Robert, 33, 35, 36, 47, 101, 102, 104, 112, 113, 129
Hollywood Steps Out, 18
Honolulu, 18
horror genre, 19, 33, 43, 44, 47, 52, 53, 55, 58, 84, 88, 97, 104, 115, 117, 120, 121, 126
Hot Shots!, 6, 24, 45, 52, 56, 58, 59, 61, 69, 77, 80, 81, 85, 114, 116, 118, 131
Hot Shots! Part Deux, 56, 131
humor, 12, 17, 27, 49, 111, 112, 125, 126
Hutcheon, Linda, 5, 8, 24, 30, 32, 35, 37, 55, 106, 107, 109, 110, 112, 118, 120, 121, 124, 125, 128
hypothesis formation, 108

'ideal reader', 108, 109
I Haven't Got a Hat, 17
I'm Gonna Git You Sucka, 46, 56, 57, 61, 66, 69, 75, 84, 114, 118, 123
iconography, 8, 47, 58, 59, 60, 66, 85, 94
intentionality, 105, 106, 107
Intolerance, 14
irony, 3, 21, 22, 24, 30, 32, 58, 73, 85, 106, 108, 109, 112, 119, 120, 126
Iser, Wolfgang, 101, 103, 108

James Bond films, 24, 38, 67, 71, 79, 86, 111
Jameson, Fredric, 31, 133
Jaws, 81
John Travolta, 64, 79, 80
Johnny Dangerously, 36, 76, 82, 86
jokes, 36, 104, 105, 111, 115

Keaton, Buster, 3, 11, 12, 13, 14, 15, 27
Killer Klowns From Outer Space, 56, 59
Klinger, Barbara, 25, 114
Kress, Gunther, 33, 35, 36, 47, 101, 102, 104, 112, 113, 129

L'arroseur arrosé, 12
Last Remake of Beau Geste, The, 38, 48, 53, 60, 61, 62, 64, 67, 68, 69, 74, 76, 78, 83, 87, 115
Lobster Man From Mars, 66, 78, 105, 121
location, 4, 14, 29, 43, 61, 63, 64, 77, 124
logonomic systems, 33-38, 43, 46, 49, 57, 78, 79, 80, 81, 83, 84, 104-107, 108, 112, 115, 121, 123, 126, 128, 129, 134
Lone Stranger and Porky, The, 17
Love and Death, 21
Love at First Bite, 47, 55, 60, 74, 78, 88, 114
Lust in the Dust, 58, 89, 115, 116, 119

Mafia!, 115, 133
Maltese Falcon, The, 45, 52, 62, 66, 68, 104, 115
Max médecin malgré lui, 12
Medusa: Dare to be Truthful, 53, 126
MGM, 15, 18, 61
Miller, Owen, 25, 106, 116
Mouse that Jack Built, The, 20
Movie, A, 20, 50
Movie, Movie, 46, 52, 53, 54, 65, 72, 87, 118
Mud and Sand, 15
musical genre, 18, 20, 33, 34, 52, 61, 63, 69, 73, 75, 76, 81, 113
musical score, 18, 20, 32, 33, 38, 46, 50, 52, 61, 69, 75, 76, 81, 84, 89, 93, 97, 98, 110, 114, 133
Mystery Science Theater 3000, 7, 107, 127

Naked Gun: From the Files of Police Squad!, The, 3
Naked Gun 33 1/3: The Final Insult, The, 78, 93, 98-100
National Lampoon's Loaded Weapon 1, 89, 115
naturalization, 110, 123
newsreels, 17, 18, 28, 53
Nielsen, Leslie, 98, 132

On the Waterfront, 46, 97

Paleface, The (1921), 13
Paleface, The (1948), 18

INDEX

Paramount Pictures, 103, 111, 117
Pardners, 20
pastiche, 30, 31
plagiarism, 26
Play it Again, Sam, 21
Plump Fiction, 114
Popovic, Anton, 25, 26, 30, 50, 122
Porklips Now, 21, 34, 93-98, 103, 111, 114
Porky's Movie Mystery, 16
posters, 14, 105, 116, 117, 133
props, 14, 29, 59
Psycho, 29, 50, 65, 116
puns, 13, 38, 71, 74, 95
Purple Rose of Cairo, The, 12
Pyramid Films, 103

quotation, 26, 27, 34, 43, 110, 113, 127

Repossessed, 25, 27, 46, 65, 72, 73, 76, 80, 82, 87, 118, 126, 132
Ride Him, Bosko, 16
Robin Hood: Men in Tights, 21, 64, 65, 124, 133
Rocky Horror Picture Show, The, 33, 55, 78
Rose, Margaret A., 5, 8, 12, 24, 26, 30, 32, 65, 108, 113
Rustler's Rhapsody, 6, 27, 33, 43, 46, 58, 66, 76, 83, 108, 110, 123

Saps in Chaps, 17
satire, 5, 11, 31, 32
Saturday the 14th, 84, 115, 116
Schatz, Thomas, 18, 37, 47, 122
Schlock, 116
science-fiction, 33, 89, 105, 121

Sennett, Mack, 13
setting, 8, 9, 12, 14, 18, 25, 33, 37, 43, 55, 62, 76, 77, 79, 80, 94, 97, 98
Sgt. Kabukiman N.Y.P.D., 131
Sherlock Jr., 3, 12, 14, 125
Silence of the Hams, The, 46, 61, 72, 77, 122
Silent Movie, 6, 29, 52, 68, 73, 84, 86, 111, 125
'singing cowboy' Westerns, 33, 58, 108, 110, 123
Sleeper, 20
Soapdish, 21
Son of Paleface, 18
soundtrack, 18, 27, 29, 38, 39, 52, 63, 64, 69, 70, 72, 74, 75, 76, 80, 81, 88, 89, 94, 95, 98, 110, 114
sound effects, 69, 81, 88
Spaceballs, 4, 21, 27, 38, 46, 56, 57, 59, 60, 63, 67, 69, 71, 72, 73, 81, 84, 85, 88, 89, 102
Spy Hard, 24, 38, 58, 61, 64, 67, 87, 111, 132
Star is Hatched, A, 17
Star Wars, 38, 59, 65, 71, 78, 81, 84, 88, 89, 102, 104
subtitles, 51, 68
Sunbonnet Blue, A, 17

Take the Money and Run, 21, 29
Tale of Two Kitties, A, 19
They Call Me Bruce?, 80, 115
This is Spinal Tap, 29, 45, 46, 47, 51, 52, 53, 54, 66, 81, 116, 117, 118, 131, 133
Three Ages, The, 14, 27
Top Gun, 6, 24, 52, 85, 116
Top Secret!, 63, 65, 70, 80, 111, 114
Transylvania 6-5000 (1963), 9, 47, 55, 71

Transylvania 6-5000 (1985), 17

UHF, 33, 74, 93, 94
Uncensored Movies, 16
Uncle Josh at the Moving Picture Show, 9, 12
Universal Pictures, 19, 28, 67, 103, 114
Untouchables, The, 98, 99

Valentino, Rudolph, 15, 69
Vieira, João Luiz, 4, 112, 125

Warner Bros., 3, 16, 17, 19, 28, 29, 52, 61, 63, 80, 117
Way Out West, 15
Weakly Reporter, 18
Western, 6, 8, 9, 11, 15, 17, 18, 19, 21, 29, 33, 34, 45, 46, 47, 48, 52, 55, 56, 58, 61, 63, 77, 78, 83, 86, 88, 104, 108, 110, 111, 113, 115, 121, 123, 126, 128, 129, 134
What's Opera, Doc?, 17
Who Framed Roger Rabbit, 53
Wollen, Peter, 24, 124

Yacowar, Maurice, 20, 44, 45, 48
Young Frankenstein, 5, 21, 26, 43, 44, 47, 52, 53, 54, 55, 59, 60, 64, 74, 103, 110, 112, 115, 117, 123, 126, 131

Zelig, 21, 27, 32, 33, 45, 47, 49, 51, 52, 53, 84, 109, 126
Zorro, the Gay Blade, 5, 50, 123